C# 7 and .NET Core 2.0 Blueprints

Build effective applications that meet modern software requirements

Dirk Strauss
Jas Rademeyer

BIRMINGHAM - MUMBAI

C# 7 and .NET Core 2.0 Blueprints

Commissioning Editor: Merint Mathew
Acquisition Editor: Alok Dhuri
Content Development Editor: Akshada Iyer
Technical Editor: Supriya Thabe
Copy Editor: Safis Editing
Project Coordinator: Prajakta Naik
Proofreader: Safis Editing
Indexer: Tejal Daruwale Soni
Graphics: Jisha Chirayil
Production Coordinator: Aparna Bhagat

First published: March 2018

Production reference: 1230318

Published by Packt Publishing Ltd.
Livery Place
35 Livery Street
Birmingham
B3 2PB, UK.

ISBN 978-1-78839-619-6

www.packtpub.com

To my children, Irénéé and Tristan
I dedicate this book to you
I love you

-Dirk Strauss

To my wife, Janati, for her love and support ever since I met her
To my kids, Xander and Lana, for always showing me the lighter side of life

-Jas Rademeyer

`mapt.io`

Mapt is an online digital library that gives you full access to over 5,000 books and videos, as well as industry leading tools to help you plan your personal development and advance your career. For more information, please visit our website.

Why subscribe?

- Spend less time learning and more time coding with practical eBooks and Videos from over 4,000 industry professionals

- Improve your learning with Skill Plans built especially for you

- Get a free eBook or video every month

- Mapt is fully searchable

- Copy and paste, print, and bookmark content

PacktPub.com

Did you know that Packt offers eBook versions of every book published, with PDF and ePub files available? You can upgrade to the eBook version at `www.PacktPub.com` and as a print book customer, you are entitled to a discount on the eBook copy. Get in touch with us at `service@packtpub.com` for more details.

At `www.PacktPub.com`, you can also read a collection of free technical articles, sign up for a range of free newsletters, and receive exclusive discounts and offers on Packt books and eBooks.

Contributors

About the authors

Dirk Strauss is a full stack developer with Embrace. He enjoys learning and sharing what he learns with others. Dirk has published books on C# for Packt as well as ebooks for Syncfusion. In his spare time, he relaxes by playing guitar and trying to learn Jimi Hendrix licks. You can find him at @DirkStrauss on Twitter.

> *I would like to thank my wife, my son, and my daughter for supporting me and always being there for me. I love you with all that I am.*

Jas Rademeyer has been a part of the IT industry for over 15 years, focusing on the software side of things for most of his career. With a degree in information science, specializing in multimedia, he has been involved in all facets of development, ranging from architecture and solution design to user experience and training.

He is currently plying his trade as a technical solutions manager, where he manages development teams on various projects in the Microsoft space.

A family man and a musician at heart, he spends his free time with his wife and two kids and serves in the worship band at church.

About the reviewer

Prakash Tripathi is a technical lead in an MNC by profession and author and speaker by passion. He has extensive experience in the design, development, maintenance, and support of enterprise applications, primarily using Microsoft technologies and platforms.

He has been awarded MVP (Most Valuable Professional) by Microsoft in the years 2016 and 2017 and by another leading developers' portal (c-sharpcorner) in 2016, 2017, and 2018. He holds a master's degree in computer applications from MANIT, Bhopal.

I would like to thank my wife, Aradhana, for her continuous support throughout the journey of the book. I cannot forget to thank the Microsoft and c-sharpcorner technical communities for providing a platform in order for me to demonstrate and excel in the fast-growing and ever-changing field.

Packt is searching for authors like you

If you're interested in becoming an author for Packt, please visit `authors.packtpub.com` and apply today. We have worked with thousands of developers and tech professionals, just like you, to help them share their insight with the global tech community. You can make a general application, apply for a specific hot topic that we are recruiting an author for, or submit your own idea.

Table of Contents

Preface

Welcome to *C# 7 and .NET Core 2.0 Blueprints*. The power of .NET Core 2.0 is illustrated by taking a *blueprint* approach to common everyday applications. You will learn how to work with .NET Core 2.0 while creating exciting applications that you can use.

Who this book is for

This book is aimed at developers who have a good grasp of C# as a programming language but might need to learn more about .NET Core in general.

What this book covers

Chapter 1, *eBook Manager and Catalogue App*, covers the new features introduced in C# 7, which allow developers to write less code and be more productive. We will create an eBook manager application. If you are like me, you have eBooks scattered all over your hard drive and some external drives as well. This application will provide a mechanism to bring all these various locations together into a virtual storage space. The application is functional, but it can be further enhanced to suit your needs.

Chapter 2, *Cricket Score Calculator and Tracker*, says that object-oriented programming (OOP) is a crucial element of writing .NET applications. Proper OOP ensures that developers can easily share code between projects. You don't have to rewrite code that has already been written. In this chapter, we will create an ASP.NET Bootstrap web application that keeps track of the cricket score of your two favorite teams. It is also with this application that the principles of object-oriented programming will become evident.

Chapter 3, *Cross Platform .NET Core System Info Manager*, is all about what .NET Core is; .NET Core allows us to create applications that will run on Windows, macOS, and Linux. To illustrate this in this chapter, we will be creating a simple Information Dashboard application that displays information about the computer we are running on as well as the weather conditions at the location of that machine.

Chapter 4, *Task Bug Logging ASP .NET Core MVC App*, takes a look at using MongoDB with ASP.NET Core MVC by creating a task/bug logging application. MongoDB allows developers to be more productive and can easily be added to .NET Core.

Chapter 5, *ASP.NET SignalR Chat Application*, begins by getting you to imagine having the ability to have your server-side code push data to your web page in real time, without the user needing to refresh the page. The ASP.NET SignalR library provides developers with a simplified method to add real-time web functionality to applications. FYI, keep this chapter in mind when going through Chapter 8, *Twitter Clone Using OAuth*. This is a perfect application to integrate SignalR into.

Chapter 6, *Web Research Tool with Entity Framework Core*, discusses Entity Framework Core, which is an essential piece in our .NET Core education. One of the most frustrating parts of developing an application that needs to read data from and write data to some sort of database is trying to get the communication layer between your code and the database established. Entity Framework Core solves this easily in .NET Core applications, and this chapter shows you how.

Chapter 7, *A Serverless Email Validation Azure Function*, shows you how to create an Azure Function and how to call that function from an ASP.NET Core MVC application. The Azure Function will just be validating an email address. Serverless computing is illustrated here, and the benefits will become clear while working through the chapter.

Chapter 8, *Twitter Clone Using OAuth*, expresses that sometimes I wish I could tweak Twitter a bit to suit my own needs, for example, saving favorite tweets. In this chapter, we will take a look at how easy it is to create a basic Twitter clone using ASP.NET Core MVC. You can then easily add functionality to your application to customize it to your specific requirements.

Chapter 9, *Using Docker and ASP.NET Core*, explores Docker, which is all the rage these days, and for very good reason. This chapter illustrates how Docker can benefit developers. I will also show you how to create an ASP.NET Core MVC application and run it inside a Docker Container. In the last part of the chapter, we will see how we can use Docker Hub with GitHub to set up automated builds.

To get the most out of this book

The assumption is that you will have a good understanding of C# 6.0 at least. All the examples in this book will make use of C# 7 where relevant.

You will need to have Visual Studio 2017 installed with the latest patch. If you do not have Visual Studio 2017, you can install Visual Studio Community 2017 for free from https://www.visualstudio.com/downloads/.

Download the example code files

You can download the example code files for this book from your account at
www.packtpub.com. If you purchased this book elsewhere, you can visit
www.packtpub.com/support and register to have the files emailed directly to you.

You can download the code files by following these steps:

1. Log in or register at www.packtpub.com.
2. Select the **SUPPORT** tab.
3. Click on **Code Downloads & Errata**.
4. Enter the name of the book in the **Search** box and follow the onscreen instructions.

Once the file is downloaded, please make sure that you unzip or extract the folder using the latest version of:

- WinRAR/7-Zip for Windows
- Zipeg/iZip/UnRarX for Mac
- 7-Zip/PeaZip for Linux

The code bundle for the book is also hosted on GitHub at https://github.com/
PacktPublishing/CSharp7-and-.NET-Core-2.0-Blueprints. In case there's an update to the code, it will be updated on the existing GitHub repository.

We also have other code bundles from our rich catalog of books and videos available at https://github.com/PacktPublishing/. Check them out!

Conventions used

There are a number of text conventions used throughout this book.

CodeInText: Indicates code words in text, database table names, folder names, filenames, file extensions, pathnames, dummy URLs, user input, and Twitter handles. Here is an example: "You can call the application anything you like, but I called mine eBookManager."

A block of code is set as follows:

```
namespace eBookManager.Engine
{
    public class DeweyDecimal
    {
        public string ComputerScience { get; set; } = "000";
        public string DataProcessing { get; set; } = "004";
        public string ComputerProgramming { get; set; } = "005";
    }
}
```

Any command-line input or output is written as follows:

```
mongod -dbpath D:MongoTask
```

Bold: Indicates a new term, an important word, or words that you see onscreen. For example, words in menus or dialog boxes appear in the text like this. Here is an example: "After you have added all the storage spaces and eBooks, you will see the **Virtual Storage Spaces** listed."

Warnings or important notes appear like this.

Tips and tricks appear like this.

Get in touch

Feedback from our readers is always welcome.

General feedback: Email feedback@packtpub.com and mention the book title in the subject of your message. If you have questions about any aspect of this book, please email us at questions@packtpub.com.

Errata: Although we have taken every care to ensure the accuracy of our content, mistakes do happen. If you have found a mistake in this book, we would be grateful if you would report this to us. Please visit www.packtpub.com/submit-errata, selecting your book, clicking on the Errata Submission Form link, and entering the details.

Piracy: If you come across any illegal copies of our works in any form on the Internet, we would be grateful if you would provide us with the location address or website name. Please contact us at `copyright@packtpub.com` with a link to the material.

If you are interested in becoming an author: If there is a topic that you have expertise in and you are interested in either writing or contributing to a book, please visit `authors.packtpub.com`.

Reviews

Please leave a review. Once you have read and used this book, why not leave a review on the site that you purchased it from? Potential readers can then see and use your unbiased opinion to make purchase decisions, we at Packt can understand what you think about our products, and our authors can see your feedback on their book. Thank you!

For more information about Packt, please visit `packtpub.com`.

1

eBook Manager and Catalogue App

C# 7 is a fantastic release and is available in Visual Studio 2017. It introduces developers to a lot of powerful features, some of which were previously only available in other languages. The new features introduced in C# 7 allow developers to write less code and be more productive.

The features available are:

- Tuples
- Pattern matching
- Out variables
- Deconstruction
- Local functions
- Improvements to literals
- Ref returns and locals
- Generalized async and return types
- Expression bodies for accessors, constructors, and finalizers
- Throw expressions

This chapter will take you through some of these features, while the rest of the book will introduce you to some of the other features as we go along. In this chapter, we will create an `eBookManager` application. If you are like me, you have eBooks scattered all over your hard drives and some external drives as well. This application will provide a mechanism to bring all these various locations together into a Virtual Storage Space. The application is functional, but can be further enhanced to suit your needs. The scope for an application such as this is vast. You can download the source code from GitHub (`https://github.com/PacktPublishing/CSharp7-and-.NET-Core-2.0-Blueprints`) and follow it to see some of the new features of C# 7 in action.

Let's begin!

Setting up the project

Using Visual Studio 2017, we will create a simple **Windows Forms App** template project. You can call the application anything you like, but I called mine `eBookManager`:

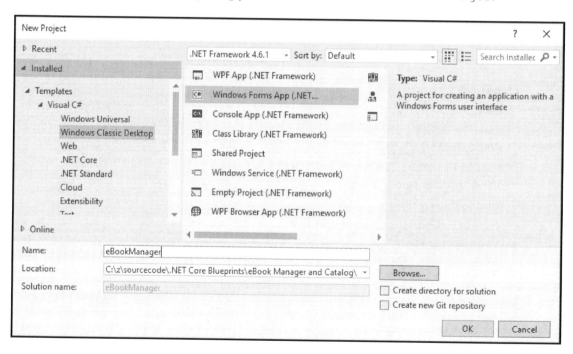

The project will be created and will look as follows:

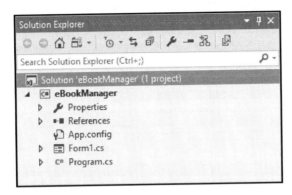

Our **Solution** needs a **Class Library** project to contain the classes that drive the eBookManager application. Add a new **Class Library** project to your **Solution** and call it eBookManager.Engine:

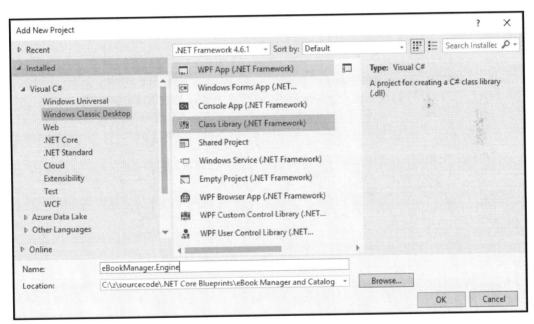

A **Class Library** project is added to the **Solution** with the default class name. Change this class to `Document`:

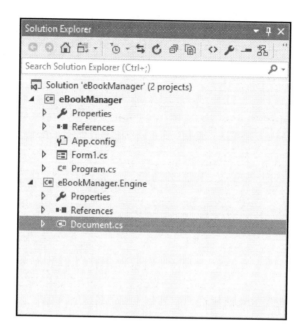

The `Document` class will represent a single eBook. Thinking of a book, we can have multiple properties that would represent a single book, but be representative of all books. An example of this would be the author. All books must have an author, otherwise it would not exist.

 I know some of you might be thinking that machines could generate documents too, but the information it generates was probably originally written by a person. Take code comments for example. A developer writes the comments in code, and a tool generates a document from that. The developer is still the author.

The properties I have added to the class are merely my interpretation of what might represent a book. Feel free to add additional code to make this your own.

Open the `Document.cs` file and add the following code to the class:

```
namespace eBookManager.Engine
{
    public class Document
    {
```

```
        public string Title { get; set; }
        public string FileName { get; set; }
        public string Extension { get; set; }
        public DateTime LastAccessed { get; set; }
        public DateTime Created { get; set; }
        public string FilePath { get; set; }
        public string FileSize { get; set; }
        public string ISBN { get; set; }
        public string Price { get; set; }
        public string Publisher { get; set; }
        public string Author { get; set; }
        public DateTime PublishDate { get; set; }
        public DeweyDecimal Classification { get; set; }
        public string Category { get; set; }
    }
}
```

You will notice that I have included a property called `Classification` of type `DeweyDecimal`. We have not added this class yet, and will do so next.

To the `eBookManager.Engine` project, add a class called `DeweyDecimal`. If you don't want to go to this level of classification for your eBooks, you can leave this class out. I have included it for the sake of completeness:

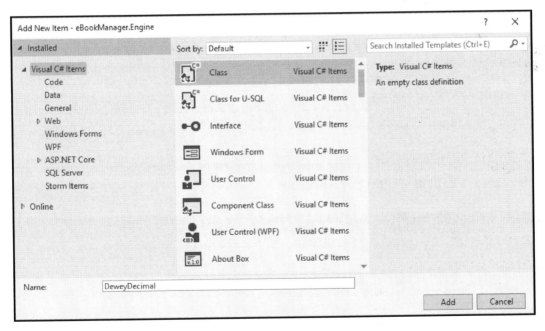

Your `DeweyDecimal` class must be in the same project as the `Document` class added earlier:

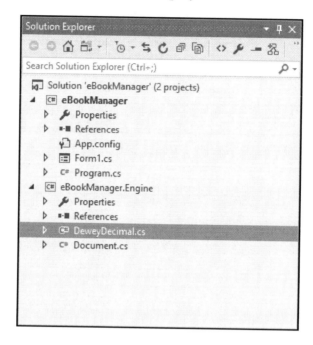

The `DeweyDecimal` system is quite big. For this reason, I have not catered for every book classification available. I have also only assumed that you would want to be working with programming eBooks. In reality, however, you may want to add in other classifications, such as literature, the sciences, the arts, and so on. It is up to you.

So let's create a class to represent the Dewey Decimal system::

1. Open up the `DeweyDecimal` class and add the following code to the class:

```
namespace eBookManager.Engine
{
    public class DeweyDecimal
    {
        public string ComputerScience { get; set; } = "000";
        public string DataProcessing { get; set; } = "004";
        public string ComputerProgramming { get; set; } = "005";
    }
}
```

Word nerds may disagree with me here, but I would like to remind them that I'm a code nerd. The classifications represented here are just so that I can catalog programming and computer science-related eBooks. As mentioned earlier, you can change this to suit your needs.

2. We now need to add in the heart of the `eBookManager.Engine` Solution. This is a class called `DocumentEngine` and it will be a class that will contain the methods you need to work with the documents:

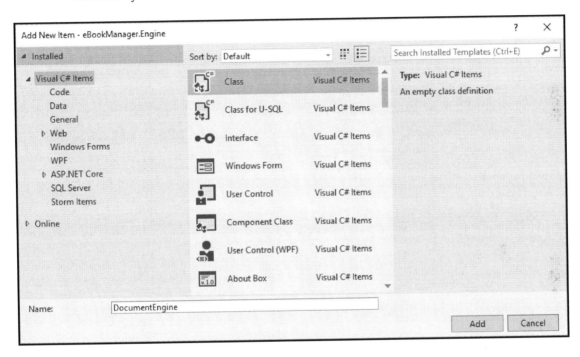

Your `eBookManager.Engine` Solution will now contain the following classes:

- `DeweyDecimal`
- `Document`
- `DocumentEngine`

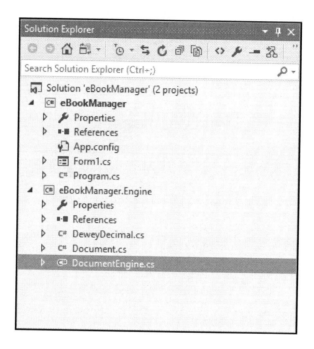

3. We now need to add a reference to `eBookManager.Engine` from the `eBookManager` project. I'm sure that you all know how to do this:

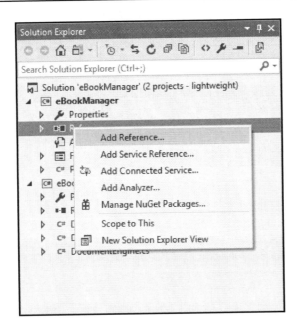

The `eBookManager.Engine` project will be available under the **Projects** section in the **Reference Manager** screen:

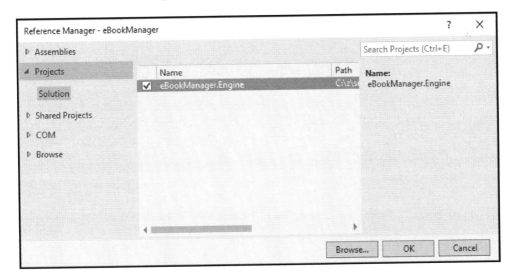

4. Once we have added the reference, we need a **Windows Form** that will be responsible for importing new books. Add a new form called `ImportBooks` to the `eBookManager` Solution:

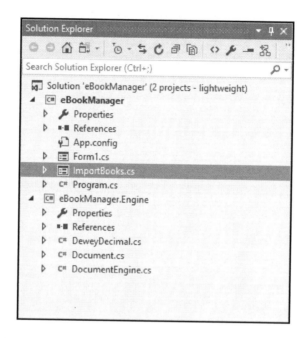

5. Before we forget, add an `ImageList` control to the `ImportBooks` form and call it `tvImages`. This will contain the images for the different types of documents we want to catalog.

The `ImageList` is a control you add from the **Toolbox** on to the `ImportBooks` form. You can access the **Images Collection Editor** from the `ImageList` properties.

The icons can be found in the `img` folder in the source code downloadable from GitHub at the following URL—`https://github.com/PacktPublishing/CSharp7-and-.NET-Core-2.0-Blueprints`.

The icons here are catering for PDF, MS Word, and ePub file types. It also contains folder images:

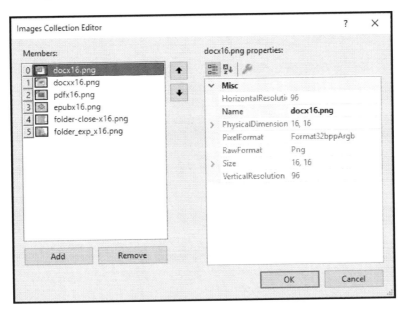

6. Now, to use tuples in C# 7, you need to add the `System.ValueTuple` NuGet package. Right-click on your **Solution** and select **Manage NuGet Packages for Solution...**

Please note that if you are running the .NET Framework 4.7, `System.ValueTuple` is included in this version of the framework. You will therefore not need to get it from NuGet.

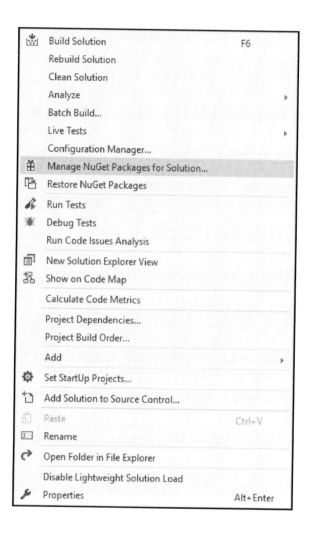

7. Search for `System.ValueTuple` and add it to your **Solution** projects. Then click **Install** and let the process complete (you will see the progress in the output window in Visual Studio):

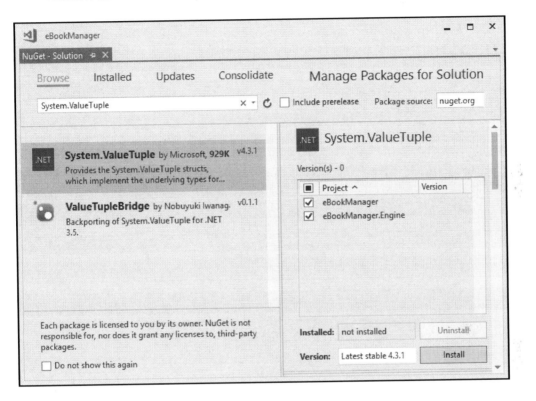

I love making use of extension methods in my projects. I usually add a separate project and/or class for this purpose. In this application, I added an `eBookManager.Helper` class library project:

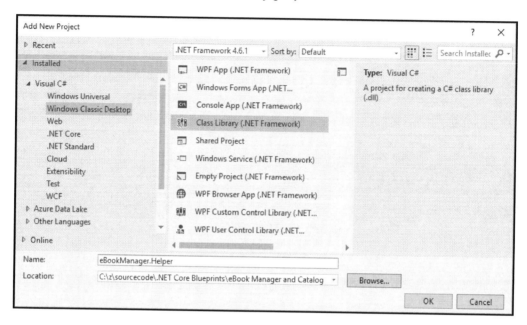

8. This helper class must also be added to the `eBookManager` Solution as a reference:

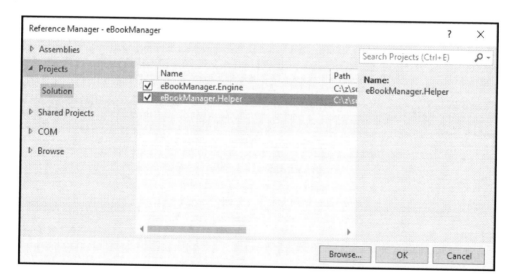

Lastly, I will be using JSON as a simple file store for my eBook catalogue. JSON is really flexible and can be consumed by various programming languages. What makes JSON so nice is the fact that it is relatively light weight and the output it generates is human-readable:

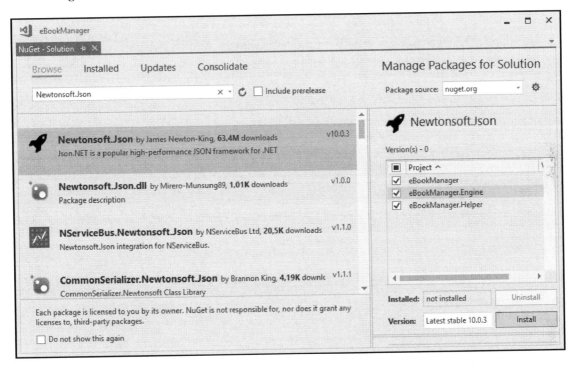

9. Go to **Manage the NuGet packages** for your **Solution** and search for Newtonsoft.Json. Add this then to the projects in your **Solution** and click the **Install** button.

You have now set up the basics needed for your eBookManager application. Next, we will venture further into the guts of the application by writing some code.

Virtual Storage Spaces and extension methods

Let's start by discussing the logic behind a Virtual Storage Space. This is a single virtual representation of several physical spaces on your hard drive (or hard drives). A storage space will be seen as a single area where a specific group of eBooks are *stored*. I use the term *stored* loosely because the storage space doesn't exist. It represents more of a grouping than a physical space on the hard drive:

1. To start creating Virtual Storage Spaces, add a new class called `StorageSpace` to the `eBookManager.Engine` project. Open the `StorageSpace.cs` file and add the following code to it:

```
using System;
using System.Collections.Generic;

namespace eBookManager.Engine
{
    [Serializable]
    public class StorageSpace
    {
        public int ID { get; set; }
        public string Name { get; set; }
        public string Description { get; set; }
        public List<Document> BookList { get; set; }
    }
}
```

 Note that you need to include the `System.Collections.Generic` namespace here, because the `StorageSpace` class contains a property called `BookList` of type `List<Document>` that will contain all the books in that particular storage space.

Now we need to focus our attention on the `ExtensionMethods` class in the `eBookManager.Helper` project. This will be a static class, because extension methods need to be static in nature in order to act on the various objects defined by the extension methods.

2. Add a new class to the `eBookManager.Helper` project and modify the `ExtensionMethods` class as follows:

```
public static class ExtensionMethods
{


}
```

Let's add the first extension method to the class called `ToInt()`. What this extension method does is take a `string` value and try to parse it to an `integer` value. I am too lazy to type `Convert.ToInt32(stringVariable)` whenever I need to convert a `string` to an `integer`. It is for this reason that I use an extension method.

3. Add the following static method to the `ExtensionMethods` class:

```
public static int ToInt(this string value, int defaultInteger =
0)
{
    try
    {
        if (int.TryParse(value, out int validInteger))
          // Out variables
         return validInteger;
        else
         return defaultInteger;
    }
    catch
    {
        return defaultInteger;
    }
}
```

The `ToInt()` extension method acts only on `string`. This is defined by the code `this string value` in the method signature where `value` is the variable name that will contain the `string` you are trying to convert to an `integer`. It also has a default parameter called `defaultInteger`, which is set to `0`. Unless the developer calling the extension method wants to return a default integer value of `0`, they can pass a different integer to this extension method (−1, for example).

It is also here that we find our first feature of C# 7. The improvement to out variables. In previous iterations of C#, we had to do the following with out variables:

```
int validInteger;
if (int.TryParse(value, out validInteger))
{

}
```

There was this predeclared integer variable hanging around and it gets its value if the string value parsed to an integer. C# 7 simplifies the code a lot more:

```
if (int.TryParse(value, out int validInteger))
```

C# 7 allows developers to declare an out variable right there where it is passed as an out argument. Moving along to the other methods of the ExtensionMethods class, these methods are used to provide the following logic:

- Read and write to the data source

- Check whether a storage space exists

- Convert bytes to megabytes

- Convert a string to an integer (as discussed previously)

The ToMegabytes method is quite easy. Not having to write this calculation all over the place, defining it inside an extension method makes sense:

```
public static double ToMegabytes(this long bytes)
{
    return (bytes > 0) ? (bytes / 1024f) / 1024f : bytes;
}
```

We also need a way to check if a particular storage space already exists.

 Be sure to add a project reference to eBookManager.Engine from the eBookManager.Helper project.

What this extension method also does is to return the next storage space ID to the calling code. If the storage space does not exist, the returned ID will be the next ID that can be used when creating a new storage space:

```
public static bool StorageSpaceExists(this List<StorageSpace>
space, string nameValueToCheck, out int storageSpaceId)
{
    bool exists = false;
    storageSpaceId = 0;

    if (space.Count() != 0)
    {
        int count = (from r in space
                        where r.Name.Equals(nameValueToCheck)
                        select r).Count();

        if (count > 0)
            exists = true;

        storageSpaceId = (from r in space
                            select r.ID).Max() + 1;
    }
    return exists;
}
```

We also need to create a method that will `write` the data we have to a file after converting it to JSON:

```
public static void WriteToDataStore(this List<StorageSpace> value,
string storagePath, bool appendToExistingFile = false)
{
    JsonSerializer json = new JsonSerializer();
    json.Formatting = Formatting.Indented;
    using (StreamWriter sw = new StreamWriter(storagePath,
     appendToExistingFile))
    {
        using (JsonWriter writer = new JsonTextWriter(sw))
        {
            json.Serialize(writer, value);
        }
    }
}
```

This method is rather self-explanatory. It acts on a List<StorageSpace> object and will create the JSON data, overwriting a file defined in the storagePath variable.

Lastly, we need to be able to read the data back again into a List<StorageSpace> object and return that to the calling code:

```
public static List<StorageSpace> ReadFromDataStore(this
List<StorageSpace> value, string storagePath)
{
    JsonSerializer json = new JsonSerializer();
    if (!File.Exists(storagePath))
    {
        var newFile = File.Create(storagePath);
        newFile.Close();
    }
    using (StreamReader sr = new StreamReader(storagePath))
    {
        using (JsonReader reader = new JsonTextReader(sr))
        {
            var retVal =
             json.Deserialize<List<StorageSpace>>(reader);
            if (retVal is null)
                retVal = new List<StorageSpace>();

            return retVal;
        }
    }
}
```

The method will return an empty List<StorageSpace> object and nothing is contained in the file. The ExtensionMethods class can contain many more extension methods that you might use often. It is a great way to separate often-used code.

The DocumentEngine class

The purpose of this class is merely to provide supporting code to a document. In the eBookManager application, I am going to use a single method called GetFileProperties() that will (you guessed it) return the properties of a selected file. This class also only contains this single method. As the application is modified for your specific purposes, you can modify this class and add additional methods specific to documents.

The `DocumentEngine` class introduces us to the next feature of C# 7 called **tuples**. What do tuples do exactly? It is often a requirement for a developer to return more than a single value from a method. Among other Solutions, you can of course use `out` parameters, but these do not work in `async` methods. Tuples provide a better way to do this.

Inside the `DocumentEngine` class, add the following code:

```
public (DateTime dateCreated, DateTime dateLastAccessed, string
fileName, string fileExtension, long fileLength, bool error)
GetFileProperties(string filePath)
{
    var returnTuple = (created: DateTime.MinValue,
    lastDateAccessed: DateTime.MinValue, name: "", ext: "",
    fileSize: 0L, error: false);
    try
    {
        FileInfo fi = new FileInfo(filePath);
        fi.Refresh();
        returnTuple = (fi.CreationTime, fi.LastAccessTime, fi.Name,
        fi.Extension, fi.Length, false);
    }
    catch
    {
        returnTuple.error = true;
    }
    return returnTuple;
}
```

The `GetFileProperties()` method returns a tuple as `(DateTime dateCreated, DateTime dateLastAccessed, string fileName, string fileExtension, long fileLength, bool error)` and allows us to inspect the values returned from the calling code easily.

Before I try to get the properties of the specific file, I initialize the `tuple` by doing the following:

```
var returnTuple = (created: DateTime.MinValue, lastDateAccessed:
DateTime.MinValue, name: "", ext: "", fileSize: 0L, error: false);
```

If there is an exception, I can return default values. Reading the file properties is simple enough using the `FileInfo` class. I can then assign the file properties to the `tuple` by doing this:

```
returnTuple = (fi.CreationTime, fi.LastAccessTime, fi.Name, fi.Extension,
fi.Length, false);
```

The `tuple` is then returned to the calling code where it will be used as required. We will have a look at the calling code next.

The ImportBooks form

The `ImportBooks` form does exactly what the name suggests. It allows us to create Virtual Storage Spaces and to import books into those spaces. The form design is as follows:

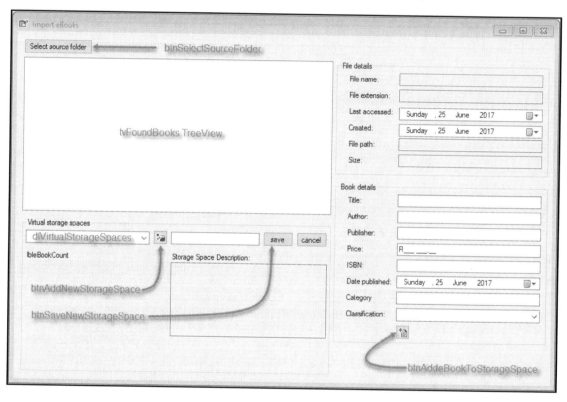

The `TreeView` controls are prefixed with `tv`, buttons with `btn`, combo boxes with `dl`, textboxes with `txt`, and date time pickers with `dt`. When this form loads, if there are any storage spaces defined then these will be listed in the `dlVirtualStorageSpaces` combo box. Clicking on the **Select source folder** button will allow us to select a source folder to look for eBooks.

If a storage space does not exist, we can add a new Virtual Storage Space by clicking the `btnAddNewStorageSpace` button. This will allow us to add a name and description for the new storage space and click on the `btnSaveNewStorageSpace` button.

Selecting an eBook from the `tvFoundBooks` TreeView will populate the **File details** group of controls to the right of the form. You can then add additional **Book details** and click on the `btnAddeBookToStorageSpace` button to add the book to our space:

1. You need to ensure that the following namespaces are added to your `ImportBooks` class:

```
using eBookManager.Engine;
using System;
using System.Collections.Generic;
using System.IO;
using System.Linq;
using System.Windows.Forms;
using static eBookManager.Helper.ExtensionMethods;
using static System.Math;
```

2. Next, let's start at the most logical place to begin with, which is the constructor `ImportBooks()` and the form variables. Add the following code above the constructor:

```
private string _jsonPath;
private List<StorageSpace> spaces;
private enum StorageSpaceSelection { New = -9999, NoSelection = -1
}
```

The usefulness of the enumerator will become evident later on in code. The `_jsonPath` variable will contain the path to the file used to store our eBook information.

3. Modify the constructor as follows:

```
public ImportBooks()
{
    InitializeComponent();
    _jsonPath = Path.Combine(Application.StartupPath,
    "bookData.txt");
    spaces = spaces.ReadFromDataStore(_jsonPath);
}
```

The `_jsonPath` is initialized to the executing folder for the application and the file hard coded to `bookData.txt`. You could provide a settings screen if you wanted to configure these settings, but I just decided to make the application use a hard-coded setting.

4. Next, we need to add another enumerator that defines the file extensions that we will be able to save in our application. It is here that we will see another feature of C# 7 called `expression-bodied` properties.

Expression-bodied accessors, constructors, and finalizers

If the following expression looks intimidating, it's because it is using a feature introduced in C# 6 and expanded in C# 7:

```
private HashSet<string> AllowedExtensions => new
HashSet<string>(StringComparer.InvariantCultureIgnoreCase) {
".doc",".docx",".pdf", ".epub" };
private enum Extention { doc = 0, docx = 1, pdf = 2, epub = 3 }
```

The preceding example returns a `HashSet` of allowed file extensions for our application. These have been around since C# 6, but have been extended in C# 7 to include *accessors*, *constructors*, and *finalizers*. Let's simplify the examples a bit.

Assume that we had to modify the `Document` class to set a field for `_defaultDate` inside the class; traditionally, we would need to do this:

```
private DateTime _defaultDate;

public Document()
{
    _defaultDate = DateTime.Now;
}
```

In C# 7, we can greatly simplify this code by simply doing the following:

```
private DateTime _defaultDate;
public Document() => _defaultDate = DateTime.Now;
```

This is perfectly legal and compiles correctly. Similarly, the same can be done with finalizers (or deconstructors). Another nice implementation of this is expression-bodied properties as seen with the `AllowedExtensions` property. The expression-bodied properties have actually been around since C# 6, but who's counting?

Suppose that we wanted to just return the `string` value of the `Extension` enumeration for PDFs, we could do something such as the following:

```
public string PDFExtension
{
    get
    {
        return nameof(Extention.pdf);
    }
}
```

That property only has a get accessor and will never return anything other than the `string` value of `Extension.pdf`. Simplify that by changing the code to:

```
public string PDFExtension => nameof(Extention.pdf);
```

That's it. A single line of code does exactly the same thing as the previous seven lines of code. Falling into the same category, expression-bodied property accessors are also simplified. Consider the following 11 lines of code:

```
public string DefaultSavePath
{
    get
    {
        return _jsonPath;
    }
    set
    {
        _jsonPath = value;
    }
}
```

With C# 7, we can simplify this to the following:

```
public string DefaultSavePath
{
    get => _jsonPath;
    set => _jsonPath = value;
}
```

This makes our code a lot more readable and quicker to write. Swing back to our `AllowedExtensions` property; traditionally, it would be written as follows:

```
private HashSet<string> AllowedExtensions
{
    get
    {
        return new HashSet<string>
        (StringComparer.InvariantCultureIgnoreCase) { ".doc",
        ".docx", ".pdf", ".epub" };
    }
}
```

Since C# 6, we have been able to simplify this, as we saw previously. This gives developers a great way to reduce unnecessary code.

Populating the TreeView control

We can see the implementation of the `AllowedExtensions` property when we look at the `PopulateBookList()` method. All that this method does is populate the `TreeView` control with files and folders found at the selected source location. Consider the following code:

```
public void PopulateBookList(string paramDir, TreeNode paramNode)
{
    DirectoryInfo dir = new DirectoryInfo(paramDir);
    foreach (DirectoryInfo dirInfo in dir.GetDirectories())
    {
        TreeNode node = new TreeNode(dirInfo.Name);
        node.ImageIndex = 4;
        node.SelectedImageIndex = 5;

        if (paramNode != null)
            paramNode.Nodes.Add(node);
        else
            tvFoundBooks.Nodes.Add(node);
        PopulateBookList(dirInfo.FullName, node);
    }
    foreach (FileInfo fleInfo in dir.GetFiles().Where
    (x => AllowedExtensions.Contains(x.Extension)).ToList())
    {
        TreeNode node = new TreeNode(fleInfo.Name);
        node.Tag = fleInfo.FullName;
        int iconIndex = Enum.Parse(typeof(Extention),
          fleInfo.Extension.TrimStart('.'), true).GetHashCode();
```

```
        node.ImageIndex = iconIndex;
        node.SelectedImageIndex = iconIndex;
        if (paramNode != null)
            paramNode.Nodes.Add(node);
        else
            tvFoundBooks.Nodes.Add(node);
    }
}
```

The first place we need to call this method is obviously from within itself, as this is a recursive method. The second place we need to call it is from the btnSelectSourceFolder button click event:

```
private void btnSelectSourceFolder_Click(object sender, EventArgs e)
{
    try
    {
        FolderBrowserDialog fbd = new FolderBrowserDialog();
        fbd.Description = "Select the location of your eBooks and documents";

        DialogResult dlgResult = fbd.ShowDialog();
        if (dlgResult == DialogResult.OK)
        {
            tvFoundBooks.Nodes.Clear();
            tvFoundBooks.ImageList = tvImages;

            string path = fbd.SelectedPath;
            DirectoryInfo di = new DirectoryInfo(path);
            TreeNode root = new TreeNode(di.Name);
            root.ImageIndex = 4;
            root.SelectedImageIndex = 5;
            tvFoundBooks.Nodes.Add(root);
            PopulateBookList(di.FullName, root);
            tvFoundBooks.Sort();

            root.Expand();
        }
    }
    catch (Exception ex)
    {
        MessageBox.Show(ex.Message);
    }
}
```

This is all quite straightforward code. Select the folder to recurse and populate the `TreeView` control with all the files found that match the file extension contained in our `AllowedExtensions` property.

We also need to look at the code when someone selects a book in the `tvFoundBooks` `TreeView` control. When a book is selected, we need to read the properties of the selected file and return those properties to the file details section:

```
private void tvFoundBooks_AfterSelect(object sender,
TreeViewEventArgs e)
{
    DocumentEngine engine = new DocumentEngine();
    string path = e.Node.Tag?.ToString() ?? "";

    if (File.Exists(path))
    {
        var (dateCreated, dateLastAccessed, fileName,
        fileExtention, fileLength, hasError) =
        engine.GetFileProperties(e.Node.Tag.ToString());

        if (!hasError)
        {
            txtFileName.Text = fileName;
            txtExtension.Text = fileExtention;
            dtCreated.Value = dateCreated;
            dtLastAccessed.Value = dateLastAccessed;
            txtFilePath.Text = e.Node.Tag.ToString();
            txtFileSize.Text = $"{Round(fileLength.ToMegabytes(),
            2).ToString()} MB";
        }
    }
}
```

You will notice that it is here that we are calling the method `GetFileProperties()` on the `DocumentEngine` class that returns the tuple.

Local functions

This is one of those features in C# 7 that I truly wondered where I would ever find a use for. As it turns out, local functions are extremely useful indeed. Also called *nested functions* by some, these functions are nested within another parent function. It is obviously only within scope inside the parent function and adds a useful way to call code that otherwise wouldn't have any real purpose outside the parent function. Consider the `PopulateStorageSpacesList()` method:

```
private void PopulateStorageSpacesList()
{
    List<KeyValuePair<int, string>> lstSpaces =
    new List<KeyValuePair<int, string>>();
    BindStorageSpaceList((int)StorageSpaceSelection.NoSelection,
    "Select Storage Space");

    void BindStorageSpaceList(int key, string value)
    // Local function
    {
        lstSpaces.Add(new KeyValuePair<int, string>(key, value));
    }

    if (spaces is null || spaces.Count() == 0) // Pattern matching
    {
        BindStorageSpaceList((int)StorageSpaceSelection.New, "
        <create new>");
    }
    else
    {
        foreach (var space in spaces)
        {
            BindStorageSpaceList(space.ID, space.Name);
        }
    }

    dlVirtualStorageSpaces.DataSource = new
    BindingSource(lstSpaces, null);
    dlVirtualStorageSpaces.DisplayMember = "Value";
    dlVirtualStorageSpaces.ValueMember = "Key";
}
```

To see how `PopulateStorageSpacesList()` calls the local function `BindStorageSpaceList()`, have a look at the following screenshot:

```
3 references | dirkstrauss, 2 days ago | 1 author, 1 change
private void PopulateStorageSpacesList()
{
    List<KeyValuePair<int, string>> lstSpaces = new List<KeyValuePair<int, string>>();
    BindStorageSpaceList((int)StorageSpaceSelection.NoSelection, "Select Storage Space");

    void BindStorageSpaceList(int key, string value) // Local function
    {
        lstSpaces.Add(new KeyValuePair<int, string>(key, value));
    }

    if (spaces is null || spaces.Count() == 0) // Pattern matching
    {
        BindStorageSpaceList((int)StorageSpaceSelection.New, "<create new>");
    }
    else
    {
        foreach (var space in spaces)
        {
            BindStorageSpaceList(space.ID, space.Name);
        }
    }

    dlVirtualStorageSpaces.DataSource = new BindingSource(lstSpaces, null);
    dlVirtualStorageSpaces.DisplayMember = "Value";
    dlVirtualStorageSpaces.ValueMember = "Key";
}
```

You will notice that the local function can be called from anywhere within the parent function. In this case, the `BindStorageSpaceList()` local function does not return anything, but you can return whatever you like from a local function. You could just as well have done the following:

```
private void SomeMethod()
{
    int currentYear = GetCurrentYear();

    int GetCurrentYear(int iAddYears = 0)
    {
        return DateTime.Now.Year + iAddYears;
    }

    int nextYear = GetCurrentYear(1);
}
```

The local function is accessible from anywhere within the parent function.

Pattern matching

Staying with the `PopulateStorageSpacesList()` method, we can see the use of another C# 7 feature called **pattern matching**. The `spaces is null` line of code is probably the simplest form of pattern matching. In reality, pattern matching supports several patterns.

Consider a `switch` statement:

```
switch (objObject)
{
    case null:
        WriteLine("null"); // Constant pattern
        break;

    case Document doc when doc.Author.Equals("Stephen King"):
        WriteLine("Stephen King is the author");
        break;

    case Document doc when doc.Author.StartsWith("Stephen"):
        WriteLine("Stephen is the author");
        break;

    default:
        break;
}
```

Pattern matching allows developers to use the `is` expression to see whether something matches a specific pattern. Bear in mind that the pattern needs to check for the most specific to the most general pattern. If you simply started the case with `case Document doc:` then all the objects passed to the `switch` statement of type `Document` would match. You would never find specific documents where the author is `Stephen King` or starts with `Stephen`.

For a construct inherited by C# from the C language, it hasn't changed much since the '70s. C# 7 changes all that with pattern matching.

Finishing up the ImportBooks code

Let's have a look at the rest of the code in the `ImportBooks` form. The form load just populates the storage spaces list, if any existing storage spaces have been previously saved:

```
private void ImportBooks_Load(object sender, EventArgs e)
{
    PopulateStorageSpacesList();
    if (dlVirtualStorageSpaces.Items.Count == 0)
```

```
    {
        dlVirtualStorageSpaces.Items.Add("<create new storage
        space>");
    }

    lblEbookCount.Text = "";
}
```

We now need to add the logic for changing the selected storage space. The `SelectedIndexChanged()` event of the `dlVirtualStorageSpaces` control is modified as follows:

```
private void dlVirtualStorageSpaces_SelectedIndexChanged(object
sender, EventArgs e)
{
    int selectedValue =
    dlVirtualStorageSpaces.SelectedValue.ToString().ToInt();

    if (selectedValue == (int)StorageSpaceSelection.New) // -9999
    {
        txtNewStorageSpaceName.Visible = true;
        lblStorageSpaceDescription.Visible = true;
        txtStorageSpaceDescription.ReadOnly = false;
        btnSaveNewStorageSpace.Visible = true;
        btnCancelNewStorageSpaceSave.Visible = true;
        dlVirtualStorageSpaces.Enabled = false;
        btnAddNewStorageSpace.Enabled = false;
        lblEbookCount.Text = "";
    }
    else if (selectedValue !=
    (int)StorageSpaceSelection.NoSelection)
    {
        // Find the contents of the selected storage space
        int contentCount = (from c in spaces
                            where c.ID == selectedValue
                            select c).Count();
        if (contentCount > 0)
        {
            StorageSpace selectedSpace = (from c in spaces
                                        where c.ID ==
                                        selectedValue
                                        select c).First();

            txtStorageSpaceDescription.Text =
            selectedSpace.Description;

            List<Document> eBooks = (selectedSpace.BookList ==
```

```
        null)
            ? new List<Document> { } : selectedSpace.BookList;
        lblEbookCount.Text = $"Storage Space contains
        {eBooks.Count()} {(eBooks.Count() == 1 ? "eBook" :
        "eBooks")}";
        }
    }
    else
    {
        lblEbookCount.Text = "";
    }
}
```

I will not go into any detailed explanation of the code here as it is relatively obvious what it is doing.

Throw expressions

We also need to add the code to save a new storage space. Add the following code to the `Click` event of the `btnSaveNewStorageSpace` button:

```
private void btnSaveNewStorageSpace_Click(object sender,
    EventArgs e)
{
    try
    {
        if (txtNewStorageSpaceName.Text.Length != 0)
        {
            string newName = txtNewStorageSpaceName.Text;

            // throw expressions: bool spaceExists =
            (space exists = false) ? return false : throw exception
            // Out variables
            bool spaceExists = (!spaces.StorageSpaceExists
            (newName, out int nextID)) ? false : throw new
            Exception("The storage space you are
             trying to add already exists.");

            if (!spaceExists)
            {
                StorageSpace newSpace = new StorageSpace();
                newSpace.Name = newName;
                newSpace.ID = nextID;
                newSpace.Description =
                txtStorageSpaceDescription.Text;
                spaces.Add(newSpace);
```

```
                          PopulateStorageSpacesList();
                          // Save new Storage Space Name
                          txtNewStorageSpaceName.Clear();
                          txtNewStorageSpaceName.Visible = false;
                          lblStorageSpaceDescription.Visible = false;
                          txtStorageSpaceDescription.ReadOnly = true;
                          txtStorageSpaceDescription.Clear();
                          btnSaveNewStorageSpace.Visible = false;
                          btnCancelNewStorageSpaceSave.Visible = false;
                          dlVirtualStorageSpaces.Enabled = true;
                          btnAddNewStorageSpace.Enabled = true;
                      }
                  }
              }
              catch (Exception ex)
              {
                  txtNewStorageSpaceName.SelectAll();
                  MessageBox.Show(ex.Message);
              }
          }
```

Here, we can see another new feature in the C# 7 language called **throw expressions**. This gives developers the ability to throw exceptions from expressions. The code in question is this code:

```
bool spaceExists = (!spaces.StorageSpaceExists(newName, out int
nextID)) ? false : throw new Exception("The storage space you are
trying to add already exists.");
```

I always like to remember the structure of the code as follows:

The last few methods deal with saving eBooks in the selected Virtual Storage Space. Modify the `Click` event of the `btnAddBookToStorageSpace` button. This code also contains a throw expression. If you haven't selected a storage space from the combo box, a new exception is thrown:

```
private void btnAddeBookToStorageSpace_Click(object sender,
EventArgs e)
{
    try
    {
        int selectedStorageSpaceID =
        dlVirtualStorageSpaces.SelectedValue.ToString().ToInt();
        if ((selectedStorageSpaceID !=
         (int)StorageSpaceSelection.NoSelection)
        && (selectedStorageSpaceID !=
          (int)StorageSpaceSelection.New))
        {
            UpdateStorageSpaceBooks(selectedStorageSpaceID);
        }
        else throw new Exception("Please select a Storage
        Space to add your eBook to"); // throw expressions
    }
    catch (Exception ex)
    {
        MessageBox.Show(ex.Message);
    }
}
```

Developers can now immediately throw exceptions in code right there where they occur. This is rather nice and makes code cleaner and its intent clearer.

Saving a selected book to a storage space

The following code basically updates the book list in the selected storage space if it already contains the specific book (after confirming with the user). Otherwise, it will add the book to the book list as a new book:

```
private void UpdateStorageSpaceBooks(int storageSpaceId)
{
    try
    {
        int iCount = (from s in spaces
                      where s.ID == storageSpaceId
                      select s).Count();
        if (iCount > 0) // The space will always exist
```

```
        {
            // Update
            StorageSpace existingSpace = (from s in spaces
              where s.ID == storageSpaceId select s).First();

            List<Document> ebooks = existingSpace.BookList;

            int iBooksExist = (ebooks != null) ? (from b in ebooks
              where $"{b.FileName}".Equals($"
                {txtFileName.Text.Trim()}")
                  select b).Count() : 0;

            if (iBooksExist > 0)
            {
                // Update existing book
                DialogResult dlgResult = MessageBox.Show($"A book
                with the same name has been found in Storage Space
                {existingSpace.Name}.
                Do you want to replace the existing book
                entry with this one?",
                "Duplicate Title", MessageBoxButtons.YesNo,
                 MessageBoxIcon.Warning,
                 MessageBoxDefaultButton.Button2);
                if (dlgResult == DialogResult.Yes)
                {
                    Document existingBook = (from b in ebooks
                        where $"
                        {b.FileName}".Equals($"
                        {txtFileName.Text.Trim()}")
                          select b).First();

                    existingBook.FileName = txtFileName.Text;
                    existingBook.Extension = txtExtension.Text;
                    existingBook.LastAccessed =
                    dtLastAccessed.Value;
                    existingBook.Created = dtCreated.Value;
                    existingBook.FilePath = txtFilePath.Text;
                    existingBook.FileSize = txtFileSize.Text;
                    existingBook.Title = txtTitle.Text;
                    existingBook.Author = txtAuthor.Text;
                    existingBook.Publisher = txtPublisher.Text;
                    existingBook.Price = txtPrice.Text;
                    existingBook.ISBN = txtISBN.Text;
                    existingBook.PublishDate =
                    dtDatePublished.Value;
                    existingBook.Category = txtCategory.Text;
                }
            }
```

```
            else
            {
                // Insert new book
                Document newBook = new Document();
                newBook.FileName = txtFileName.Text;
                newBook.Extension = txtExtension.Text;
                newBook.LastAccessed = dtLastAccessed.Value;
                newBook.Created = dtCreated.Value;
                newBook.FilePath = txtFilePath.Text;
                newBook.FileSize = txtFileSize.Text;
                newBook.Title = txtTitle.Text;
                newBook.Author = txtAuthor.Text;
                newBook.Publisher = txtPublisher.Text;
                newBook.Price = txtPrice.Text;
                newBook.ISBN = txtISBN.Text;
                newBook.PublishDate = dtDatePublished.Value;
                newBook.Category = txtCategory.Text;
                if (ebooks == null)
                    ebooks = new List<Document>();
                ebooks.Add(newBook);
                existingSpace.BookList = ebooks;
            }
        }
        spaces.WriteToDataStore(_jsonPath);
        PopulateStorageSpacesList();
        MessageBox.Show("Book added");
    }
    catch (Exception ex)
    {
        MessageBox.Show(ex.Message);
    }
}
```

Lastly, as a matter of housekeeping, the ImportBooks form contains the following code for displaying and enabling controls based on the button click events of btnCancelNewStorageSpace and btnAddNewStorageSpace buttons:

```
private void btnCancelNewStorageSpaceSave_Click(object sender,
EventArgs e)
{
    txtNewStorageSpaceName.Clear();
    txtNewStorageSpaceName.Visible = false;
    lblStorageSpaceDescription.Visible = false;
    txtStorageSpaceDescription.ReadOnly = true;
    txtStorageSpaceDescription.Clear();
    btnSaveNewStorageSpace.Visible = false;
    btnCancelNewStorageSpaceSave.Visible = false;
```

```
            dlVirtualStorageSpaces.Enabled = true;
            btnAddNewStorageSpace.Enabled = true;
        }

        private void btnAddNewStorageSpace_Click(object sender, EventArgs
        e)
        {
            txtNewStorageSpaceName.Visible = true;
            lblStorageSpaceDescription.Visible = true;
            txtStorageSpaceDescription.ReadOnly = false;
            btnSaveNewStorageSpace.Visible = true;
            btnCancelNewStorageSpaceSave.Visible = true;
            dlVirtualStorageSpaces.Enabled = false;
            btnAddNewStorageSpace.Enabled = false;
        }
```

All that remains now is for us to complete the code in the `Form1.cs` form, which is the start-up form.

Main eBookManager form

Start off by renaming `Form1.cs` to `eBookManager.cs`. This is the start-up form for the application and it will list all the existing storage spaces previously saved:

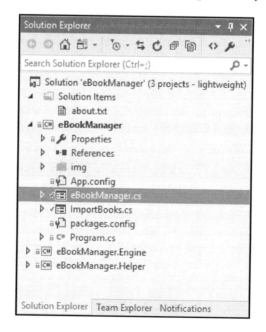

Design your `eBookManager` form as follows:

- `ListView` control for existing storage spaces
- `ListView` for eBooks contained in selected storage space
- Button that opens the file location of the eBook
- A menu control to navigate to the `ImportBooks.cs` form
- Various read-only fields to display the selected eBook information

When you have added the controls, your **eBook Manager** form will look as follows:

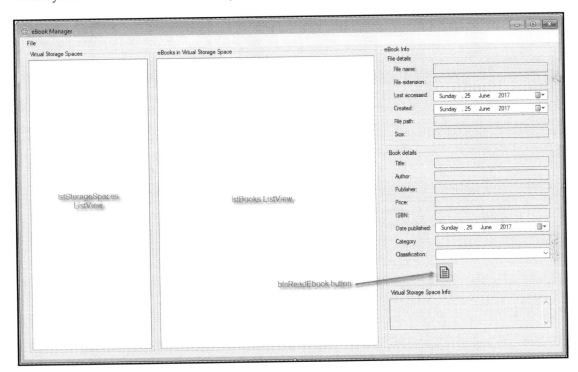

Looking at the code we used earlier, you need to ensure that the following `using` statements are imported:

```
using eBookManager.Engine;
using eBookManager.Helper;
using System;
using System.Collections.Generic;
using System.IO;
using System.Windows.Forms;
using System.Linq;
```

```
using System.Diagnostics;
```

The constructor is quite similar to the `ImportBooks.cs` form's constructor. It reads any available storage spaces and populates the storage spaces list view control with the previously saved storage spaces:

```
private string _jsonPath;
private List<StorageSpace> spaces;

public eBookManager()
{
    InitializeComponent();
    _jsonPath = Path.Combine(Application.StartupPath,
    "bookData.txt");
    spaces = spaces.ReadFromDataStore(_jsonPath);
}

private void Form1_Load(object sender, EventArgs e)
{
    PopulateStorageSpaceList();
}

private void PopulateStorageSpaceList()
{
    lstStorageSpaces.Clear();
    if (!(spaces == null))
    {
        foreach (StorageSpace space in spaces)
        {
            ListViewItem lvItem = new ListViewItem(space.Name, 0);
            lvItem.Tag = space.BookList;
            lvItem.Name = space.ID.ToString();
            lstStorageSpaces.Items.Add(lvItem);
        }
    }
}
```

If the user clicks on a storage space, we need to be able to read the books contained in that selected space:

```
private void lstStorageSpaces_MouseClick(object sender,
MouseEventArgs e)
{
    ListViewItem selectedStorageSpace =
    lstStorageSpaces.SelectedItems[0];
    int spaceID = selectedStorageSpace.Name.ToInt();
```

```
txtStorageSpaceDescription.Text = (from d in spaces
                                   where d.ID == spaceID
                                   select
                                   d.Description).First();

List<Document> ebookList =
 (List<Document>)selectedStorageSpace.Tag;
PopulateContainedEbooks(ebookList);
}
```

We now need to create the method that will populate the `lstBooks` list view with the books contained in the selected storage space:

```
private void PopulateContainedEbooks(List<Document> ebookList)
{
    lstBooks.Clear();
    ClearSelectedBook();

    if (ebookList != null)
    {
        foreach (Document eBook in ebookList)
        {
            ListViewItem book = new ListViewItem(eBook.Title, 1);
            book.Tag = eBook;
            lstBooks.Items.Add(book);
        }
    }
    else
    {
        ListViewItem book = new ListViewItem("This storage space
        contains no eBooks", 2);
        book.Tag = "";
        lstBooks.Items.Add(book);
    }
}
```

You will notice that each `ListViewItem` is populated with the title of the eBook and the index of an image in an `ImageList` control that I added to the form. To find the images in the GitHub repository, browse to the following path:

https://github.com/PacktPublishing/CSharp7-and-.NET-Core-2.0-Blueprints/tree/master/eBookManager/eBookManager/img

Looking at the **Images Collection Editor**, you will see that I have added them as follows:

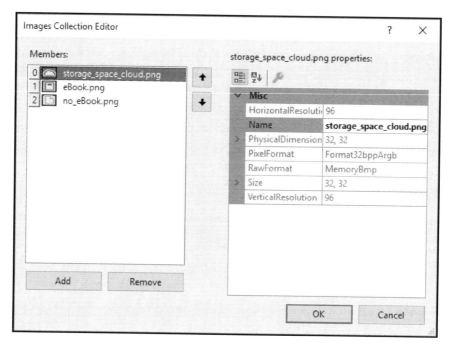

We also need to clear the selected book's details when the selected storage space is changed. I have created two group controls around the file and book details. This code just loops through all the child controls, and if the child control is a textbox, it clears it:

```csharp
private void ClearSelectedBook()
{
    foreach (Control ctrl in gbBookDetails.Controls)
    {
        if (ctrl is TextBox)
            ctrl.Text = "";
    }

    foreach (Control ctrl in gbFileDetails.Controls)
    {
        if (ctrl is TextBox)
            ctrl.Text = "";
    }

    dtLastAccessed.Value = DateTime.Now;
    dtCreated.Value = DateTime.Now;
    dtDatePublished.Value = DateTime.Now;
```

}

The `MenuStrip` that was added to the form has a click event on the `ImportEBooks` menu item. It simply opens up the `ImportBooks` form:

```
private void mnuImportEbooks_Click(object sender, EventArgs e)
{
    ImportBooks import = new ImportBooks();
    import.ShowDialog();
    spaces = spaces.ReadFromDataStore(_jsonPath);
    PopulateStorageSpaceList();
}
```

The following method wraps up the logic to select a specific eBook and populate the file and eBook details on the `eBookManager` form:

```
private void lstBooks_MouseClick(object sender, MouseEventArgs e)
{
    ListViewItem selectedBook = lstBooks.SelectedItems[0];
    if (!String.IsNullOrEmpty(selectedBook.Tag.ToString()))
    {
        Document ebook = (Document)selectedBook.Tag;
        txtFileName.Text = ebook.FileName;
        txtExtension.Text = ebook.Extension;
        dtLastAccessed.Value = ebook.LastAccessed;
        dtCreated.Value = ebook.Created;
        txtFilePath.Text = ebook.FilePath;
        txtFileSize.Text = ebook.FileSize;
        txtTitle.Text = ebook.Title;
        txtAuthor.Text = ebook.Author;
        txtPublisher.Text = ebook.Publisher;
        txtPrice.Text = ebook.Price;
        txtISBN.Text = ebook.ISBN;
        dtDatePublished.Value = ebook.PublishDate;
        txtCategory.Text = ebook.Category;
    }
}
```

Lastly, when the book selected is the one you wish to read, click on the **Read eBook** button to open the file location of the selected eBook:

```
private void btnReadEbook_Click(object sender, EventArgs e)
{
    string filePath = txtFilePath.Text;
    FileInfo fi = new FileInfo(filePath);
    if (fi.Exists)
    {
        Process.Start(Path.GetDirectoryName(filePath));
    }
}
```

This completes the code logic contained in the `eBookManager` application.

You can further modify the code to open the required application for the selected eBook instead of just the file location. In other words, if you click on a PDF document, the application can launch a PDF reader with the document loaded. Lastly, note that the classification has not been implemented in this version of the application.

It is time to fire up the application and test it out.

Running the eBookManager application

When the application starts for the first time, there will be no Virtual Storage Spaces available. To create one, we will need to import some books. Click on the **Import eBooks** menu item:

The **Import eBooks** screen opens where you can add a new storage space and **Select source folder** for eBooks:

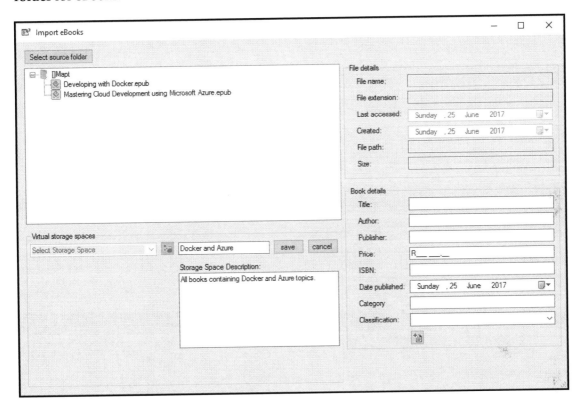

Once you have selected an eBook, add the applicable information regarding the book and save it to the storage space:

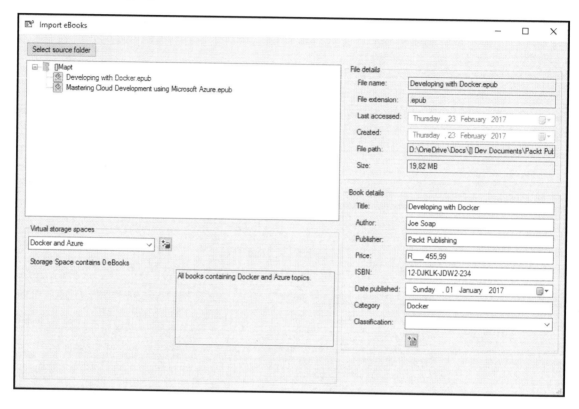

After you have added all the storage spaces and eBooks, you will see the **Virtual Storage Spaces** listed. As you click on a **storage space**, the books it contains will be listed:

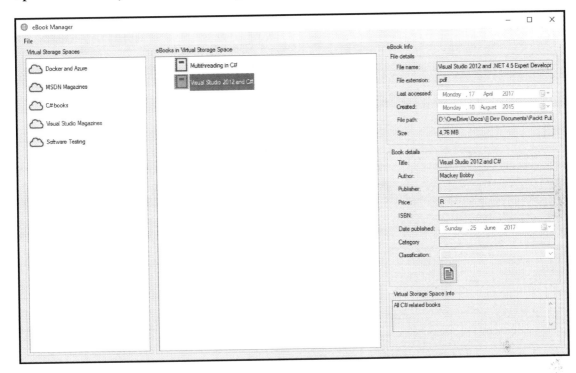

Selecting an eBook and clicking on the **Read eBook** button will open up the file location containing the selected eBook:

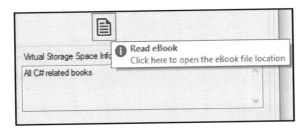

Lastly, let's have a look at the **JSON** file generated for the `eBook Manager` application:

As you can see, the JSON file is quite nicely laid out and it is easily readable.

Summary

C# 7 is a fantastic version of the language. In this chapter, we had a look at out variables. You will remember that with C# 7 we now have the ability to declare the variable right at the point it is passed as an out argument. We then looked at tuples, which provide an elegant way to return multiple values from a method.

Moving, on we looked at expression-bodied properties, which is a more succinct way to write your code. Then, we discussed local functions (one of my favorite features) and its ability to create a helper function inside another function. This makes sense if the function that uses the local function is the only code that uses it.

Pattern matching was up next and are syntactic elements that look to see if a specific value has a certain *shape*. This makes switch statements (for example) nicer to use. Lastly, we looked at throw expressions. This makes it possible to add exception throwing to our expression-bodied members, conditional and null-coalescing expressions.

As you continue to use C# 7, you will discover more opportunities to use these new features. At first (for me anyway) I had to purposefully condition myself to write code using a new feature (out variables being a perfect example).

After a while, the convenience of doing that becomes second nature. You will soon start to automatically write code using the new features available to you.

2

Cricket Score Calculator and Tracker

Object-oriented programming (OOP) is a crucial element of writing .NET applications. Proper OOP ensures that developers can share code easily between projects. You don't have to rewrite code that has already been written. This is called **inheritance**.

A lot has been written throughout the years on the topic of OOP. In fact, doing a search on the internet on the benefits of OOP will return countless results. The fundamental benefits of OOP, however, are the modular approach to writing code, the ease with which code can be shared, and the ability to extend the functionality of shared code.

These little building blocks (or classes) are self-contained units of code that each perform a function. Developers do not need to know what goes on inside the class when they use it. They can just assume that the class will function on its own and will always work. Should the class they implement not provide a specific functionality, the developer is free to extend the functionality of the class.

We will have a look at the features that define OOP, which are:

- Inheritance
- Abstraction
- Encapsulation
- Polymorphism

We will also have a look at:

- Single responsibility
- The open/closed principle

In this chapter, we will have a little fun. We will create an ASP.NET Bootstrap web application that keeps track of the cricket scores of your two favorite teams. It is with this app that the principles of OOP will become evident.

The *Cricket Score Tracker* app can be found on GitHub, and I encourage you to download the source code and make it your own. The GitHub repository URL is—`https://github.com/PacktPublishing/CSharp7-and-.NET-Core-2.0-Blueprints/tree/master/cricketScoreTrack`.

There are so many features that a person can build into an application such as this, but the topic of OOP has only a single chapter in this book to convey this topic. Therefore, the focus is on OOP (more than the hard and fast rules of cricket) and some liberties have been taken with certain functionalities.

Let the games begin!

Setting up the project

Using Visual Studio 2017, we will create an ASP.NET Web Application project. You can call the application anything you like, but I called mine `cricketScoreTrack`. When you click on the new **ASP.NET Web Application** template, you will be presented with a few ASP.NET templates.

The ASP.NET templates are:

- **Empty**
- **Web Forms**
- **MVC**
- **Web API**
- **Single Page Application**
- **Azure API App**
- **Azure Mobile App**

We are just going to select the **Web Forms** template. For this application, we don't need authentication, so don't change this setting:

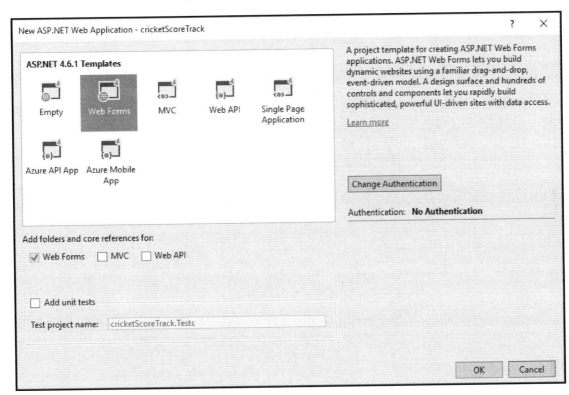

I will assume that you have also downloaded the application from GitHub for this chapter, because you will need it as we discuss the architecture. The URL is—`https://github.com/PacktPublishing/CSharp7-and-.NET-Core-2.0-Blueprints/tree/master/cricketScoreTrack`.

Click on **OK** to create the web application. The project will be created and will look as follows:

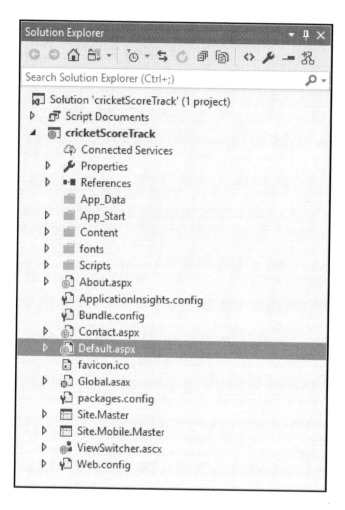

To give you an idea of what we are building, the UI will look as follows:

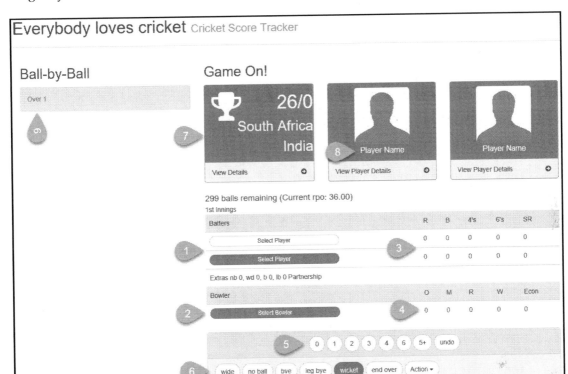

The various sections are as follows:

- Batsmen selection (**1** in the preceding screenshot)
- Bowler selection (**2** in the preceding screenshot)
- Batsmen game statistics—Runs, Balls, 4's, 6's, Strike Rate (**3** in the preceding screenshot)
- Bowler game statistics—Overs, Maidens, Runs, Wickets, Economy (**4** in the preceding screenshot)
- Batsmen runs (**5** in the preceding screenshot)
- Game actions (**6** in the preceding screenshot)
- Game score and teams (**7** in the preceding screenshot)
- Current batsmen details (**8** in the preceding screenshot)
- Runs per ball and over (**9** in the preceding screenshot)

As you can see, there is a lot going on here. There are obviously a lot of areas that you can still expand on. Another fun idea is to have an in-game statistics panel and even a Duckworth-Lewis calculation, if you have the time to try and implement it. I say try, because the actual algorithm of the calculation is a secret.

There are, however, a lot of implementations online, and one of particular interest to me was the article by Sarvashrestha Paliwal, *Azure Business Lead for Microsoft India*. They used machine learning to analyze historical cricket games and thereby provide a continually improving Duckworth-Lewis calculation.

 You can read his article at the following link—https://azure.microsoft.com/en-us/blog/improving-the-d-l-me thod-using-machine-learning/.

Let's have a closer look at the application structure. Expanding the Scripts folder, you will notice that the application uses jQuery and Bootstrap:

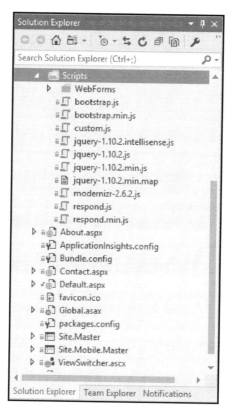

Expanding the `Content` folder, you will see the CSS files in use:

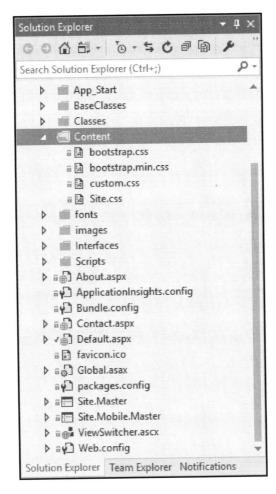

Note that there is a `custom.css` file in this folder that I added:

```
.score {
    font-size: 40px;
}
.team {
    font-size: 30px;
}
.player {
    font-size: 16.5px;
}
.info {
```

```
        font-size: 18px;
    }
    .btn-round-xs {
        border-radius: 11px;
        padding-left: 10px;
        padding-right: 10px;
        width: 100%;
    }
    .btn-round {
        border-radius: 17px;
    }
    .navbar-top-links {
        margin-right: 0;
    }
    .nav {
        padding-left: 0;
        margin-bottom: 0;
        list-style: none;
    }
```

This CSS file basically styles the buttons and some other text font on the form. There is nothing complicated about this CSS. The reason for the Bootstrap, jQuery, JavaScript, and CSS files is to enable the Bootstrap functionality on the web page.

To see Bootstrap in action, we will use Chrome to run the web application.

The version of Chrome used for this book was Version 60.0.3112.90 (Official Build) (64-bit).

Run the Cricket Score Tracker Bootstrap web application by going to **Debug** on the menu and clicking on **Start Without Debugging** or by pressing *Ctrl + F5*. When the web application has loaded in Chrome, press *Ctrl + Shift + I* to open the developer tools:

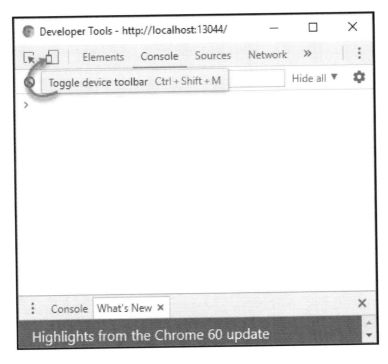

At the top left of the screen, click on the **Toggle device toolbar** button or press *Ctrl + Shift + M.*

Chrome will then render the application as it would look on a mobile device. From the toolbar to the top, you will see that the application has been rendered as it would appear on an iPhone 6 Plus:

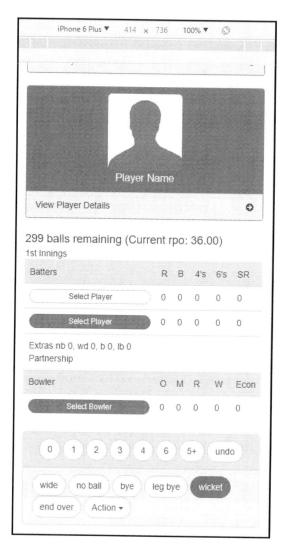

Clicking on the device type, you can change the device you want to render the page for. Changing it to an iPad Pro renders the page accordingly. You can also simulate the rotation of the device:

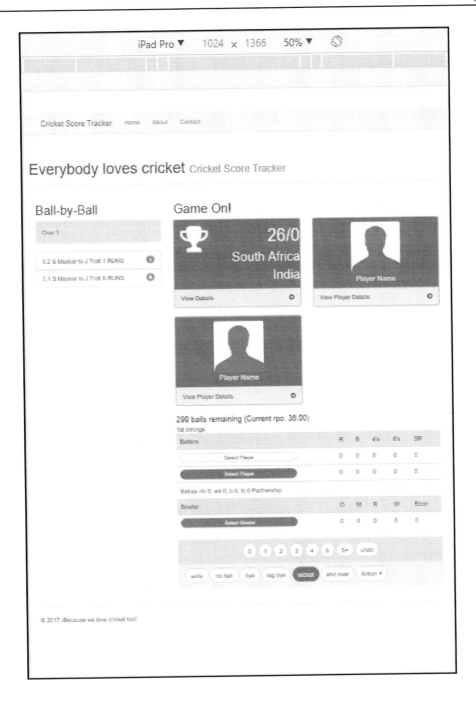

This feature is very powerful and allows modern web developers to test the responsiveness of their web applications. If something doesn't look quite right after you have rendered your application for a particular device, you need to go and investigate where you went wrong.

At the time of writing, the devices supported were:

- BlackBerry Z30 and PlayBook
- Galaxy Note 3, Note II, S3, and S5
- Kindle Fire HDX
- LG Optimus L70
- Laptop with HiDPI screen and MDPI screen
- Laptop with touch
- Microsoft Lumina 550 and 950
- Nexus 7, 6, 5, 4, 10, 5X, and 6P
- Nokia Lumina 520
- Nokia N9
- iPad Mini
- iPhone 4, 5, 6, and 6 Plus
- iPad and iPad Pro

To add devices, go to the bottom of the device menu. Following the separator, there is an **Edit...** menu item. Clicking that will take you to the **Emulated Devices** screen.

Looking at the **Emulated Devices** screen, you will notice that there are additional **Settings** to the right of the form:

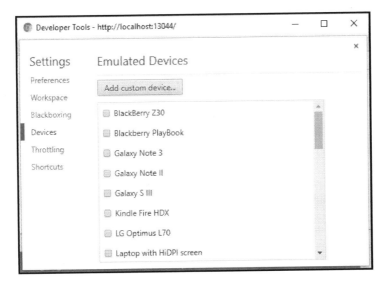

One that stands out for a developer should be the **Throttling** setting:

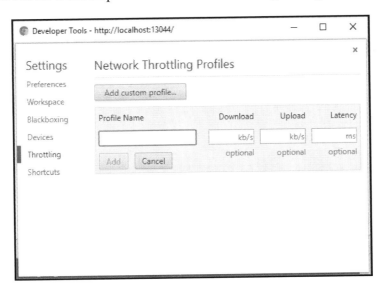

As the name suggests, **Throttling** allows you to test your application as if it were running on a slower connection. You can then test functionality and ensure that your web application is as optimized as possible to allow it to work well on slower connections.

Swing back to the **Solution Explorer** in Visual Studio 2017 and have a look at the folders called `BaseClasses`, `Classes`, and `Interfaces`:

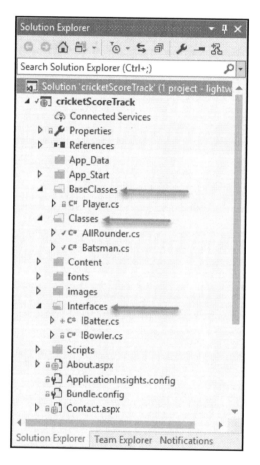

These folders contain the crux of this whole chapter. It is here where we will see what OOP is all about and how OOP works to provide a better approach to modeling a real-world scenario (a cricket match) in code.

Object-oriented programming

As briefly mentioned earlier, OOP provides a modular approach to writing self-contained units of code. The concept of OOP centers around what we call the **four pillars of object-oriented programming**.

They are as follows:

- Abstraction
- Polymorphism
- Inheritance
- Encapsulation

The order doesn't really matter, but I always write the four pillars in this order because I use the mnemonic **A PIE** to remember each one. Let's discuss each of these concepts in more detail.

Abstraction

An abstraction describes what something should do without actually showing you how to do it. According to the Microsoft documentation:

> *"An abstraction is a type that describes a contract but does not provide a full implementation of the contract."*

Included as examples of abstractions are **abstract classes** and **interfaces**. Examples of abstractions in the .NET Framework include `Stream`, `IEnumerable<T>`, and `Object`. If the topic of abstraction seems a bit fuzzy now, don't worry. I will go into much more detail in the section on encapsulation and the difference between encapsulation and abstraction.

Polymorphism

You might hear of polymorphism referred to as the third pillar of OOP. But if I wrote it in that order above, my mnemonic would no longer work!

Polymorphism is a Greek word that refers to something that has many shapes or forms. We will see an example of this in the *Cricket Score Tracking* app later on. Just remember that it has two distinct aspects:

- During runtime, a class that is derived from a base class may be treated as an object of the class it inherits. This is seen in parameters, collections, and arrays.
- The base class can define **virtual methods** that the derived class would then override. The derived class then provides their own implementation of the overridden methods.

Polymorphism is a very powerful feature in OOP.

Compile-time polymorphism versus run-time polymorphism

Before we go further, let me pause for a minute and explain the previous two bullet points on polymorphism.

When we say **compile-time polymorphism**, we are saying that we will be declaring methods with the same name but with different signatures. Therefore, the same method can perform different functions based on the signature (parameters) it receives. This is also known as early binding, overloading, or static binding.

When we say **run-time polymorphism**, we are saying that we will be declaring methods with the same name and with the same signature. In a base class, for example, the method is overridden by the method in a derived class. This is achieved by what we call inheritance and by using the `virtual` or `override` keywords. Run-time polymorphism is also known as *late binding, overriding,* or *dynamic binding*.

Inheritance

The ability to be able to create your own classes that reuse, extend, and modify the behavior that the base class defines is called **inheritance**. Another important aspect to understand is that a derived class can only directly inherit a single base class.

Does this then mean that you can only inherit the behavior defined in a single base class? Well, yes and no. Inheritance is transitive in nature.

To explain this, imagine that you have three classes:

- Person
- Pedestrian
- Driver

The Person class is the base class. Pedestrian inherits from the Person class and therefore Pedestrian inherits the members declared in the Person class. The Driver class inherits from the Pedestrian class and therefore Driver inherits the members declared in Pedestrian and Person:

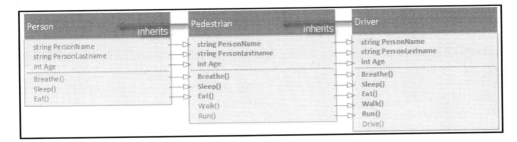

This is what is meant when we say that inheritance is transitive. You can only inherit from a single class, but you get all the members that the class you inherit from, inherits itself. You can only inherit from a single class, but you get all the members that the class you are inheriting from, inherits from its base class. Put another way, the Driver class can only inherit from a single base class (in the preceding image, the Pedestrian class). This means that because the Pedestrian class inherits from the Person class, and the Driver class inherits from the Pedestrian class, that the Driver class also inherits the members in the Person class.

Encapsulation

Simply put, this means that the inner workings of the class (the implementation details) are not necessarily shared with outside code. Remember that we mentioned earlier that a class is something that you just want to use and expect it to work. The class exposes what it needs to to the calling code, but it maintains tight control over the inner workings it implements.

You can, therefore, hide the variables, properties, and methods by scoping them as private. This way, you protect the data contained inside the class from accidental corruption.

Encapsulation versus abstraction

Let's pause for a minute again to have a look at this concept, as it confuses developers (and it is a bit confusing, so examples help a lot). Part of the problem stems from the definitions:

- **Abstraction**: only showing what is necessary
- **Encapsulation**: hiding complexity

If we had to think of a basic class to encrypt some text, we'd need to take a minute to decide exactly what the class must do. I would imagine that the class needs to:

- Take a string value for the text
- Have a method to encrypt the text

So, let's code this:

```
public class EncryptionHelper
{
  public string TextToEncrypt = "";
  public void Encrypt()
  {
  }
}
```

I also know that if I wanted to encrypt some text, that I would need a randomly generated byte array to salt the text to be encrypted. Let's add that method:

```
public class EncryptionHelper
{
  public string TextToEncrypt = "";
  public void Encrypt()
  {
  }
  public string GenerateSalt()
  {
    Return "";
  }
}
```

Now, taking a look at the class again, I realize that the encrypted text will need to be saved in a database. So, I add a method to do just that:

```
public class EncryptionHelper
{
  public string TextToEncrypt = "";
  public void Encrypt()
```

```
  {
  }
  public string GenerateSalt()
  {
     return "";
  }
  public void SaveToDatabase()
  {
  }
}
```

If we had to implement this class, it would look something like this:

```
EncryptionHelper encr = new EncryptionHelper();
encr.TextToEncrypt = "Secret Text";
string salt = encr.GenerateSalt();
encr.Encrypt();
encr.SaveToDatabase();
```

Okay, but now we see that there is a problem. The salt needs to be used by the encryption method, so naturally we would think to add a parameter to the Encrypt() method to take the salt. We would therefore do the following:

```
public void Encrypt(string salt)
{
}
```

It is here that the code starts to become a bit blurred. We are calling a method on the class to generate a salt. We are then passing the salt we generated from the class, back to the class. Imagine a class with many more methods. Which methods need to be called when, and in what order?

So, let's take a step back and think. What exactly are we wanting to do here? We want to encrypt some text. Therefore, we just want the following:

```
public class EncryptionHelper
{
   public string TextToEncrypt = "";
   public void Encrypt()
   {
   }
}
```

This is what we call **abstraction**. Looking back at the definition of abstraction, what we are doing in code fits with the definition because we are only showing what is necessary.

Then what about the other methods in the class? Well, quite simply put...make them `private`. The developer implementing your class does not need to know how to encrypt a string of text. The developer implementing your class just wants to encrypt the string and have it saved. The code can then be **encapsulated** as follows:

```
public class EncryptionHelper
{
  public string TextToEncrypt = "";
  public void Encrypt()
  {
    string salt = GenerateSalt();
    // Encrypt the text in the TextToEncrypt variable
    SaveToDatabase();
  }
  private string GenerateSalt()
  {
    return "";
  }
  private void SaveToDatabase()
  {
  }
}
```

The code that calls the encrypt class is now also much simpler. It looks like this:

```
EncryptionHelper encr = new EncryptionHelper();
encr.TextToEncrypt = "Secret Text";
encr.Encrypt();
```

Again, this fits with the definition of **encapsulation**, which is to hide complexity.

 Please note that the code in the preceding encryption example does not have any implementation. I was only illustrating a concept here. You are free to add your own implementation, should you want to.

Lastly, do not confuse abstraction with abstract classes. These are different things. Abstraction is a way of thinking. We will take a look at abstract classes in the next section.

So, take a 5-minute break, grab some fresh air or a cup of coffee, come back, and buckle up! It's about to get interesting.

Classes in Cricket Score Tracker

Taking what we have already learned about the four pillars of OOP, we will have a look at the areas in our application that make use of these concepts to provide the building blocks of *Cricket Score Tracker*.

Abstract classes

Open up the BaseClasses folder and double click on the Player.cs file. You will see the following code:

```
namespace cricketScoreTrack.BaseClasses
{
    public abstract class Player
    {
        public abstract string FirstName { get; set; }
        public abstract string LastName { get; set; }
        public abstract int Age { get; set; }
        public abstract string Bio { get; set; }
    }
}
```

This is our **abstract class**. The abstract modifier in the class declaration and the properties tells us that this thing we are going to modify has missing or incomplete implementation. It, therefore, is only intended for use as a base class. Any member marked as abstract must be implemented by classes that are derived from our Player abstract class.

The abstract modifier is used with:

- Classes
- Methods
- Properties
- Indexers
- Events

If we had to include a method called CalculatePlayerRank() in our abstract Player class, then we would need to provide an implementation of this method in any class that is derived from Player.

Therefore, in the `Player` abstract class, this method would be defined as follows:

```
abstract public int CalculatePlayerRank();
```

In any derived classes, Visual Studio 2017 will be running code analyzers to determine if all the members of the abstract class have been implemented by the derived classes. When you let Visual Studio 2017 implement the abstract class in a derived class, it is defaulted with `NotImplementedException()` in the method body:

```
public override int CalculatePlayerRank()
{
    throw new NotImplementedException();
}
```

This is done because you haven't actually provided any implementation for the `CalculatePlayerRank()` method yet. To do this, you need to replace `throw new NotImplementedException();` with actual working code to calculate the rank of the current player.

 It is interesting to note is that while `NotImplementedException()` is within the body of the `CalculatePlayerRank()` method, it does not warn you that the method isn't returning an int value.

Abstract classes can be seen as a blueprint of what needs to be done. The way you do it is up to you as a developer.

Interfaces

Open up the `Interfaces` folder and have a look at the `IBatter.cs` and `IBowler.cs` files. The `IBatter` interface looks as follows:

```
namespace cricketScoreTrack.Interfaces
{
    interface IBatter
    {
        int BatsmanRuns { get; set; }
        int BatsmanBallsFaced { get; set; }
        int BatsmanMatch4s { get; set; }
        int BatsmanMatch6s { get; set; }
        double BatsmanBattingStrikeRate { get; }
    }
}
```

Looking at the `IBowler` interface, you will see the following:

```
namespace cricketScoreTrack.Interfaces
{
    interface IBowler
    {
        double BowlerSpeed { get; set; }
        string BowlerType { get; set; }
        int BowlerBallsBowled { get; set; }
        int BowlerMaidens { get; set; }
        int BowlerWickets { get; set; }
        double BowlerStrikeRate { get; }
        double BowlerEconomy { get; }
        int BowlerRunsConceded { get; set; }
        int BowlerOversBowled { get; set; }
    }
}
```

An interface will only contain the signatures of methods, properties, events, or indexers. If we had to add a method to the interface to calculate the spin of the ball, it would look something like this:

```
void CalculateBallSpin();
```

On the implementation, we would see the code implemented as follows:

```
void CalculateBallSpin()
{
}
```

The next logical question would probably be what the difference is between an **abstract class** and an **interface**. Let's turn to the excellent Microsoft documentation at—https://docs.microsoft.com/en-us/.

After opening Microsoft Docs, try the dark theme. The theme toggle is to the right of the page, just below the Comments, Edit, and Share links. It's really great for us night owls.

Microsoft sums up an interface very nicely with the following statement:

An interface is like an abstract base class. Any class or struct that implements the interface must implement all its members.

Think of interfaces as verbs; that is to say, interfaces describe some sort of action. Something that a cricket player does. In this case, the actions are batting and bowling. The interfaces in *Cricket Score Tracker* are therefore IBatter and IBowler. Note that convention dictates that interfaces begin with the letter I.

Abstract classes on the other hand, act as a noun that tells you what something is. We have Batsmen and All-Rounders. We can say that both these cricketers are players. That is the common noun that describes the cricketers in a cricket match. Therefore, the Player abstract class makes sense here.

Classes

The classes used in the *Cricket Score Tracker* app are then created in the Classes folder. Here you will see a Batsman class and an AllRounder class. For the sake of simplicity, I only created these two classes. In cricket, all bowlers must bat, but not all batsmen have to bowl. You then get bowlers who can bowl and bat equally well, and they are defined as all-rounders. This is what I have modeled here.

Let's have a look at the Batsman class first. We want a batsman to have the abstract properties of a player, but he must also be a batter. Our class, therefore, inherits the Player base class (remember, we can only inherit from a single class) and implements the properties of the IBatter interface:

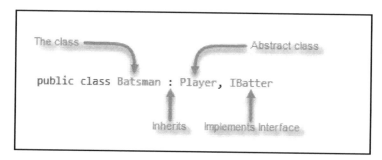

The class definition, therefore, reads as a Batsman public class, inherits a Player, and implements the IBatter interface. The Batsman class, therefore, looks as follows:

```
using cricketScoreTrack.BaseClasses;
using cricketScoreTrack.Interfaces;

namespace cricketScoreTrack.Classes
{
```

```
public class Batsman : Player, IBatter
{
    #region Player
    public override string FirstName { get; set; }
    public override string LastName { get; set; }
    public override int Age { get; set; }
    public override string Bio { get; set; }
    #endregion

    #region IBatsman
    public int BatsmanRuns { get; set; }
    public int BatsmanBallsFaced { get; set; }
    public int BatsmanMatch4s { get; set; }
    public int BatsmanMatch6s { get; set; }

    public double BatsmanBattingStrikeRate => (BatsmanRuns * 100)
      / BatsmanBallsFaced;

    public override int CalculatePlayerRank()
    {
        return 0;
    }
    #endregion
}
}
```

Note that the Batsman class implements the properties of the abstract class and the interface. Also note that, at this point in time, I do not want to add an implementation for the CalculatePlayerRank() method.

Let's have a look at the AllRounder class. We want the all-rounders to also have the abstract properties of a player, but they must also be a batter and a bowler. Our class, therefore, inherits the Player base class but now implements the properties of the IBatter and the IBowler interfaces:

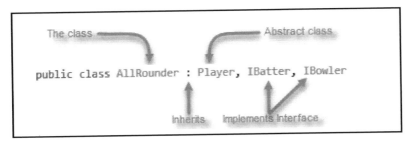

The class definition, therefore, reads as an `AllRounder` public class, inherits a `Player`, and implements the `IBatter` and `IBowler` interfaces. The `AllRounder` class, therefore, looks as follows:

```
using cricketScoreTrack.BaseClasses;
using cricketScoreTrack.Interfaces;
using System;

namespace cricketScoreTrack.Classes
{
    public class AllRounder : Player, IBatter, IBowler
    {
        #region enums
        public enum StrikeRate { Bowling = 0, Batting = 1 }
        #endregion

        #region Player
        public override string FirstName { get; set; }
        public override string LastName { get; set; }
        public override int Age { get; set; }
        public override string Bio { get; set; }
        #endregion

        #region IBatsman
        public int BatsmanRuns { get; set; }
        public int BatsmanBallsFaced { get; set; }
        public int BatsmanMatch4s { get; set; }
        public int BatsmanMatch6s { get; set; }
        public double BatsmanBattingStrikeRate =>
         CalculateStrikeRate(StrikeRate.Batting);
        #endregion

        #region IBowler
        public double BowlerSpeed { get; set; }
        public string BowlerType { get; set; }
        public int BowlerBallsBowled { get; set; }
        public int BowlerMaidens { get; set; }
        public int BowlerWickets { get; set; }
        public double BowlerStrikeRate =>
         CalculateStrikeRate(StrikeRate.Bowling);
        public double BowlerEconomy => BowlerRunsConceded /
         BowlerOversBowled;
        public int BowlerRunsConceded  { get; set; }
        public int BowlerOversBowled { get; set; }
        #endregion
        private double CalculateStrikeRate(StrikeRate strikeRateType)
        {
```

```
        switch (strikeRateType)
        {
            case StrikeRate.Bowling:
                return (BowlerBallsBowled / BowlerWickets);
            case StrikeRate.Batting:
                return (BatsmanRuns * 100) / BatsmanBallsFaced;
            default:
                throw new Exception("Invalid enum");
        }
    }

    public override int CalculatePlayerRank()
    {
        return 0;
    }
    }
}
```

You will notice once again that I didn't add in any implementation for the
CalculatePlayerRank() method. Because the abstract class defines this method, all
classes that inherit from the abstract class must implement this method.

You now also see that this AllRounder class must implement the properties of both
IBowler and IBatter.

Putting it all together

Now, let's have a look how we use the classes to create the *Cricket Score Tracker* app. The
buttons below the **Batters** section and **Bowler** section are used to select batsmen and a
bowler for the specific over.

While each button is taken care of by its own click event, they all call the exact same method. We will have a look at how that is accomplished in a moment:

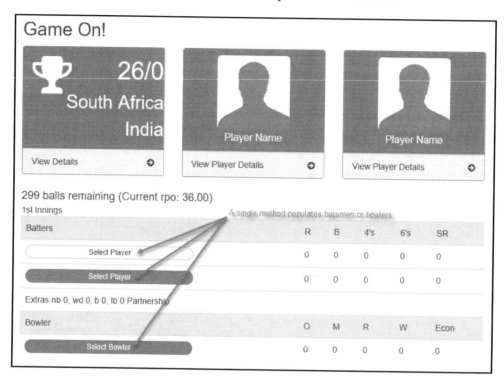

Clicking on either button under the **Batsmen** section will display a modal dialog with a drop-down list populated with the batsmen in the team:

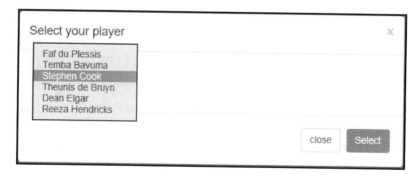

Similarly, when we click on the **Select Bowler** button, we will see the exact same modal dialog screen displayed. This time, however, it will be a list of bowlers displayed for selection:

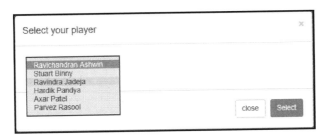

Selecting players from the drop-down lists will populate the text on the button clicked with that player's name. This then sets up the current over with the players involved.

 Take note that we are talking in terms of the classes here. We have players, but they can be batsmen or all-rounders (bowlers).

Each player will be either a batsman or a bowler (`AllRounder` class):

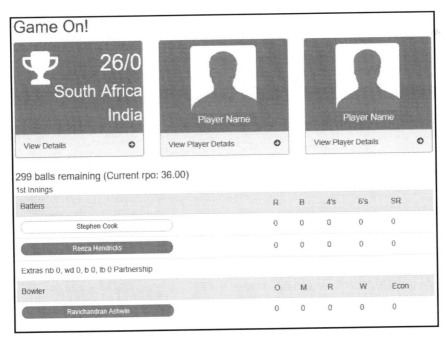

So how did we manage to make a single method return two different players? I used a method called `GeneratePlayerList()`. This method is responsible for creating the player list in the modal dialog that pops up. That is all that method is responsible for. In other words, it performs no other function apart from generating the player list.

Let's look at how the `Default.aspx.cs` file is created. For simplicity's sake, I just created two lists for each team. I also created an `enum` for the player selection. The code looks as follows:

```
public enum SelectedPlayer { Batsman1 = 1, Batsman2 = 2, Bowler = 3 }
List<Player> southAfrica;
List<Player> india;
```

In reality, however, you would probably make the list names `team1` and `team2`, and allow the user to select the teams from a setup screen for this game. I have not added this functionality as I am merely trying to illustrate the concepts of OOP here.

In `Page_Load`, I then populate the lists with players, as follows:

```
protected void Page_Load(object sender, EventArgs e)
{
    southAfrica = Get_SA_Players();
    india = Get_India_Players();
}
```

Again, for simplicity, I have hard-coded the player names and manually added them to the lists.

 The `Get_India_Players()` method is identical to that of the `Get_SA_Players()` method. You can then just copy the method and change the names to your favorite cricket players or favorite cricket teams.

In reality, you would probably read this from a database of teams and players. So instead of `Get_SA_Players()` and `Get_India_Players()`, you would have a single `Get_Players()` method that would be responsible for reading the players into the lists.

For now, looking at the `Get_SA_Players()` method, we simply do the following:

```
private List<Player> Get_SA_Players()
{
    List<Player> players = new List<Player>();

    #region Batsmen
    Batsman b1 = new Batsman();
```

```
        b1.FirstName = "Faf";
        b1.LastName = "du Plessis";
        b1.Age = 33;
        players.Add(b1);
        // Rest omitted for brevity
        #endregion

        #region All Rounders
        AllRounder ar1 = new AllRounder();
        ar1.FirstName = "Farhaan";
        ar1.LastName = "Behardien";
        ar1.Age = 33;
        players.Add(ar1);
        // Rest omitted for brevity
        #endregion

        return players;
    }
```

Notice now that the `players` list is of type `List<Player>`, and that we are adding `Batsman` and `AllRounder` types to it. This is what the term **polymorphism** means. Remember that one of the aspects of polymorphism we mentioned earlier was:

> *During run time, a class that is derived from a base class may be treated as an object of the class it inherits. This is seen in parameters, collections or arrays.*

Therefore, because `Batsman` and `AllRounder` inherit from the `Player` abstract class, they are treated as objects of `Player` for the `List<Player>`.

 If you swing back to the section on polymorphism earlier in the chapter, you will see that this is an example of run-time polymorphism.

Moving back to the logic to select the batsman or bowler, we look to a method to generate the player list called `GeneratePlayerList()`:

```
private void GeneratePlayerList(List<Player> team, Type type)
{
    List<string> players = new List<string>();

    if (type == typeof(Batsman))
        players = (from r in team.OfType<Batsman>()
                    select $"{r.FirstName} {r.LastName}").ToList();

    if (type == typeof(AllRounder))
```

```
        players = (from r in team.OfType<AllRounder>()
                    select $"{r.FirstName} {r.LastName}").ToList();

    int liVal = 0;
    if (ddlPlayersSelect.Items.Count > 0)
        ddlPlayersSelect.Items.Clear();

    foreach (string player in players)
    {
        ListItem li = new ListItem();
        li.Text = player.ToString();
        li.Value = liVal.ToString();
        ddlPlayersSelect.Items.Add(li);

        liVal += 1;
    }
}
```

You will notice that the method takes a `List<Player>` argument as well as a `Type`. The method checks whether `type` is a `Batsman` or `AllRounder` and based on that, reads the first and last names of the players in the list.

 I believe that this method can be simplified even further, but I wanted to illustrate the concept of polymorphism at work.

The actual aim is to try and write the least amount of code for the maximum required effect. As a rule of thumb, some developers maintain that if a method's length is longer than the code page you are looking at in the IDE, you need to do some refactoring.

Having less code and smaller methods allows the code to be easier to read and understand. It also allows better maintainability of that code because smaller sections of code are easier to debug. In fact, you might experience fewer bugs because you are writing smaller, more manageable pieces of code.

Many years ago, I was part of a team that worked on a project for a large corporation in Cape Town. They had a systems architect called *Uthmaan Hendrix*. I will never forget this guy. He was the humblest bloke I had ever come across. The documentation he created for the system we worked on was simply incredible. It took almost all the think work out of the code we had to write. The developers didn't have to decide how to architect the project at all.

This project implemented SOLID principles, and understanding the code was really easy. I still have a copy of that document. I still refer to it from time to time. Unfortunately, not all developers have the luxury of having a dedicated systems architect on the project they are working with. It is, however, good for developers to understand what the SOLID design principles are.

SOLID design principles

This brings us to another interesting concept in OOP called **SOLID** design principles. These design principles apply to any OOP design and are intended to make software easier to understand, more flexible, and easily maintainable.

The term SOLID is a mnemonic for:

- Single responsibility principle
- Open/closed principle
- Liskov substitution principle
- Interface segregation principle
- Dependency inversion principle

In this chapter, we will only take a look at the first two principles—the **single responsibility principle** and the **open/closed principle**. Let's look at the single responsibility principle next.

Single responsibility principle

Simply put, a module or class should have the following characteristics only:

- It should do one single thing and only have a single reason to change
- It should do its one single thing well
- The functionality provided needs to be entirely encapsulated by that class or module

What is meant when saying that a module must be responsible for a single thing? The Google definition of a module is:

"Each of a set of standardized parts or independent units that can be used to construct a more complex structure, such as an item of furniture or a building."

From this, we can understand that a module is a simple building block. It can be used or reused to create something bigger and more complex when used with other modules. In C# therefore, the module does closely resemble a class, but I will go so far as to say that a module can also be extended to be a method.

The function that the class or module performs can only be one thing. That is to say that it has a **narrow responsibility**. It is not concerned with anything else other than doing that one thing it was designed to do.

If we had to apply the single responsibility principle to a person, then that person would be only a software developer, for example. But what if a software developer also was a doctor and a mechanic and a school teacher? Would that person be effective in any of those roles? That would contravene the single responsibility principle. The same is true for code.

Having a look at our `AllRounder` and `Batsman` classes, you will notice that in `AllRounder`, we have the following code:

```
private double CalculateStrikeRate(StrikeRate strikeRateType)
{
    switch (strikeRateType)
    {
        case StrikeRate.Bowling:
            return (BowlerBallsBowled / BowlerWickets);
        case StrikeRate.Batting:
            return (BatsmanRuns * 100) / BatsmanBallsFaced;
        default:
            throw new Exception("Invalid enum");
    }
}

public override int CalculatePlayerRank()
{
    return 0;
}
```

In `Batsman`, we have the following code:

```
public double BatsmanBattingStrikeRate => (BatsmanRuns * 100) /
BatsmanBallsFaced;

public override int CalculatePlayerRank()
{
    return 0;
}
```

Using what we have learned about the single responsibility principle, we notice that there is an issue here. To illustrate the problem, let's compare the code side by side:

```
2 references | dirkstrauss, 6 days ago | 1 author, 1 change
public double BatsmanBattingStrikeRate => (BatsmanRuns * 100) / BatsmanBallsFaced;

2 references | dirkstrauss, 13 hours ago | 1 author, 1 change
public override int CalculatePlayerRank()
{
    return 0;
}

references | dirkstrauss, 6 days ago | 1 author, 1 change
private double CalculateStrikeRate(StrikeRate strikeRateType)
{
    switch (strikeRateType)
    {
        case StrikeRate.Bowling:
            // Balls Bowled / Wickets Taken
            return (BowlerBallsBowled / BowlerWickets);
        case StrikeRate.Batting:
            // (Runs Scored x 100) / Balls Faced
            return (BatsmanRuns * 100) / BatsmanBallsFaced;
        default:
            throw new Exception("Invalid enum");
    }
}

2 references | dirkstrauss, 13 hours ago | 1 author, 1 change
public override int CalculatePlayerRank()
{
    return 0;
}
```

We are essentially repeating code in the `Batsman` and `AllRounder` classes. This doesn't really bode well for single responsibility, does it? I mean, the one principle is that a class must only have a single function to perform. At the moment, both the `Batsman` and `AllRounder` classes are taking care of calculating strike rates. They also both take care of calculating the player rank. They even both have exactly the same code for calculating the strike rate of a batsman!

The problem comes in when the strike rate calculation changes (not that it easily would, but let's assume it does). We now know that we have to change the calculation in both places. As soon as the developer changes one calculation and not the other, a bug is introduced into our application.

Let's simplify our classes. In the `BaseClasses` folder, create a new abstract class called `Statistics`. The code should look as follows:

```
namespace cricketScoreTrack.BaseClasses
{
    public abstract class Statistics
    {
        public abstract double CalculateStrikeRate(Player player);
        public abstract int CalculatePlayerRank(Player player);
    }
}
```

In the `Classes` folder, create a new derived class called `PlayerStatistics` (that is to say it inherits from the `Statistics` abstract class). The code should look as follows:

```
using cricketScoreTrack.BaseClasses;
using System;

namespace cricketScoreTrack.Classes
{
    public class PlayerStatistics : Statistics
    {
        public override int CalculatePlayerRank(Player player)
        {
            return 1;
        }
        public override double CalculateStrikeRate(Player player)
        {
            switch (player)
            {
                case AllRounder allrounder:
                    return (allrounder.BowlerBallsBowled /
                    allrounder.BowlerWickets);
                case Batsman batsman:
                    return (batsman.BatsmanRuns * 100) /
                    batsman.BatsmanBallsFaced;
                default:
                    throw new ArgumentException("Incorrect argument
                    supplied");
            }
        }
    }
}
```

You will see that the `PlayerStatistics` class is now solely responsible for calculating player statistics for the player's rank and the player's strike rate.

 You will see that I have not included much of an implementation for calculating the player's rank. I briefly commented the code on GitHub for this method on how a player's rank is determined. It is quite a complicated calculation and differs for batsmen and bowlers. I have therefore omitted it for the purposes of this chapter on OOP.

Your **Solution** should now look as follows:

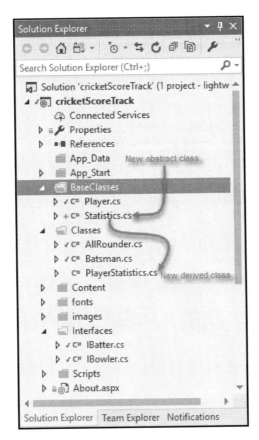

Swing back over to your `Player` abstract class and remove `abstract public int CalculatePlayerRank();` from the class. In the `IBowler` interface, remove the `double BowlerStrikeRate { get; }` property. In the `IBatter` interface, remove the `double BatsmanBattingStrikeRate { get; }` property.

In the `Batsman` class, remove `public double BatsmanBattingStrikeRate` and `public override int CalculatePlayerRank()` from the class. The code in the `Batsman` class will now look as follows:

```
using cricketScoreTrack.BaseClasses;
using cricketScoreTrack.Interfaces;

namespace cricketScoreTrack.Classes
{
    public class Batsman : Player, IBatter
    {
        #region Player
        public override string FirstName { get; set; }
        public override string LastName { get; set; }
        public override int Age { get; set; }
        public override string Bio { get; set; }
        #endregion

        #region IBatsman
        public int BatsmanRuns { get; set; }
        public int BatsmanBallsFaced { get; set; }
        public int BatsmanMatch4s { get; set; }
        public int BatsmanMatch6s { get; set; }
        #endregion
    }
}
```

Looking at the `AllRounder` class, remove the `public enum StrikeRate { Bowling = 0, Batting = 1 }` enum as well as the `public double BatsmanBattingStrikeRate` and `public double BowlerStrikeRate` properties.

Lastly, remove the `private double CalculateStrikeRate(StrikeRate strikeRateType)` and `public override int CalculatePlayerRank()` methods. The code for the `AllRounder` class now looks as follows:

```
using cricketScoreTrack.BaseClasses;
using cricketScoreTrack.Interfaces;
using System;

namespace cricketScoreTrack.Classes
{
    public class AllRounder : Player, IBatter, IBowler
    {
        #region Player
        public override string FirstName { get; set; }
        public override string LastName { get; set; }
```

```
        public override int Age { get; set; }
        public override string Bio { get; set; }
        #endregion

        #region IBatsman
        public int BatsmanRuns { get; set; }
        public int BatsmanBallsFaced { get; set; }
        public int BatsmanMatch4s { get; set; }
        public int BatsmanMatch6s { get; set; }
        #endregion

        #region IBowler
        public double BowlerSpeed { get; set; }
        public string BowlerType { get; set; }
        public int BowlerBallsBowled { get; set; }
        public int BowlerMaidens { get; set; }
        public int BowlerWickets { get; set; }
        public double BowlerEconomy => BowlerRunsConceded /
          BowlerOversBowled;
        public int BowlerRunsConceded  { get; set; }
        public int BowlerOversBowled { get; set; }
        #endregion
    }
}
```

Looking back at our `AllRounder` and `Batsman` classes, the code is clearly simplified. It is definitely more flexible and is starting to look like a well-constructed set of classes. Give your solution a rebuild and make sure that it is all working.

Open/closed principle

Previously, we had a look at the **single responsibility principle**. Hand in hand with this is the **open/closed principle**.

Bertrand Meyer stated that software entities (classes, modules, functions, and so on):

- Should be open for extension
- Should be closed for modification

What exactly does this mean? Let's take the `PlayerStatistics` class as an example. Inside this class, you know that we have a method to calculate the strike rate of a particular player. This is included in the class because it inherits from the `Statistics` abstract class. That is correct, but the fact that the `CalculateStrikeRate(Player player)` method caters for two player types (all-rounders and batsmen) is already a hint of a problem.

Let's assume that we have introduced new player types—different bowler types (for example, fast bowlers and spin bowlers). In order for us to accommodate the new player type, we must change the code in the CalculateStrikeRate() method.

What if we wanted to pass through a collection of batsmen to calculate the average strike rate between all of them? We would need to modify the CalculateStrikeRate() method again to accommodate this. As time goes by and the complexities increase, it will become very difficult to keep on catering for different player types that need the strike rate calculation. This means that our CalculateStrikeRate() method is **open for modification** and **closed for extension**. This is in contravention of the principles stated previously in the bullet list.

So, what can we do to fix this? In truth, we are already halfway there. Start by creating a new Bowler class in the Classes folder:

```
using cricketScoreTrack.BaseClasses;
using cricketScoreTrack.Interfaces;

namespace cricketScoreTrack.Classes
{
    public class Bowler : Player, IBowler
    {
        #region Player
        public override string FirstName { get; set; }
        public override string LastName { get; set; }
        public override int Age { get; set; }
        public override string Bio { get; set; }
        #endregion

        #region IBowler
        public double BowlerSpeed { get; set; }
        public string BowlerType { get; set; }
        public int BowlerBallsBowled { get; set; }
        public int BowlerMaidens { get; set; }
        public int BowlerWickets { get; set; }
        public double BowlerEconomy => BowlerRunsConceded /
          BowlerOversBowled;
        public int BowlerRunsConceded { get; set; }
        public int BowlerOversBowled { get; set; }
        #endregion
    }
}
```

You can see how easy it is to construct new player types—we have only to tell the class that it needs to inherit the `Player` abstract class and implement the `IBowler` interface.

Next, we need to create new player statistics classes—namely, `BatsmanStatistics`, `BowlerStatistics`, and `AllRounderStatistics`. The code for the `BatsmanStatistics` class will look as follows:

```
using cricketScoreTrack.BaseClasses;
using System;

namespace cricketScoreTrack.Classes
{
    public class BatsmanStatistics : Statistics
    {
        public override int CalculatePlayerRank(Player player)
        {
            return 1;
        }

        public override double CalculateStrikeRate(Player player)
        {
            if (player is Batsman batsman)
            {
                return (batsman.BatsmanRuns * 100) /
                    batsman.BatsmanBallsFaced;
            }
            else
                throw new ArgumentException("Incorrect argument
                    supplied");
        }
    }
}
```

Next, we add the `AllRounderStatistics` class:

```
using cricketScoreTrack.BaseClasses;
using System;

namespace cricketScoreTrack.Classes
{
    public class AllRounderStatistics : Statistics
    {
        public override int CalculatePlayerRank(Player player)
        {
            return 1;
```

```
        }

        public override double CalculateStrikeRate(Player player)
        {
            if (player is AllRounder allrounder)
            {
                return (allrounder.BowlerBallsBowled /
                allrounder.BowlerWickets);
            }
            else
                throw new ArgumentException("Incorrect argument
                supplied");
        }
    }
}
```

Lastly, we add the new player type statistics class called BowlerStatistics:

```
using cricketScoreTrack.BaseClasses;
using System;

namespace cricketScoreTrack.Classes
{
    public class BowlerStatistics : Statistics
    {
        public override int CalculatePlayerRank(Player player)
        {
            return 1;
        }

        public override double CalculateStrikeRate(Player player)
        {
            if (player is Bowler bowler)
            {
                return (bowler.BowlerBallsBowled /
                bowler.BowlerWickets);
            }
            else
                throw new ArgumentException("Incorrect argument
                supplied");
        }
    }
}
```

Moving the responsibility of calculating the strike rates for all players away from the PlayerStatistics class makes our code cleaner and more robust. In fact, the PlayerStatistics class is all but obsolete.

By adding another player type, we were able to easily define the logic of this new player by implementing the correct interface. Our code is smaller and easier to maintain. We can see this by comparing the previous code for `CalculateStrikeRate()` with the new code we wrote.

To illustrate more clearly, take a look at the following code:

```
public override double CalculateStrikeRate(Player player)
{
    switch (player)
    {
        case AllRounder allrounder:
            return (allrounder.BowlerBallsBowled /
                allrounder.BowlerWickets);

        case Batsman batsman:
            return (batsman.BatsmanRuns * 100) /
                batsman.BatsmanBallsFaced;

        case Bowler bowler:
            return (bowler.BowlerBallsBowled / bowler.BowlerWickets);

        default:
            throw new ArgumentException("Incorrect argument
                supplied");
    }
}
```

The preceding code is much more complex and less maintainable than the following:

```
public override double CalculateStrikeRate(Player player)
{
    if (player is Bowler bowler)
    {
        return (bowler.BowlerBallsBowled / bowler.BowlerWickets);
    }
    else
        throw new ArgumentException("Incorrect argument supplied");
}
```

The benefit of creating a `BowlerStatistics` class, for example, is that you know that throughout the class we are only dealing with a bowler and nothing else...a single responsibility that is open for extension without having to modify the code.

Summary

While the principles of SOLID programming are great guidelines to follow, very few systems that you come across will actually implement them throughout the application. This is especially true if you inherit a system and that system has been in production for a number of years.

I will admit that I have come across applications designed with SOLID in mind. These were really easy to work on and the bar is set high for other developers in a team to maintain the same level of code quality.

Peer code reviews and a thorough understanding of SOLID principles by every developer on the team ensure that the same level of code is maintained.

This chapter has had a lot going on. Apart from laying the foundation for a really nice *Cricket Score Tracking* app, we have had a look at what OOP really means.

We had a look at abstraction and the difference between abstraction and encapsulation. We discussed polymorphism, and we looked at what run-time polymorphism is versus compile-time polymorphism. We also had a look at inheritance, which was creating a derived class by inheriting a base class.

We then discussed classes, abstract classes (which are not to be confused with abstraction), and interfaces. The difference between abstract classes and interfaces were (hopefully) clearly explained. Remember, an interface acts as a verb or action whereas an abstract class acts as a noun which states what something is.

In the last section, we briefly discussed SOLID design principles and highlighted the single responsibility and open/closed principles.

In the next chapter, we will be delving into cross-platform development using .NET Core. You will see that .NET Core is a very important skill to master and that it will be with us for a long time to come. As .NET Core and the .NET Standard evolve, developers will be empowered to create—well, I will leave that up to you to imagine. The sky's the limit.

3

Cross Platform .NET Core System Info Manager

In this chapter, we will be creating a simple *Information Dashboard* application that displays information about the computer we are running on as well as the weather conditions at the location of that machine. This is done using the IP address, and while perhaps not 100% accurate (seeing as the location given for me was a town or so away), the concept I want to prove here is not location accuracy.

Regarding the application we're creating, we will be doing the following:

- Setting up the application on Windows
- Having a look at the `Startup.cs` file and adding controllers and views
- Running the application on Windows
- Running the application on macOS
- Setting up and running the application on Linux

This chapter is all about what ASP.NET Core is. For those of you who don't know, .NET Core allows us to create applications that will run on Windows, macOS, and Linux.

 .NET Core includes ASP.NET Core and EF Core.

Microsoft defines ASP.NET Core as follows:

"ASP.NET Core is a cross-platform, high-performance, open-source framework for building modern, cloud-based, Internet-connected applications."

Yes, .NET Core is open source. You can find it on GitHub at—https://github.com/dotnet/core. The benefits of using .NET Core are listed on the document site—https://docs.microsoft.com/en-us/aspnet/core/. These are as follows:

- A unified story for building web UI and web APIs
- Integration of modern client-side frameworks and development workflows
- A cloud-ready, environment-based configuration system
- Built-in dependency injection
- A lightweight, high-performance, and modular HTTP request pipeline
- Ability to host on **IIS (Internet Information Services)** or self-host in your own process
- Can run on .NET Core, which supports true side-by-side app versioning
- Tooling that simplifies modern web development
- Ability to build and run on Windows, macOS, and Linux
- Open source and community-focused

 I encourage you to have a look at the Microsoft document site for this topic at—https://docs.microsoft.com/en-us/aspnet/core/.

In reality, ASP.NET Core includes just the NuGet packages applicable to your project. This means smaller and better-performing applications. The use of NuGet will become evident in this chapter.

So, let's get to it. Let's create our first cross-platform ASP.NET Core MVC application next.

Setting up the project on Windows

The first thing we need to do is set up .NET Core 2.0 on our development machine. For the purposes of this book, I am using a Windows PC to illustrate this step but, in reality, you would be able to set up a .NET Core application on macOS or on Linux.

I will be illustrating how to set up .NET Core on Linux later on in this chapter. The process is similar for macOS, but I find that it is a bit trickier on Linux. Therefore, I have opted to show this step by step for Linux.

For macOS, I will show you how to run this application created on a Windows PC. This is the true beauty of .NET Core. It is a truly cross-platform technology capable of performing flawlessly on any of the three platforms (Windows, macOS, and Linux):

1. Point your browser to `https://www.microsoft.com/net/core` and download the .NET Core SDK:

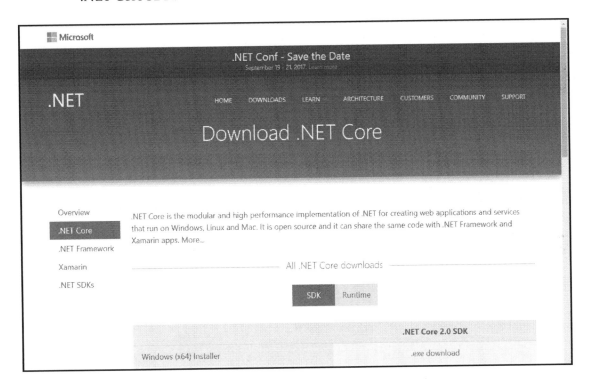

The installation is also quite straightforward. If you have a look at this screen, you will notice similarities between this and the Linux installation. Both have a note that informs you that it will run a command during the installation process to improve the project restore speed:

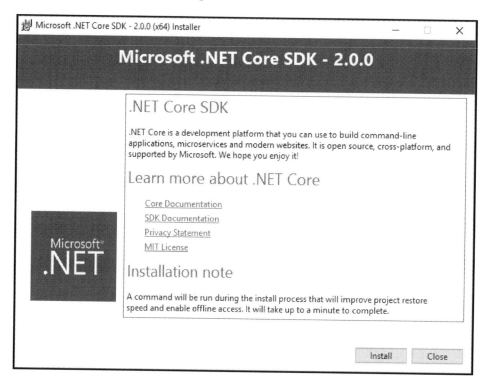

After the installation is complete, you will find some links to resources, documentation, tutorials, and release notes:

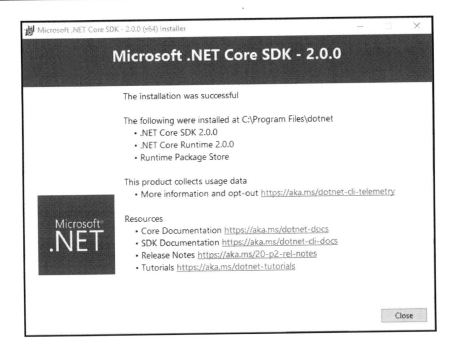

2. Start Visual Studio and create a new **ASP.NET Core Web Application**. Also, select **.NET Framework 4.6.2**:

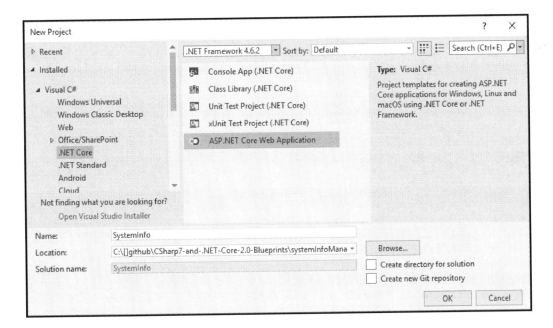

3. On the next screen, select the **Web Application (Model-View-Controller)** from the templates and ensure that you have selected **ASP.NET Core 2.0.** When you are ready, click on the **OK** button to create your ASP.NET Core project:

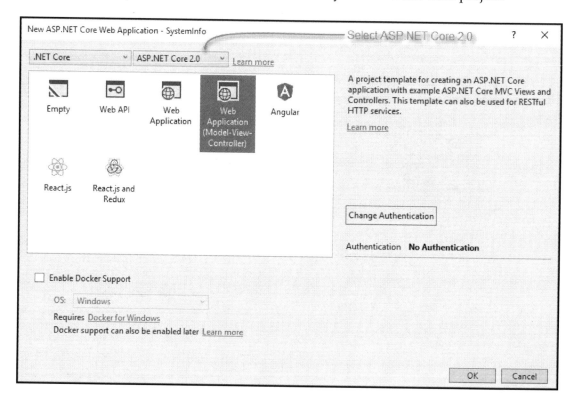

After your project is created, you will see the familiar MVC structure in **Solution Explorer**. The Model-View-Controller architectural pattern takes a bit of getting used to, especially if you are a web developer coming from the traditional ASP.NET Web Forms approach.

I guarantee you that after a while of working with MVC, you will not want to go back to ASP.NET Web Forms. Working with MVC is a lot of fun and in many ways more rewarding, especially if this is still all new to you:

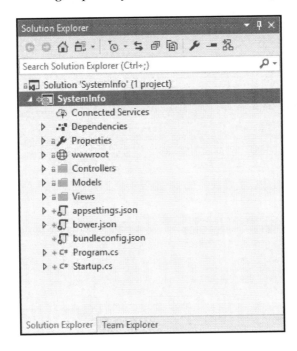

4. As the application is now, you can run it by holding down *Ctrl + F5* or hitting the debug button in Visual Studio. When the application starts up, the browser will display the standard view for your MVC application:

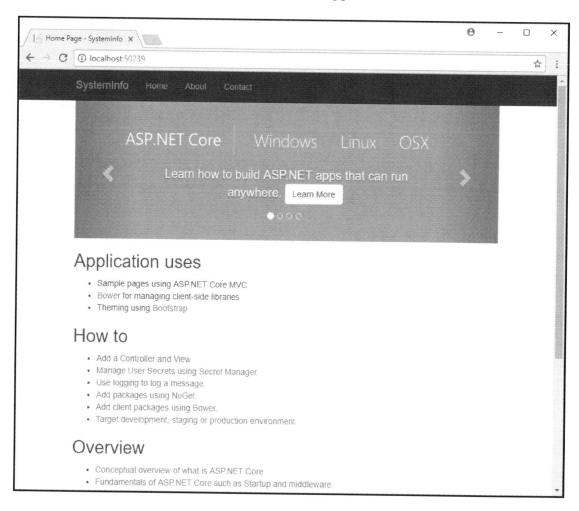

5. Stop the debug session and right-click on the project in **Solution Explorer**. From the context menu that pops up, click on **ManageNuGetPackages...**, which will open the NuGet form.

The first NuGet package we are going to add is Newtonsoft.Json. This is to enable us to work with JSON in our application.

6. Click on the **Install** button to add the latest version to your application:

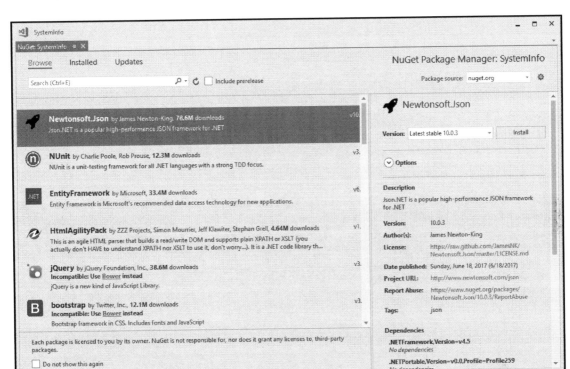

The next NuGet package we are going to add is called `DarkSkyCore`. This is a .NET Standard library for using the Dark Sky API.

I can already see the question marks popping up at the statement **a .NET Standard library**. We are dealing with .NET Core here, right? What, then, is the .NET Standard?

The following website (.NET Core Tutorials) explains it really well (`https://dotnetcoretutorials.com/2017/01/13/net-standard-vs-net-core-wh ats-difference/`):

> *"If you write a library that you want working on .net Core, UWP, Windows Phone and .net Framework, you will need to only use classes that are available on all of those platforms. How do you know what classes are available on all platforms? The .net Standard!"*

The .NET Standard is exactly that, a standard. If you want to target more platforms, you need to target a lower version of the standard. If you want more APIs available to you, you need to target a higher version of the standard. There is a GitHub repository, `https://github.com/dotnet/standard`, that you can check out, and for a handy chart that shows you which version of each platform implements each version of the standard, swing over to—`https://github.com/dotnet/standard/blob/master/docs/versions.md` and check it out.

7. Back to `DarkSkyCore`. Click on the **Install** button to get the latest version:

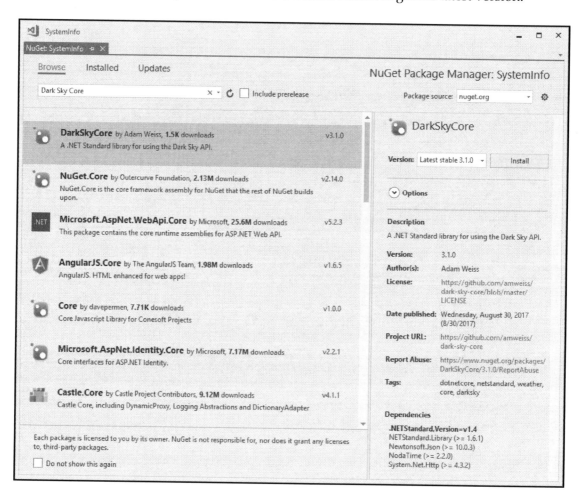

Now that we have our NuGet packages in place, let's have a look at the project in more detail.

The project in detail

Looking at the project after I have added all the required resources, controllers, views, and models, you will notice that I have added some extra folders.

My solution will look as follows:

- _docs (marked **1** in the following screenshot): A personal preference of mine is to keep a folder where I can make notes and keep relevant links I find useful for the project
- climacons(**2**): This is the folder containing the SVG files that will serve as the weather icon
- InformationController(**3**): This is the controller for the project
- InformationModel(**4**): This is the model for the project
- GetInfo(**5**): This is the view corresponding to the GetInfo() method on my controller

Apart from the `Models`, `Views`, and `Controllers` folders, you can place the other folders where you see fit. Just remember to keep references to them relevant to your solution:

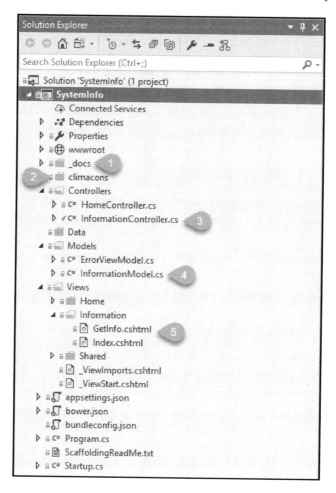

Climacons

Adam Whitcroft has created 75 climatically categorized pictographs for web applications and UI designers. We will need to download them to use in our application:

1. Head on over to `http://adamwhitcroft.com/climacons/` and download the set to include them in your project.

Always remember to provide attribution back to the creators of resources you use in your applications.

2. To include the folder in the project, simply place the SVG files in a folder in your project:

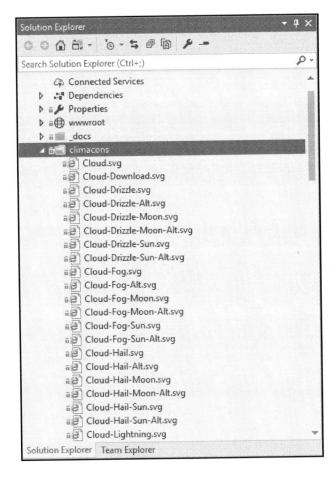

The Startup.cs file

Digging deeper into the code, let's start at the `Startup.cs` file. It should have been created by default as in the following code listings, but for the sake of completeness, I have included it here too.

> As a standard naming convention, the name `Startup` is used for this file. In reality, though, you can call it whatever you like. Just be sure to rename it in the `Program.cs` file too.

The following `using` statements should be included in the `Startup.cs` file:

```
using Microsoft.AspNetCore.Builder;
using Microsoft.AspNetCore.Hosting;
using Microsoft.Extensions.Configuration;
using Microsoft.Extensions.DependencyInjection;
```

The code contained in the `Startup` file will be the same for you and is generated by default when creating the application. We will not be modifying this file for this chapter but, typically, if you wanted to add any middleware, you would come here to the `Configure()` method:

```
public class Startup
{
    public Startup(IConfiguration configuration)
    {
        Configuration = configuration;
    }

    public IConfiguration Configuration { get; }

    // This method gets called by the runtime. Use this method to add
       services to the container.
    public void ConfigureServices(IServiceCollection services)
    {
        services.AddMvc();
    }

    // This method gets called by the runtime. Use this method
      to configure the HTTP request pipeline.
    public void Configure(IApplicationBuilder app, IHostingEnvironment
    env)
    {
        if (env.IsDevelopment())
        {
```

```
        app.UseDeveloperExceptionPage();
        app.UseBrowserLink();
    }
    else
    {
        app.UseExceptionHandler("/Home/Error");
    }

    app.UseStaticFiles();

    app.UseMvc(routes =>
    {
        routes.MapRoute(
            name: "default",
            template: "{controller=Home}/{action=Index}/{id?}");
    });
    }
}
```

The InformationModel class

The model for this application is pretty straightforward. All this will do is expose the values obtained in our controller and provide the view access to these values. To add the model, right-click the Models folder and add a new class called InformationModel:

```
public class InformationModel
{
    public string OperatingSystem { get; set; }
    public string InfoTitle { get; set; }
    public string FrameworkDescription { get; set; }
    public string OSArchitecture { get; set; }
    public string ProcessArchitecture { get; set; }
    public string Memory { get; set; }
    public string IPAddressString { get; set; }
    public string WeatherBy { get; set; }
    public string CurrentTemperature { get; set; }
    public string CurrentIcon { get; set; }
    public string DailySummary { get; set; }
    public string CurrentCity { get; set; }
    public string UnitOfMeasure { get; set; }
}
```

You can then add the properties, as illustrated in the preceding code listing.

The InformationController class

The next step we need to take is to add the controller for our application:

1. Right-click the `Controllers` folder and select **Add**, and then click on **Controller** from the context menu:

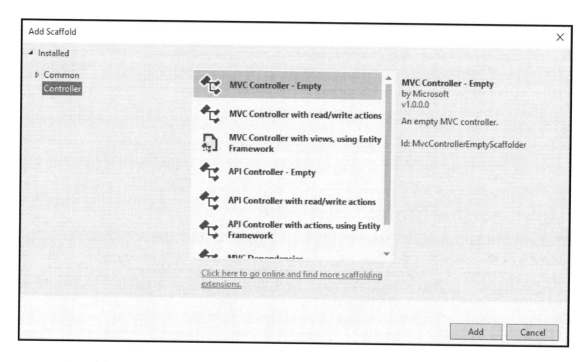

2. Add a new controller called `InformationController` by selecting **MVC Controller - Empty** from the **Add Scaffold** screen. The following `using` statements need to be added to the controller:

```
using DarkSky.Models;
using DarkSky.Services;
using Microsoft.AspNetCore.Hosting;
using Microsoft.AspNetCore.Mvc;
using Newtonsoft.Json;
using System.Globalization;
using System.IO;
using System.Net.Http;
using System.Runtime.InteropServices;
using System.Threading.Tasks;
using static System.Math;
```

The Microsoft documentation says the following:

> *"The IHostingEnvironment service provides the core abstraction for working with environments. This service is provided by the ASP.NET hosting layer, and can be injected into your startup logic via Dependency Injection."*

To read more on this, browse to
`https://docs.microsoft.com/en-us/aspnet/core/fundamentals/environ`
`ments` and check out the documentation.

3. Add the following properties to the preceding constructor in our controller. You will notice that we have added the `IHostingEnvironment` interface to the class:

```
public string PublicIP { get; set; } = "IP Lookup Failed";
public double Long { get; set; }
public double Latt { get; set; }
public string City { get; set; }
public string CurrentWeatherIcon { get; set; }
public string WeatherAttribution { get; set; }
public string CurrentTemp { get; set; } = "undetermined";
public string DayWeatherSummary { get; set; }
public string TempUnitOfMeasure { get; set; }
private readonly IHostingEnvironment _hostEnv;

public InformationController(IHostingEnvironment
hostingEnvironment)
{
    _hostEnv = hostingEnvironment;
}
```

4. Create an empty method called `GetInfo()`. The naming of the controllers (and the methods contained inside them), views, and models is quite deliberate. The MVC design pattern follows a set of conventions that, if adhered to, make binding this altogether quite easy:

```
public IActionResult GetInfo()
{
}
```

5. If you recall, the `Startup` class defined a `MapRoute` call in the `Configure()` method:

```
app.UseMvc(routes =>
{
    routes.MapRoute(
        name: "default",
        template: "{controller=Home}/{action=Index}/{id?}");
});
```

This section of code `{controller=Home}/{action=Index}/{id?}` is called the **route template**. The MVC application uses tokenizing to extract the route values.

This means the following:

- `{controller=Home}` defines the name of the controller with a default of `Home`
- `{action=Index}` defines the method of the controller with a default of `Index`
- Lastly, `{id?}` is defined as an optional by the `?` and can be used to pass around parameters

This means that if I don't give the application a route (or URL), it will use the defaults which have been set up in the `MapRoute` call.

If, however, I give the application a route of `http://localhost:50239/Information/GetInfo`, it will redirect to the `GetInfo()` method on the `InformationController`.

 For more information on routing, go to—`https://docs.microsoft.com/en-us/aspnet/core/mvc/controllers/routing` and read through the documentation.

6. Staying inside our `Controllers` folder, add a class called `LocationInfo`. We will use this to bind the JSON string to it after calling the location info API:

```
public class LocationInfo
{
    public string ip { get; set; }
    public string city { get; set; }
    public string region { get; set; }
```

```
        public string region_code { get; set; }
        public string country { get; set; }
        public string country_name { get; set; }
        public string postal { get; set; }
        public double latitude { get; set; }
        public double longitude { get; set; }
        public string timezone { get; set; }
        public string asn { get; set; }
        public string org { get; set; }
    }
```

To get the location information, you can use one of many location APIs. I used an API over at `https://ipapi.co` to provide the location information for me. The `GetLocationInfo()` method simply calls the API and deserializes the JSON returned into the `LocationInfo` class created a moment ago.

Personally, I think that the name `ipapi` is really clever. It is something one will not easily forget. They also provide a free tier in their pricing which is for 1,000 requests per day. This is perfect for personal use:

```
    private async Task GetLocationInfo()
    {
        var httpClient = new HttpClient();
        string json = await
          httpClient.GetStringAsync("https://ipapi.co/json");
        LocationInfo info = JsonConvert.DeserializeObject<LocationInfo>
        (json);

        PublicIP = info.ip;
        Long = info.longitude;
        Latt = info.latitude;
        City = info.city;
    }
```

7. The next API we will be using is **Dark Sky**. You will need to sign up for an account at `https://darksky.net/dev` in order to get your API key:

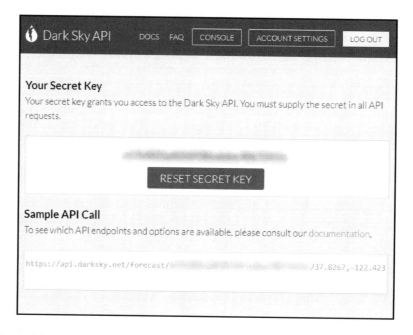

What I like about Dark Sky is that their API also allows you 1,000 free API calls every day:

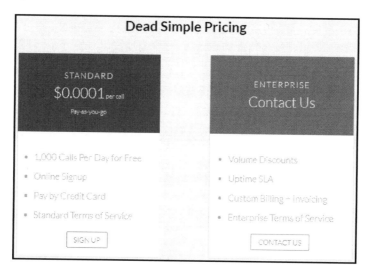

This makes it perfect for personal use. If you have high-volume users, even the pay-as-you-go option isn't expensive at all.

Please note that if you make use of the Dark Sky API for a commercial application, you cannot require each user of your application to register for a Dark Sky API key. All users of your Dark Sky application must use the specific API key you generated via the online portal.

For those who are interested, the FAQ provides clarity on this and many other important questions:

> "...your end-users should not sign up for Dark Sky API keys: the API key
> should be associated with your app or service, not your users.
> The 1,000 free calls per day are intended to facilitate personal use and
> application development, not to provide free weather data to your app. It costs
> us money to develop and maintain the infrastructure that supports the Dark Sky
> API. If your application were to grow in popularity, we would have to pay for
> the use of resources necessary to handle increased traffic (to the benefit of your
> service and your users) without the financial means to support it. For this
> reason, applications that ask users to register for an API key are prohibited by
> our terms of service."

Keeping track of the API calls is also very easy and can be viewed via the online portal:

With the Dark Sky API registration sorted, we want to see whether the application is running in a region that uses the metric system or imperial system for units of measure.

8. Create a method called `GetUnitOfMeasure()` that returns a `DarkSkyService.OptionalParameters` object. All this essentially does is use the `RegionInfo` class to check whether the current region is metric or not.

It then sets the `optParms` variable and returns it to the calling class. I also take the liberty of sneaking in the symbol for Celsius or Fahrenheit for the `TempUnitOfMeasure` property:

```
private DarkSkyService.OptionalParameters GetUnitOfMeasure()
{
    bool blnMetric = RegionInfo.CurrentRegion.IsMetric;
    DarkSkyService.OptionalParameters optParms = new
     DarkSkyService.OptionalParameters();
    if (blnMetric)
    {
        optParms.MeasurementUnits = "si";
        TempUnitOfMeasure = "C";
    }
    else
    {
        optParms.MeasurementUnits = "us";
        TempUnitOfMeasure = "F";
    }
    return optParms;
}
```

9. The next method to add is called `GetCurrentWeatherIcon()`, which will be used to determine the Dark Sky icon to display on our web page. There are many more to choose from, but I have opted, for the sake of brevity, to only include these few icon names. These icon names correspond to the fill list of SVG filenames in the `climacons` folder in our solution:

```
private string GetCurrentWeatherIcon(Icon ic)
{
    string iconFilename = string.Empty;

    switch (ic)
    {
        case Icon.ClearDay:
            iconFilename = "Sun.svg";
            break;

        case Icon.ClearNight:
            iconFilename = "Moon.svg";
            break;
```

```
        case Icon.Cloudy:
            iconFilename = "Cloud.svg";
            break;

        case Icon.Fog:
            iconFilename = "Cloud-Fog.svg";
            break;

        case Icon.PartlyCloudyDay:
            iconFilename = "Cloud-Sun.svg";
            break;

        case Icon.PartlyCloudyNight:
            iconFilename = "Cloud-Moon.svg";
            break;

        case Icon.Rain:
            iconFilename = "Cloud-Rain.svg";
            break;

        case Icon.Snow:
            iconFilename = "Snowflake.svg";
            break;

         case Icon.Wind:
            iconFilename = "Wind.svg";
            break;
         default:
            iconFilename = "Thermometer.svg";
            break;
    }
    return iconFilename;
}
```

10. The next method to create is the `GetWeatherInfo()` method. All this does is call the `DarkSkyService` class and pass it the API key you generated earlier in the Dark Sky portal. You will notice that the code is not really rocket science at all.

The steps in the class are as follows:

1. Define the API key for Dark Sky.
2. Instantiate a new `DarkSkyService` object using the API key.
3. Get the `OptionalParameters` object that determines the unit of measure.
4. We then use the latitude and longitude along with `optParms` to get the forecast.
5. Based on the forecast, I find the appropriate weather icon.
6. I do a `Path.Combine` to get the correct path to the SVG file.
7. I read all the text contained inside that SVG file.
8. Lastly, I set some properties for the attribution back to Dark Sky, the weather summary, and set the temperature value rounded up using the `Round` function in the static `Math` class. In the code, I don't need to fully qualify this because I have imported the static `Math` class earlier.

Your code therefore needs to look as follows:

```
private async Task GetWeatherInfo()
{
    string apiKey = "YOUR_API_KEY_HERE";
    DarkSkyService weather = new DarkSkyService(apiKey);
    DarkSkyService.OptionalParameters optParms =
     GetUnitOfMeasure();
    var foreCast = await weather.GetForecast(Latt, Long, optParms);
    string iconFilename =
     GetCurrentWeatherIcon(foreCast.Response.Currently.Icon);
    string svgFile = Path.Combine(_hostEnv.ContentRootPath,
     "climacons", iconFilename);
    CurrentWeatherIcon = System.IO.File.ReadAllText($"{svgFile}");

    WeatherAttribution = foreCast.AttributionLine;
    DayWeatherSummary = foreCast.Response.Daily.Summary;
    if (foreCast.Response.Currently.Temperature.HasValue)
        CurrentTemp =
     Round(foreCast.Response.Currently.Temperature.Value,
     0).ToString();
}
```

11. Last but not least, we need to add the appropriate code to the `GetInfo()` method. The first section of the method deals with finding the system information of the computer the application is running on. This will obviously change based on the operating system we are running our .NET Core app on:

```
public IActionResult GetInfo()
{
    Models.InformationModel model = new Models.InformationModel();
    model.OperatingSystem = RuntimeInformation.OSDescription;
    model.FrameworkDescription =
     RuntimeInformation.FrameworkDescription;
    model.OSArchitecture =
     RuntimeInformation.OSArchitecture.ToString();
    model.ProcessArchitecture =
     RuntimeInformation.ProcessArchitecture.ToString();
    string title = string.Empty;
    string OSArchitecture = string.Empty;

    if (model.OSArchitecture.ToUpper().Equals("X64")) {
     OSArchitecture = "64-bit"; } else { OSArchitecture =
     "32-bit"; }

    if (RuntimeInformation.IsOSPlatform(OSPlatform.Windows)) {
     title
     = $"Windows {OSArchitecture}"; }
    else if (RuntimeInformation.IsOSPlatform(OSPlatform.OSX)) {
     title = $"OSX {OSArchitecture}"; }
    else if (RuntimeInformation.IsOSPlatform(OSPlatform.Linux)) {
     title = $"Linux {OSArchitecture}"; }

    GetLocationInfo().Wait();
    model.IPAddressString = PublicIP;

    GetWeatherInfo().Wait();
    model.CurrentIcon = CurrentWeatherIcon;
    model.WeatherBy = WeatherAttribution;
    model.CurrentTemperature = CurrentTemp;
    model.DailySummary = DayWeatherSummary;
    model.CurrentCity = City;
    model.UnitOfMeasure = TempUnitOfMeasure;

    model.InfoTitle = title;
    return View(model);
}
```

The last section of the GetInfo() method deals with determining the weather information we crafted in the previous steps.

The next portion of work will entail creating our view. Once we are done with that, the real fun starts.

The GetInfo view

Putting the view together is quite straightforward. I opted for a very minimalistic approach (apart from the weather icon), but you can be as creative here as you like:

1. Right-click the `Views` folder and add a new folder called `Information`. Inside the `Information` folder, add a new view called `GetInfo` by right-clicking the folder and selecting **Add** and then clicking on **View...** from the context menu:

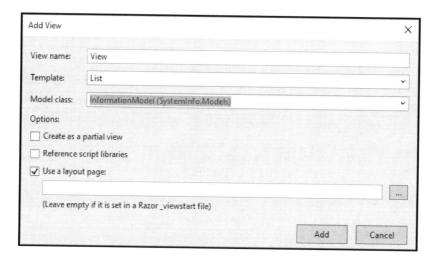

The naming of the view also adheres to the naming convention used in MVC.

Refer to the *The project in detail* section earlier in this chapter for an image of the Visual Studio solution displaying the layout of the `Views` folder.

The view which has been created uses Razor syntax. Razor is a way for developers to add C# code (server code) directly inside web pages. The code inside the `GetInfo.cshtml` page looks as follows:

```
@model SystemInfo.Models.InformationModel

@{
    ViewData["Title"] = "GetInfo";
}

<h2>
    System Information for: @Html.DisplayFor(model =>
```

```
    model.InfoTitle)
</h2>

<div>
    <hr />
    <dl class="dl-horizontal">
        <dt>
            Operating System
        </dt>
        <dd>
            @Html.DisplayFor(model => model.OperatingSystem)
        </dd>
        <dt>
            Framework Description
        </dt>
        <dd>
            @Html.DisplayFor(model => model.FrameworkDescription)
        </dd>
        <dt>
            Process Architecture
        </dt>
        <dd>
            @Html.DisplayFor(model => model.ProcessArchitecture)
        </dd>
        <dt>
            Public IP
        </dt>
        <dd>
            @Html.DisplayFor(model => model.IPAddressString)
        </dd>
    </dl>
</div>

<h2>
    Current Location: @Html.DisplayFor(model => model.CurrentCity)
</h2>
<div>
    <div
style="float:left">@Html.Raw(Model.CurrentIcon)</div><div><h3>@Mode
l.CurrentTemperature&deg;@Model.UnitOfMeasure</h3></div>
</div>

<div>
    <h4>@Html.DisplayFor(model => model.DailySummary)</h4>
</div>
<div>
    Weather Info: @Html.DisplayFor(model => model.WeatherBy)
</div>
```

As you can see, MVC adds the `@model` keyword to Razor's vernacular. By doing this, you are allowing the view to specify the type of the view's `Model` property. The syntax is `@model class` and is contained in the first line, `@model SystemInfo.Models.InformationModel`, which strongly types the view to the `InformationModel` class.

With this kind of flexibility, you can add C# expressions directly into your client-side code.

2. The last bit of code you need to add is to the `_Layout.cshtml` file in the `Views/Shared` folder:

```html
_Layout.cshtml ⌐ X
1    <!DOCTYPE html>
2    <html>
3    <head>
4        <meta charset="utf-8" />
5        <meta name="viewport" content="width=device-width, initial-scale=1.0" />
6        <title>@ViewData["Title"] - Information Dashboard</title>
7
8        <environment include="Development">
9            <link rel="stylesheet" href="~/lib/bootstrap/dist/css/bootstrap.css" />
10           <link rel="stylesheet" href="~/css/site.css" />
11       </environment>
12       <environment exclude="Development">
13           <link rel="stylesheet" href="https://ajax.aspnetcdn.com/ajax/bootstrap/3.3.7/css/bootstrap.min.css"
14               asp-fallback-href="~/lib/bootstrap/dist/css/bootstrap.min.css"
15               asp-fallback-test-class="sr-only" asp-fallback-test-property="position" asp-fallback-test-value="absolute" />
16           <link rel="stylesheet" href="~/css/site.min.css" asp-append-version="true" />
17       </environment>
18   </head>
19   <body>
20       <nav class="navbar navbar-inverse navbar-fixed-top">
21           <div class="container">
22               <div class="navbar-header">
23                   <button type="button" class="navbar-toggle" data-toggle="collapse" data-target=".navbar-collapse">
24                       <span class="sr-only">Toggle navigation</span>
25                       <span class="icon-bar"></span>
26                       <span class="icon-bar"></span>
27                       <span class="icon-bar"></span>
28                   </button>
29                   <a asp-area="" asp-controller="Home" asp-action="Index" class="navbar-brand">SystemInfo</a>
30               </div>
31               <div class="navbar-collapse collapse">
32                   <ul class="nav navbar-nav">
33                       <li><a asp-area="" asp-controller="Home" asp-action="Index">Home</a></li>
34                       <li><a asp-area="" asp-controller="Home" asp-action="About">About</a></li>
35                       <li><a asp-area="" asp-controller="Home" asp-action="Contact">Contact</a></li>
36                       <li><a asp-area="" asp-controller="Information" asp-action="GetInfo">Information Dashboard</a></li>
37                   </ul>
38               </div>
39           </div>
40       </nav>
41       <div class="container body-content">
42           @RenderBody()
43           <hr />
44           <footer>
45               <p>&copy; 2017 - Information Dashboard</p>
46           </footer>
47       </div>
```

Add List Item

We are just adding a link to the menu here to navigate to our
`InformationController` class. You will notice that the code follows the
convention of controller and action, where the `asp-controller` specifies the
`InformationController` class and the `asp-action` specifies the `GetInfo`
method inside that controller.

3. At this stage, the application should be ready to run. Build it and make sure you
   get a clean build. Run the application and click on the **Information Dashboard**
   menu item.

   The **Information Dashboard** will display the computer information it is running
   on as well as the weather information for the current location the machine is
   located at (or close thereby):

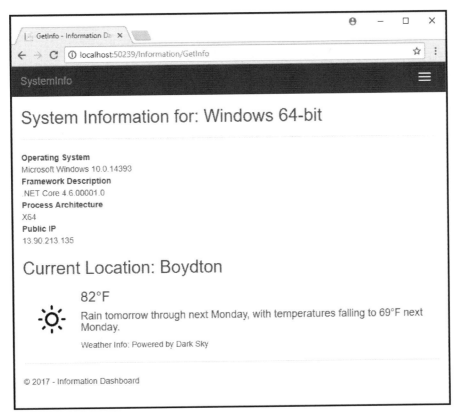

For the Windows portion of this chapter, I used Azure and therefore the server is
located in the US. That is why the information displayed is US-based.

4. Finally, let's have a peek at the generated HTML code from our Razor view. If you use the built-in developer tools (I'm using Chrome) and view the page source, you will find that the HTML created from the Razor view is quite unremarkable:

```html
<h2>
    System Information for: Windows 64-bit
</h2>

<div>
    <hr />
    <dl class="dl-horizontal">
        <dt>
            Operating System
        </dt>
        <dd>
            Microsoft Windows 10.0.14393
        </dd>
        <dt>
            Framework Description
        </dt>
        <dd>
            .NET Core 4.6.00001.0
        </dd>
        <dt>
            Process Architecture
        </dt>
        <dd>
            X64
        </dd>
        <dt>
            Public IP
        </dt>
        <dd>
            13.90.213.135
        </dd>
    </dl>
</div>
```

At the end of the day, all this is is just HTML. What is remarkable, however, is the fact that we used Razor to access properties on our model and place them directly inside the HTML of our view.

Running the application on macOS

For this portion of the chapter, I will assume that you are using a Mac that has had .NET Core 1.1 installed. If you do not have .NET Core installed on your Mac, head on over to `https://www.microsoft.com/net/core#macos` and follow the installation steps (or follow along):

1. Simply put, from your .NET Core solution in Windows, just publish the .NET Core application. Then, go ahead and copy the published files to your Mac. I just put my published files in a desktop folder called `netCoreInfoDash`:

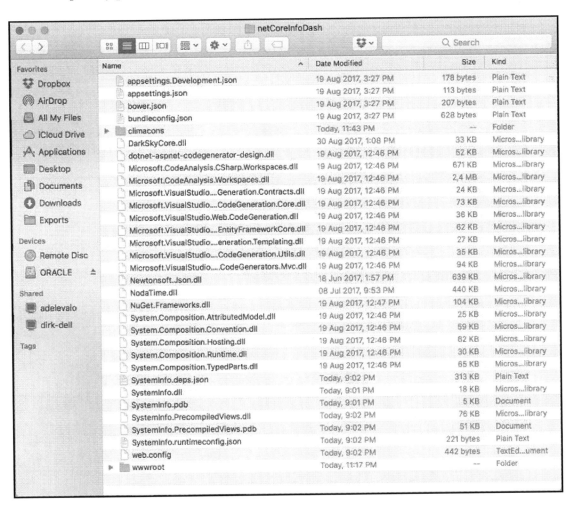

2. Open the Terminal on your Mac and change the working directory to the
   `netCoreInfoDash` folder. Type in the command `dotnet SystemInfo.dll` and
   hit *Enter*:

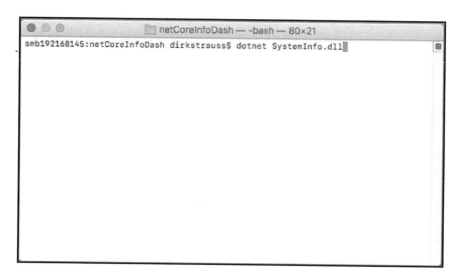

Because the project was created for .NET Core 2.0 and our Mac only has .NET
Core 1.1, we will see the following error message in the Terminal:

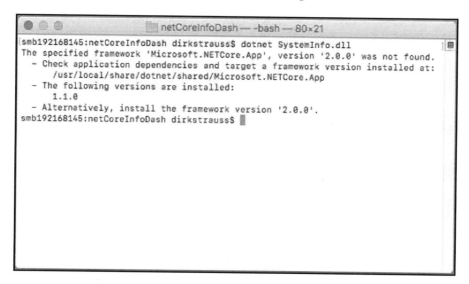

3. We need to update the version of .NET Core on the Mac to version 2.0. To do this, go to `https://www.microsoft.com/net/core#macos` and install .NET Core 2.0.

Installing the .NET Core SDK is quite straightforward:

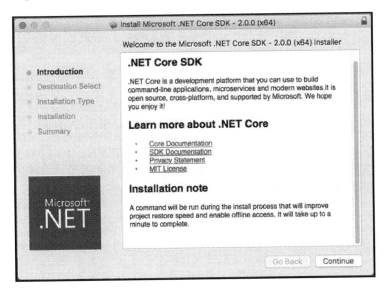

In no time at all, .NET Core 2.0 is installed on your Mac:

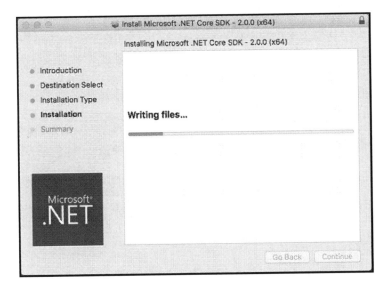

4. Back in the Terminal, type in `dotnet SystemInfo.dll` and hit *Enter*. This time, you will see the following information output in the Terminal window. You will see that the address `http://localhost:5000` is specified. The port listed for you might change, but `5000` is usually the port given:

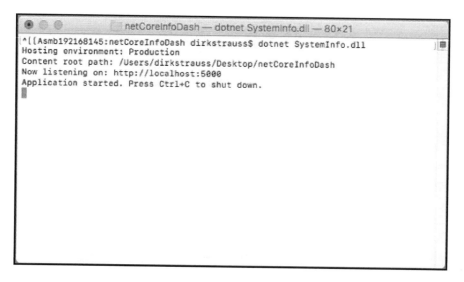

5. Open the browser on your Mac (it can be Safari, but I use Chrome) and navigate to—`http://localhost:5000`. You will see that the familiar application start page is displayed. If you click on the **Information Dashboard** menu item, you will see the page we created exactly as it was displayed on the Windows machine:

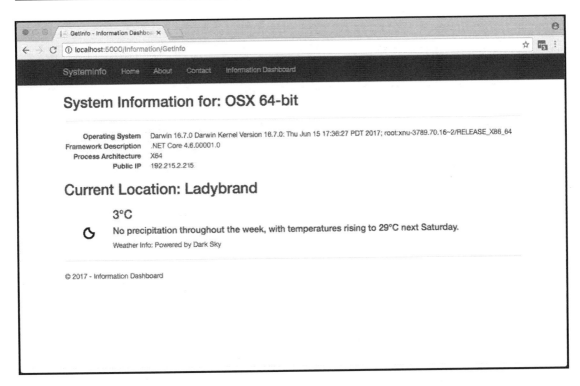

The only difference here is that the Mac is not on Azure and is in fact in my office in South Africa. The temperature information has changed to Celsius and the machine information displayed is for that of my Mac. It's a nice Spring evening here in South Africa.

Setting up the app on Linux

Everyone keeps talking about the ability of .NET Core to run cross-platform, even on Linux. I, therefore, decided to give it a try. I know that Linux might not interest many of you, but there is a definite sense of satisfaction of being able to use a powerful operating system such as Linux.

If you are developing .NET Core applications, I would encourage you to set up a Linux box for testing purposes. There are many ways that you can go about doing this. If you have access to Azure, you can set up a Linux VM on Azure.

You can also use virtualization software to provide a fully functional VM on your local machine. The option I chose was to use **VirtualBox** as well as testing out the process on **Parallels**. Both methods are really easy, but VirtualBox is free to use so this would be a good option. You can download the latest version of VirtualBox from `https://www.virtualbox.org/wiki/Downloads` for free.

You can also save yourself the setup time by downloading ready to use VirtualBox images from a variety of sites online. Just make sure they are reputable sites such as **OS Boxes** at—`http://www.osboxes.org/virtualbox-images/`.

Whatever route you choose to follow, the rest of this chapter will assume that you have already set up your Linux environment and that you are ready to set up your .NET Core application.

So let's see how to install .NET Core for Linux:

1. Find the instructions for installing .NET Core 2.0 for your particular flavor of Linux from—`https://www.microsoft.com/net/download/linux`:

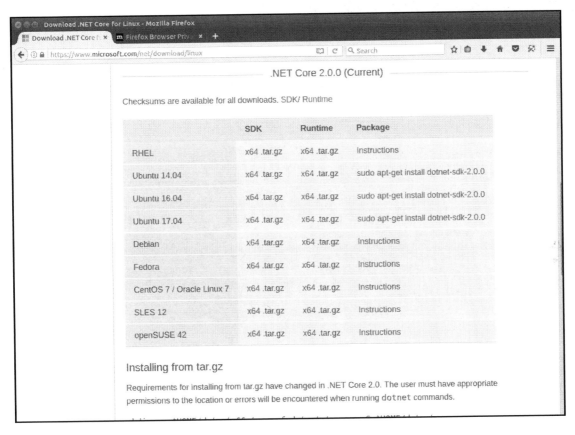

2. I am using **Ubuntu 16.04**, and clicking on the `sudo apt-get install dotnet-sdk-2.0.0` link will take me to the installation steps.

3. Open up the Terminal window on Linux Ubuntu (or Linux Mint) by typing *Ctrl + Alt + T*.

Seeing as I am running a fresh copy of Linux, I need to install **cURL** first. This tool allows me to transfer data to and from servers to my local machine.

4. Run the following command to get cURL:

```
sudo apt-get install curl
```

5. The Terminal will ask for your password. Typing in the password does nothing on the screen, but keep on typing and hit *Enter*:

 The password that doesn't display a masked output to the screen as you type is by design when working with Linux. It's a feature.

```
parallels@parallels-vm: ~
parallels@parallels-vm:~$ sudo apt-get install curl
[sudo] password for parallels:
Reading package lists... Done
Building dependency tree
Reading state information... Done
The following NEW packages will be installed:
  curl
0 upgraded, 1 newly installed, 0 to remove and 38 not upgraded.
Need to get 139 kB of archives.
After this operation, 338 kB of additional disk space will be used.
Get:1 http://us.archive.ubuntu.com/ubuntu xenial-updates/main amd64 curl amd64 7
.47.0-1ubuntu2.2 [139 kB]
Fetched 139 kB in 1s (79.7 kB/s)
Selecting previously unselected package curl.
(Reading database ... 209217 files and directories currently installed.)
Preparing to unpack .../curl_7.47.0-1ubuntu2.2_amd64.deb ...
Unpacking curl (7.47.0-1ubuntu2.2) ...
Processing triggers for man-db (2.7.5-1) ...
Setting up curl (7.47.0-1ubuntu2.2) ...
parallels@parallels-vm:~$
```

6. Now, we need to register the trusted Microsoft signature key. Type-in the following:

```
curl https://packages.microsoft.com/keys/microsoft.asc | gpg --
dearmor > microsoft.gpg
```

```
parallels@parallels-vm: ~
parallels@parallels-vm:~$ curl https://packages.microsoft.com/keys/microsoft.asc
 | gpg --dearmor > microsoft.gpg
  % Total    % Received % Xferd  Average Speed   Time    Time     Time  Current
                                 Dload  Upload   Total   Spent    Left  Speed
100   983  100   983    0     0    426      0  0:00:02  0:00:02 --:--:--   426
parallels@parallels-vm:~$ █
```

7. When this is done, type in the following:

   `sudo mv microsoft.gpg /etc/apt/trusted.gpg.d/microsoft.gpg`

8. Now, we need to register the Microsoft Product feed for Ubuntu 16.04. To do this, type in the following:

   `sudo sh -c 'echo "deb [arch=amd64]`
   `https://packages.microsoft.com/repos/microsoft-ubuntu-xenial-pr`
   `od xenial main" > /etc/apt/sources.list.d/dotnetdev.list'`

9. Then, directly after that, type in the following:

   `sudo apt-get update`

10. Now, we can install the .NET Core 2.0 SDK by typing in the following:

    `sudo apt-get install dotnet-sdk-2.0.0`

11. The Terminal asks us if we want to continue, which we do. So, type in Y and hit *Enter*:

When this process is complete, you will see the cursor ready for input next to the ~$:

12. To check which version of .NET Core is installed, type in the following command:

    ```
    dotnet --version
    ```

13. This should display **2.0.0**. We now have .NET Core 2.0 installed on our Linux machine. As a quick start, make a new directory called `testapp` and change your working directory to the `testapp` directory by typing the following:

    ```
    mkdir testapp
    cd testapp
    ```

    Consider the following screenshot:

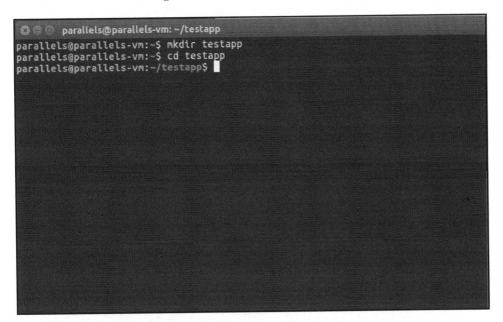

14. We just want to see whether .NET Core is working on our Linux machine, so while you're in the `testapp` directory, type in the following:

    ```
    dotnet new razor
    ```

Yes, it is that easy. This has just created a new MVC Web project for us on Linux:

```
parallels@parallels-vm: ~/testapp
parallels@parallels-vm:~/testapp$ dotnet new razor
The template "ASP.NET Core Web App" was created successfully.
This template contains technologies from parties other than Microsoft, see https
://aka.ms/template-3pn for details.

Processing post-creation actions...
Running 'dotnet restore' on /home/parallels/testapp/testapp.csproj...
  Restoring packages for /home/parallels/testapp/testapp.csproj...
  Restoring packages for /home/parallels/testapp/testapp.csproj...
  Restore completed in 28.16 sec for /home/parallels/testapp/testapp.csproj.
  Generating MSBuild file /home/parallels/testapp/obj/testapp.csproj.nuget.g.pro
ps.
  Generating MSBuild file /home/parallels/testapp/obj/testapp.csproj.nuget.g.tar
gets.
  Restore completed in 34.26 sec for /home/parallels/testapp/testapp.csproj.


Restore succeeded.

parallels@parallels-vm:~/testapp$
```

15. As we did on our Mac, type in the following command:

```
dotnet run
```

Take a look at the following screenshot:

```
parallels@parallels-vm: ~/testapp
parallels@parallels-vm:~/testapp$ dotnet run
warn: Microsoft.AspNetCore.DataProtection.KeyManagement.XmlKeyManager[35]
      No XML encryptor configured. Key {1712bdad-88d7-4b30-9b6c-2abc54472b26} ma
y be persisted to storage in unencrypted form.
Hosting environment: Production
Content root path: /home/parallels/testapp
Now listening on: http://localhost:5000
Application started. Press Ctrl+C to shut down.
```

16. In the output in the Terminal, you will notice that the same port number is displayed for localhost. Unlike macOS, on Ubuntu I can click on `http://localhost:5000` inside the Terminal window. This will open up the application we just created:

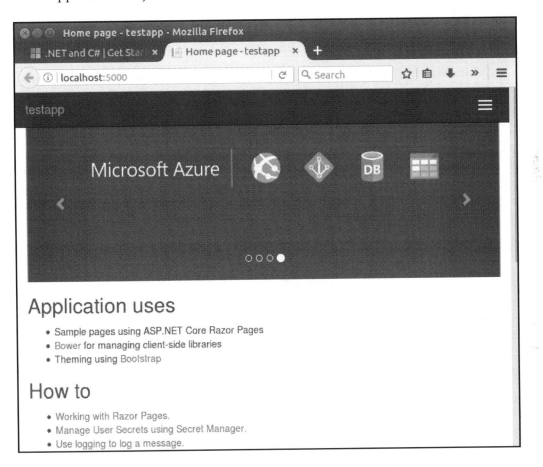

Now that we know .NET Core 2.0 is running correctly on Linux, let's copy over the project files to our Linux machine:

1. Create a folder on the desktop; you can call it whatever you like. Copy the project files for the .NET Core application into that folder (do not copy the published files into this folder):

 You will remember that on macOS, we only copied the published files. This is different on Linux. Here, you need to copy all your project files.

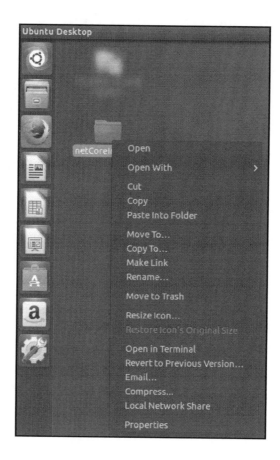

2. Right-click the folder and select **Open in Terminal.**

Now that we are in the folder containing our solution files, type in the following:

```
dotnet restore
```

This command restores the dependencies and tools of our project:

```
parallels@parallels-vm: ~/Desktop/netCoreInfoProj
parallels@parallels-vm:~/Desktop/netCoreInfoProj$ dotnet restore
  Restoring packages for /home/parallels/Desktop/netCoreInfoProj/SystemInfo/Syst
emInfo.csproj...
  Restore completed in 3.31 sec for /home/parallels/Desktop/netCoreInfoProj/Syst
emInfo/SystemInfo.csproj.
  Installing NodaTime 2.2.0.
  Installing System.Net.Http 4.3.2.
  Installing Newtonsoft.Json 10.0.3.
  Installing DarkSkyCore 3.1.0.
  Generating MSBuild file /home/parallels/Desktop/netCoreInfoProj/SystemInfo/obj
/SystemInfo.csproj.nuget.g.props.
  Generating MSBuild file /home/parallels/Desktop/netCoreInfoProj/SystemInfo/obj
/SystemInfo.csproj.nuget.g.targets.
  Restore completed in 21.13 sec for /home/parallels/Desktop/netCoreInfoProj/Sys
temInfo/SystemInfo.csproj.
parallels@parallels-vm:~/Desktop/netCoreInfoProj$
```

3. Because we are working with the solution files, I needed to navigate one folder down and type the following:

```
dotnet run
```

Take a look at the following screenshot:

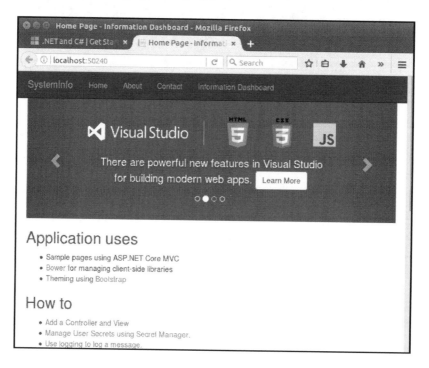

4. Navigating to `http://localhost:50240` displayed in the Terminal window takes me to the start page of my application:

5. Clicking on the **Information Dashboard** menu item will take us to the page we created:

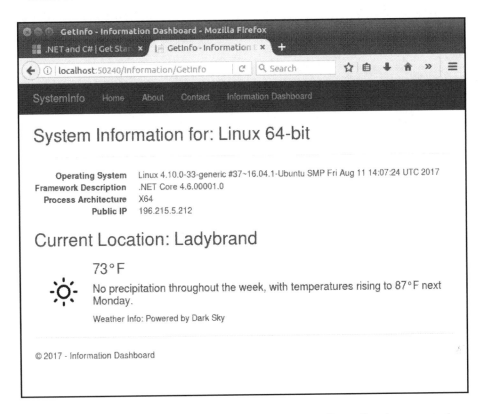

And that is all there is to it. We have an ASP.NET Core MVC application created on a Windows PC using Visual Studio 2017 Enterprise, which is running on a Linux machine. The best thing of all is that we didn't change a single line of code to get our application to run on the different platforms.

Summary

Looking back at this chapter, we had a look at setting up an ASP.NET Core application on Windows. We looked at adding views and controllers and, if you are familiar with ASP.NET MVC, then you will have felt right at home. If not, ASP.NET MVC is really very easy.

Lastly, we had a look at what makes .NET Core so powerful by running the same application on Windows, macOS, and Linux.

The power of .NET Core should be evident to you by now. It allows developers to write truly cross-platform applications using .NET. This technology is a game changer and something every developer must get to grips with.

Next, you might wonder what we need to do when we want to hook up a database to a .NET Core application. In the next chapter, we will look at using MongoDB on an ASP.NET Core MVC application.

Why do we want to use MongoDB, you might wonder? Well, MongoDB is free, open source, and flexible. Then again, why would we not want to use MongoDB? See you in the next chapter!

4
Task Bug Logging ASP .NET Core MVC App

In this chapter, we will take a look at using MongoDB with ASP.NET Core MVC by creating a task/bug logging application. A personal task manager is useful, and logging bugs is especially handy when you can't attend to them immediately.

We will cover the following topics in this chapter:

- Setting up MongoDB on your local machine
- A first look at using MongoDB Compass
- Creating an ASP.NET Core MVC application and integrating MongoDB

You might be wondering why we would choose MongoDB. The question you need to ask is, how much effort do you want to go through to create a simple application?

What are the benefits of using MongoDB?

To answer this question, let's have a look at the benefits of using MongoDB.

Faster development with MongoDB

This might become clearer during your development process, but let's just say that one part of the development process I dislike is having to create data tables for the various forms and fields. Have you ever had to create a table to store address field information? That's right, you need to add something similar to the following:

- Address1
- Address2
- Address3
- Address4
- City
- State
- Zip
- Country

This table can obviously get very large. It depends on what exactly you need to store. With MongoDB, you only need to pass it the address array. MongoDB takes care of the rest. No more mucking around with creating table statements.

Career–enhancing skillset

More and more career sites are listing MongoDB as a sought-after skillset. It is more frequently used in companies, and new developers are expected to have some experience with MongoDB. A quick search on LinkedIn's jobs portal for the MongoDB keyword returned 7,800 jobs in the US alone. Having MongoDB experience is a great career booster, especially if you are used to using SQL Server.

MongoDB is ranked well in the industry

To further prove my point, MongoDB is ranked fifth overall on the website **DB-Engines** (`https://db-engines.com/en/ranking`) and ranked first under the category of **Document Stores** (`https://db-engines.com/en/ranking/document+store`).

 These stats were correct at the time of writing. In fact, MongoDB is showing an increase in rankings consistently year on year.

It is clear that MongoDB is here to stay, and more importantly, that the community loves MongoDB. This is very important, because it creates a healthy community of developers that share knowledge and articles on MongoDB. Broad adoption of MongoDB furthers the development of the technology.

Setting up MongoDB on your local machine

Head on over to `https://www.mongodb.com/download-center#community` and download the latest version of MongoDB Community Server for Windows. The installer then gives you the option to install **MongoDB Compass**.

You can also download Compass as a separate installer from the preceding link or by navigating directly to:
`https://www.mongodb.com/download-center?jmp=nav#compass.`

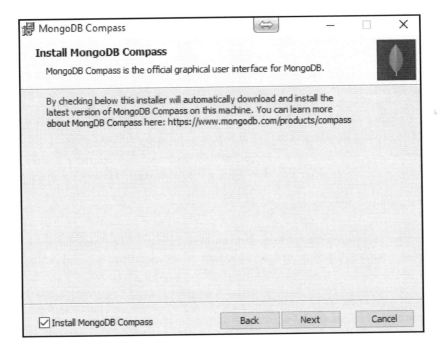

Looking at the web page for **MongoDB Compass**, at
`https://docs.mongodb.com/compass/master/`, the description of **MongoDB Compass** is quite clear:

> *"MongoDB Compass is designed to allow users to easily analyze and understand the contents of their data collections within MongoDB and perform queries, without requiring knowledge of MongoDB query syntax.*
>
> *MongoDB Compass provides users with a graphical view of their MongoDB schema by randomly sampling a subset of documents from the collection. Sampling documents minimizes performance impact on the database and can produce results quickly."*

If this is your first time working with MongoDB, I suggest that you install **MongoDB Compass** and play around with it a bit.

After installing MongoDB, you will find it under `C:\ProgramFiles\MongoDB`. What I now like to do is keep the full installation path on an environmental variable. This makes it easier to access from PowerShell or the Command Prompt. The full installation path to the `bin` folder is `C:\Program\FilesMongoDBServer3.6bin`.

To set it up, we perform the following steps:

1. Open up the **System Properties** screen and click on the **Environment Variables** button.
2. Under the **System variables** group, select the **Path** variable and click on the **Edit** button. Add the full installation path to the **Path** system variables.
3. We now need to go and create a folder on the hard drive to store the MongoDB database. You can create this folder anywhere, but wherever you do create it, you need to use it in the next step. I created my MongoDB database folder at the following path: `D:\MongoTask`.

4. In order to work with MongoDB, you must start the MongoDB server first. It doesn't matter if this is on a remote machine or on your local machine. Open PowerShell and run the following command:

```
mongod -dbpath D:MongoTask
```

5. On running the preceding command, press **Enter**. You have now started the MongoDB server. Next, start **MongoDB Compass**.

6. You will see that you don't have any databases yet. Click on the **CREATE DATABASE** button, as shown in the following screenshot:

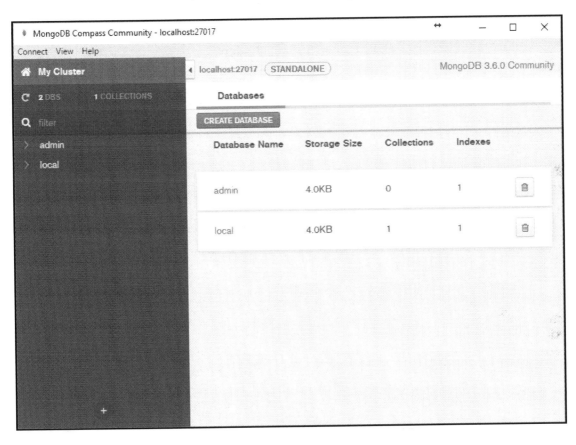

7. The **Create Database** window opens up where you can specify a database name under **Database Name** and a collection name under **Collection Name**.

8. To finish, click on the **CEATE DATABASE** button at the bottom of the screen, as shown in the following screenshot:

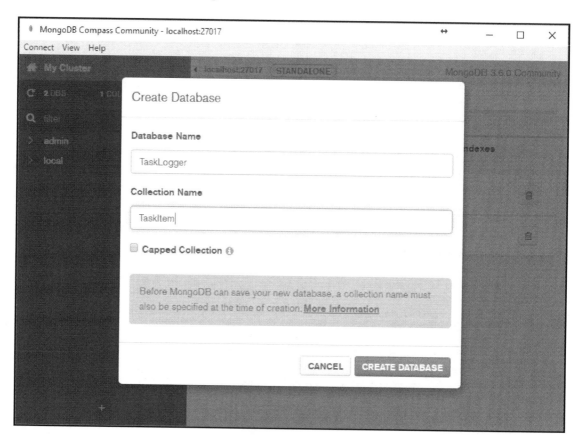

9. You will see that a new database called `TaskLogger` has been created and if you expand the `TaskLogger` database node, you will see the **TaskItem** document listed, as shown in the following screenshot:

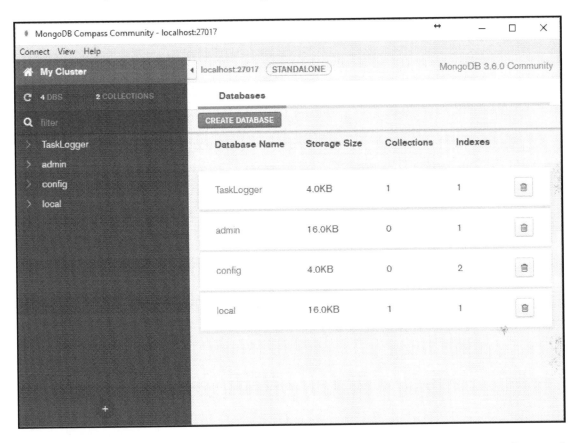

We will not be focusing too much on MongoDB Compass in this chapter. For now, I wanted to show you that there is a way to visually manage MongoDB databases by using MongoDB Compass. You can go ahead and delete the **TaskItem** document that you just created. You will see, how the application created a document for you automatically when you insert data into your MongoDB database for the first time later on.

Connecting your ASP.NET Core MVC application to MongoDB

When talking about using MongoDB in your application, one wonders how easy it will be to add this functionality to a new ASP.NET Core MVC application. The process is really easy. To start off, create a new ASP.NET Core Web application and name it `BugTracker`:

1. On the **New ASP.NET Core Web Application - BugTracker** screen, make sure that you have selected **ASP.NET Core 2.0** from the drop-down list.
2. Select **Web Application (Model-View-Controller)**.
3. Uncheck the **Enable Docker Support** option. Finally, click on the **OK** button.
4. Your new ASP.NET Core MVC application will be created with the basics, as shown in the following screenshot:

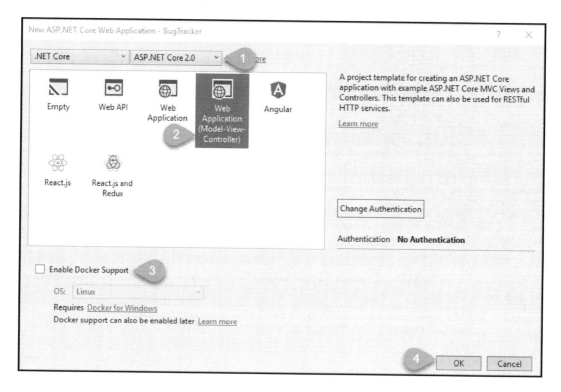

5. Enabling Docker support for your application can easily be done at creation time. You can also enable Docker support for existing applications.

I will take a look at Docker in a later chapter and how to make your application work with Docker. For now, our application does not need Docker support. Leave it unchecked and create your application as you would normally.

Adding the NuGet package

Seeing as this chapter is all about MongoDB, we need to add this to our project. The best way to do this, is by adding the NuGet package. We can do this as follows:

1. Right-click on your project and select **Manage NuGet Packages...** from the context menu, as shown in the following screenshot:

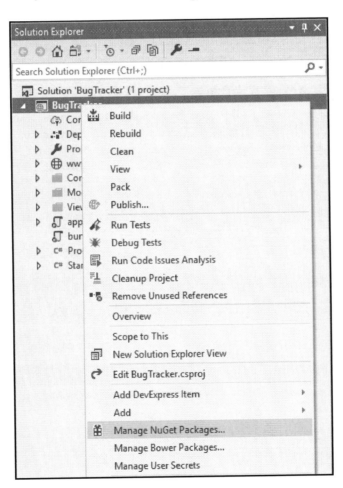

2. On the NuGet screen, you will select the **Browse** tab and enter `Mongodb.Driver` as the search term.

3. Select the **MongoDB.Driver by MongoDB** option.

4. Click on the **Install** button to add the latest stable package to your project. This is depicted in the following screenshot:

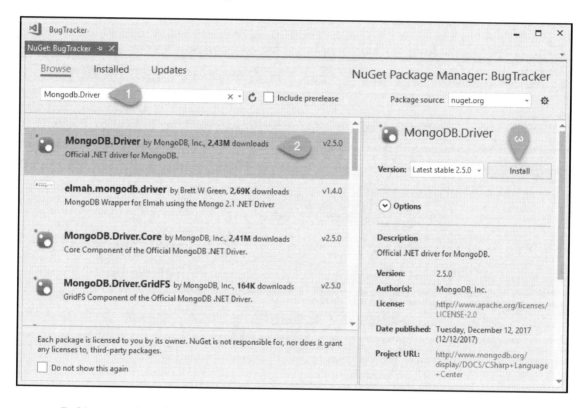

5. You can view the progress in the **Output** window of Visual Studio.

6. After MongoDB has been added to your project, you will see that **MongoDB.Driver (2.5.0)** is added under the **NuGet** dependencies of your project, as shown in the following screenshot:

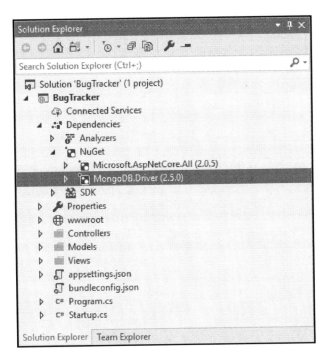

7. Expand the `Controllers` folder. You will see that by default, Visual Studio has created a `HomeController.cs` file. The code in that file should be something like the following:

```
public class HomeController : Controller
{
    public IActionResult Index()
    {
        return View();
    }

    public IActionResult About()
    {
        ViewData["Message"] = "Your application description
        page.";

        return View();
    }
}
```

```
public IActionResult Contact()
{
    ViewData["Message"] = "Your contact page.";

    return View();
}

public IActionResult Error()
{
    return View(new ErrorViewModel { RequestId =
        Activity.Current?.Id ?? HttpContext.TraceIdentifier
});
}
}
```

We want to be able to connect to MongoDB from here, so let's create some code to connect to the Mongo client.

 You will need to add a `using` statement to your class as follows:
`using MongoDB.Driver;`

The steps to connect to MongoDB are as follows:

1. Create a constructor by typing the snippet short code `ctor` and tabbing twice, or by typing in the code explicitly. Your constructor needs to create a new instance of `MongoClient`. When you have done this, your code should look as follows:

```
public HomeController()
{
    var mclient = new MongoClient();
}
```

2. For `MongoClient` to work, we need to give it a connection string to the MongoDB instance we created. Open the `appsettings.json` file in the **Solution 'Bug Tracker'** pane, as shown in the following screenshot:

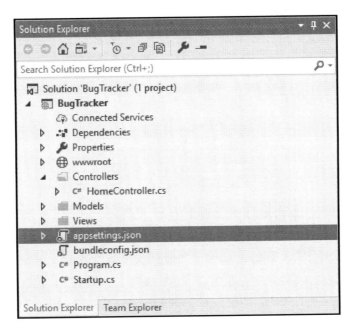

3. When you open your `appsettings.json` file, it should look as follows:

```
{
  "Logging": {
    "IncludeScopes": false,
    "LogLevel": {
      "Default": "Warning"
    }
  }
}
```

4. Modify the file and add the MongoDB connection details, as follows:

```
{
  "MongoConnection": {
    "ConnectionString": "mongodb://localhost:27017",
    "Database": "TaskLogger"
  },
  "Logging": {
    "IncludeScopes": false,
    "LogLevel": {
      "Default": "Warning"
    }
  }
}
```

5. We now want to create a `Settings.cs` file in the `Models` folder, as shown in the following screenshot:

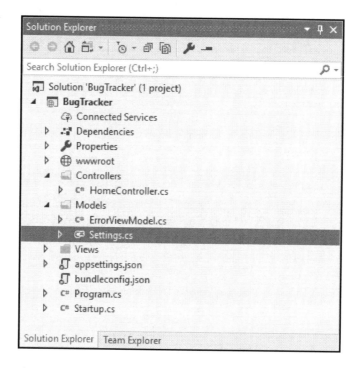

6. Open the `Settings.cs` file and add the following code to it:

```
public class Settings
{
    public string ConnectionString { get; set; }
    public string Database { get; set; }
}
```

7. We now need to open the `Startup.cs` file and modify the `ConfigureServices` method as follows to register the service:

```
public void ConfigureServices(IServiceCollection services)
{
    services.AddMvc();

    services.Configure<Settings>(Options =>
    {
        Options.ConnectionString = Configuration.GetSection
        ("MongoConnection:ConnectionString").Value;
```

```
            Options.Database = Configuration.GetSection
              ("MongoConnection:Database").Value;
        });

    }
```

8. Go back to the `HomeController.cs` file and modify the constructor to pass the connection string to `MongoClient`:

```
public HomeController(IOptions<Settings> settings)
{
    var mclient = new
      MongoClient(settings.Value.ConnectionString);
}
```

9. At this point, I want to test my code to see that it is actually accessing my MongoDB instance. To do this, modify your code to return the cluster description:

```
IMongoDatabase _database;

public HomeController(IOptions<Settings> settings)
{
    var mclient = new
      MongoClient(settings.Value.ConnectionString);
      _database = mclient.GetDatabase(settings.Value.Database);
}

public IActionResult Index()
{
    return Json(_database.Client.Cluster.Description);
}
```

10. Run your ASP.NET Core MVC application and see the information output in the browser, as shown in the following screenshot:

This is all well and good, but let's look at how to separate the logic of adding the database connection into a class of its own.

Creating the MongoDbRepository class

To create a `MongoDbRepository` class, we need to perform the following steps:

1. Create a new folder called `Data` in your solution. Inside that folder, create a new class called `MongoDBRepository`:

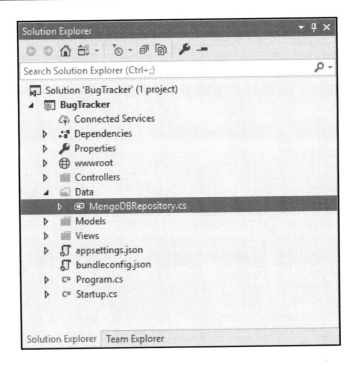

2. Inside this class, add the following code:

```csharp
public class MongoDBRepository
{
    public readonly IMongoDatabase Database;

    public MongoDBRepository(IOptions<Settings> settings)
    {
        try
        {
            var mclient = new
            MongoClient(settings.Value.ConnectionString);
            Database =
            mclient.GetDatabase(settings.Value.Database);
        }
        catch (Exception ex)
        {
            throw new Exception("There was a problem connecting
            to the MongoDB database", ex);
        }
    }
}
```

If the code looks familiar, it's because it's the same code that we wrote in the `HomeController.cs` class, only this time, it has a bit of error handling and it's in its own class. This means that we also need to modify the `HomeController` class.

3. Change the code in the constructor of the `HomeController` as well as in the `Index` action. Your code needs to look as follows:

```
public MongoDBRepository mongoDb;

public HomeController(IOptions<Settings> settings)
{
    mongoDb =  new MongoDBRepository(settings);
}
public IActionResult Index()
{
    return Json(mongoDb.Database.Client.Cluster.Description);
}
```

4. Running your application again, you will see the same information displayed earlier in the browser, so output to the browser window again.

The only difference is that the code is now separated properly and makes it easy to reuse. Therefore, if any changes happen further on down the line, it only gets updated here.

Reading and writing data to MongoDB

In this section, we will have a look at how to read a list of work items from the MongoDB database and also how to insert a new work item into the database. I call them work items, because a work item can be a task or a bug. This can be done by performing the following steps:

1. In the **Models** folder, create a new class called `WorkItem`, as shown in the following screenshot:

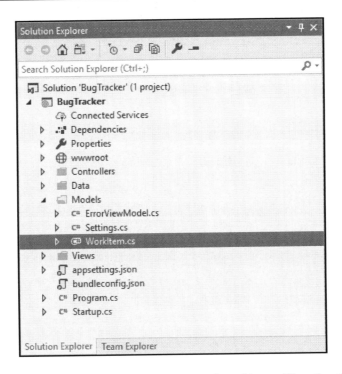

2. Add the following code to the `WorkItem` class. You will notice that `Id` is of type `ObjectId`. This represents the unique identifier in the MondoDB document that gets created.

You need to ensure that you add the following `using` statement to your `WorkItem` class using `MongoDB.Bson;`.

Take a look the following code:

```
public class WorkItem
{
    public ObjectId Id { get; set; }
    public string Title { get; set; }
    public string Description { get; set; }
    public int Severity { get; set; }
    public string WorkItemType { get; set; }
    public string AssignedTo { get; set; }
}
```

3. Next, open up the `MongoDBRepository` class and add the following property to the class:

```
public IMongoCollection<WorkItem> WorkItems
{
    get
    {
        return Database.GetCollection<WorkItem>("workitem");
    }
}
```

4. Since we are using C# 6 at least, we can further simplify the `WorkItem` property by changing it to an **Expression Bodied Property**. To do this, change the code to look as follows:

```
public IMongoCollection<WorkItem> WorkItems =>
Database.GetCollection<WorkItem>("workitem");
```

5. If this looks a bit confusing, have a look at the following screenshot:

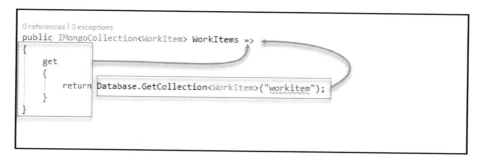

The curly braces, `get`, and `return` statements are replaced by the `=>` lambda operator. The object being returned (in this case, the collection of `WorkItem` objects) goes after the lambda operator. This results in the **Expression Bodied Property**.

Creating the interfaces and Work ItemService

Next, we need to create an interface. To do this, we need to perform the following steps:

1. Create a new folder in your solution called **Interfaces** and add an interface called `IWorkItemService` to the **Interfaces** folder, as shown in the following screenshot:

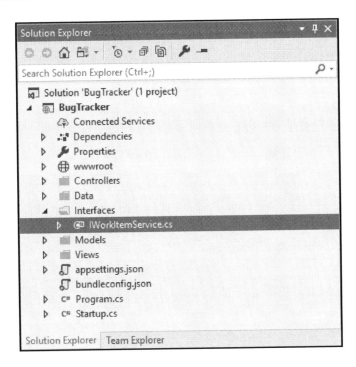

2. Add the following code to the `IWorkItemService` interface:

```
public interface IWorkItemService
{
    IEnumerable<WorkItem> GetAllWorkItems();
}
```

3. In your `Data` folder, add another class called `WorkItemService` and make it implement the `IWorkItemService` interface.

> Be sure to add the `using` statement to reference your interface. In my example, this is the `using BugTracker.Interfaces;` statement.

4. You will notice that Visual Studio prompts you to implement the interface. To do this, click on the lightbulb tip and click on **Implement interface** from the context menu, as shown in the following screenshot:

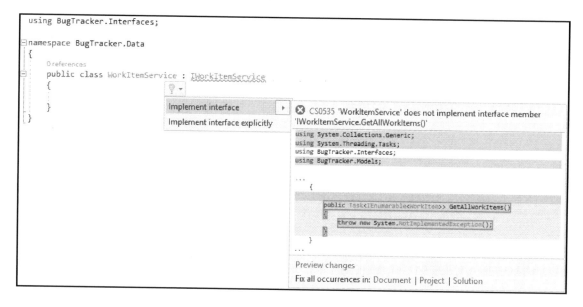

5. After you have done this, your `WorkItemService` class will look as follows:

```
public class WorkItemService : IWorkItemService
{
    public IEnumerable<WorkItem> GetAllWorkItems()
    {
        throw new System.NotImplementedException();
    }
}
```

6. Next, add a constructor and complete the `GetAllWorkItems` method so that your class looks as follows:

```
public class WorkItemService : IWorkItemService
{
    private readonly MongoDBRepository repository;

    public WorkItemService(IOptions<Settings> settings)
    {
        repository = new MongoDBRepository(settings);
    }
    public IEnumerable<WorkItem> GetAllWorkItems()
    {
        return repository.WorkItems.Find(x => true).ToList();
    }
}
```

7. You now need to open up your `Startup.cs` file and edit the `ConfigureServices` method to add the following line of code:

```
services.AddScoped<IWorkItemService, WorkItemService>();
```

8. Your `ConfigureServices` method will now look as follows:

```
public void ConfigureServices(IServiceCollection services)
{
    services.AddMvc();

    services.Configure<Settings>(Options =>
    {
        Options.ConnectionString =
Configuration.GetSection("MongoConnection:ConnectionString").Value;
        Options.Database =
Configuration.GetSection("MongoConnection:Database").Value;
    });

    services.AddScoped<IWorkItemService, WorkItemService>();
}
```

What you have done is registered the `IWorkItemService` interface into the Dependency Injection framework. For more on dependency injection, see the following article at:

https://docs.microsoft.com/en-us/aspnet/core/fundamentals/dependency-injection.

Creating the view

When we start our application, we want to see a list of work items. Therefore, we need to create a view for `HomeController` to display a list of work items by performing the following steps:

1. In the **Views** folder, expand the **Home** subfolder and delete the `Index.cshtml` file if there is one.
2. Then, right-click the **Home** folder and navigate to **Add | View** from the context menu. The **Add MVC View** window will be displayed.
3. Name the view as `Index` and select **List** as the **Template**. From the dropdown for **Model class**, select **WorkItem (BugTracker.Models)**.
4. Leave the rest of the settings as they are and click on the **Add** button:

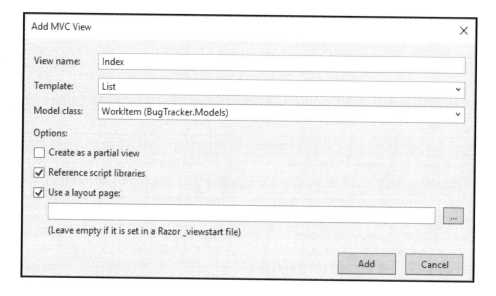

After the view has been added, your **Solution Explorer** will look as follows:

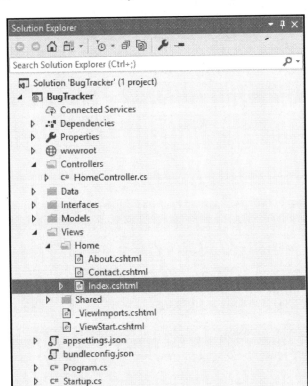

5. Taking a closer look at the view, you will notice that it uses
   `IEnumerable<BugTracker.Models.WorkItem>` as the model:

```
@model IEnumerable<BugTracker.Models.WorkItem>

@{
    ViewData["Title"] = "Work Item Listings";
}
```

This allows us to iterate the collection of the `WorkItem` objects returned and output them in the list. Also note that `ViewData["Title"]` has been updated from `Index` to `Work Item Listings`.

Modifying the HomeController

The last thing we need to do before we can run our application is to modify the
HomeController class to work with the IWorkItemService:

1. Modify the constructor and the Index action as follows:

    ```
    private readonly IWorkItemService _workItemService;

    public HomeController(IWorkItemService workItemService)
    {
        _workItemService = workItemService;
    }

    public IActionResult Index()
    {
        var workItems = _workItemService.GetAllWorkItems();
        return View(workItems);
    }
    ```

2. We are getting all the work items in the MongoDB database and passing them to
    the view for the model to work with.

Make sure that you have started the MongoDB server by using the mongod
-dbpath <path> command format, as explained earlier in the chapter.

3. When you are done, run your application, as shown in the following screenshot:

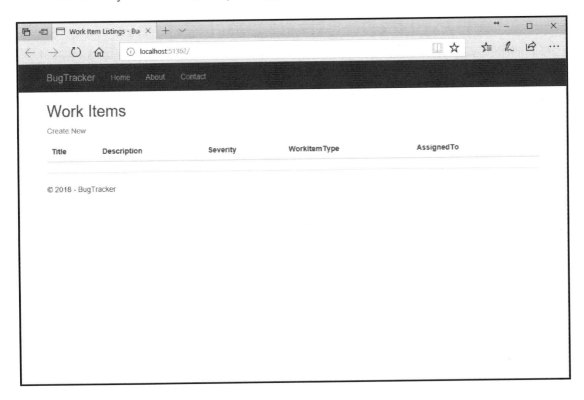

4. At this point, there are no work items in the database, so we see this empty list in the browser. Next, we will add the code to insert work items into our MongoDB database.

Adding work items

Let's add work items by performing the following steps:

1. To add work items, let's start off by adding a class to our **Models** folder called `AddWorkItem`, as shown in the following screenshot:

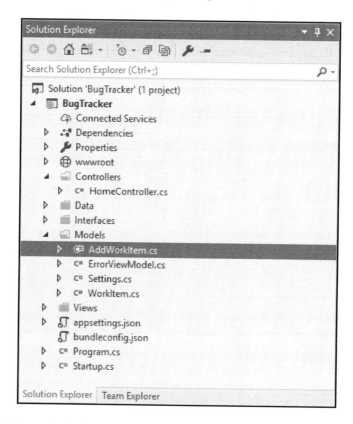

2. Modify the code in the class to essentially look like the `WorkItem` class:

```
public class AddWorkItem
{
    public string Title { get; set; }
    public string Description { get; set; }
    public int Severity { get; set; }
    public string WorkItemType { get; set; }
    public string AssignedTo { get; set; }
}
```

3. Next, create a new folder under the **Views** folder called `AddWorkItem`. Right-click the `AddWorkItem` folder and select **Add** and then click on **View** in the context menu.

4. The **Add MVC View** window will be displayed. Call the view `AddItem` and select **Create** for **Template**.

5. From the dropdown for **Model class**, select **AddWorkItem (BugTracker.Models)**.

6. Leave the rest of the settings as is and click on the **Add** button, as shown in the following screenshot:

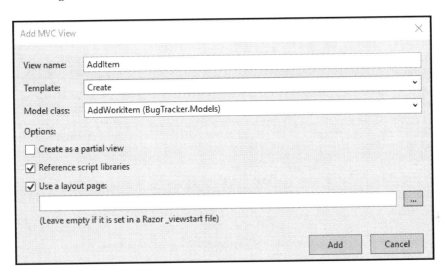

7. Open the `AddItem.cshtml` file and have a look at the form action. Ensure that it is set to `CreateWorkItem`. The following code snippet shows what the code should look like:

```
<div class="row">
  <div class="col-md-4">
    <form asp-action="CreateWorkItem">
        <div asp-validation-summary="ModelOnly" class="text-
danger"></div> @*Rest of code omitted for brevity*@
```

Your `Views` folder should now look as follows:

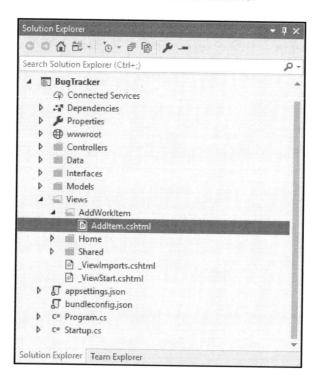

8. Now, we need to make a small change to our `IWorkItemService` interface. Modify the code in the interface to look as follows:

```
public interface IWorkItemService
{
    IEnumerable<WorkItem> GetAllWorkItems();
    void InsertWorkItem(WorkItem workItem);
}
```

We have just specified that the classes that implement the `IWorkItemService` interface must have a method called `InsertWorkItem` that takes a parameter of the `WorkItem` type. This means that we need to swing by `WorkItemService` and add a method called `InsertWorkItem`. Our code in the `WorkItemService` imterface will look as follows:

```
private readonly MongoDBRepository repository;

public WorkItemService(IOptions<Settings> settings)
{
```

```
        repository = new MongoDBRepository(settings);
    }
    public IEnumerable<WorkItem> GetAllWorkItems()
    {
        return repository.WorkItems.Find(x => true).ToList();
    }

    public void InsertWorkItem(WorkItem workItem)
    {
        throw new System.NotImplementedException();
    }
```

9. Change the `InsertWorkItem` method to add a single object of the `WorkItem` type to our MongoDB database. Change the code to look as follows:

```
    public void InsertWorkItem(WorkItem workItem)
    {
    }
```

10. Now, we need to modify our `WorkItem` class slightly. Add two constructors to the class, one that takes an `AddWorkItem` object as parameter and another that takes no parameters at all:

```
    public class WorkItem
    {
        public ObjectId Id { get; set; }
        public string Title { get; set; }
        public string Description { get; set; }
        public int Severity { get; set; }
        public string WorkItemType { get; set; }
        public string AssignedTo { get; set; }

        public WorkItem()
        {

        }

        public WorkItem(AddWorkItem addWorkItem)
        {
            Title = addWorkItem.Title;
            Description = addWorkItem.Description;
            Severity = addWorkItem.Severity;
            WorkItemType = addWorkItem.WorkItemType;
            AssignedTo = addWorkItem.AssignedTo;
        }
    }
```

The reason we have added a second constructor that takes no parameters is so that MongoDB can deserialize `WorkItem`.

 If you want to read up more regarding the reason we add a parameterless constructor for deserialization, take a look at the following URL: `https://stackoverflow.com/questions/267724/why-xml-serializable-class-need-a-parameterless-constructor`.

11. We now need to add another controller to our project. Right-click the **Controllers** folder, and add a new controller called `AddWorkItemController`. Feel free to add this as an empty controller. We will add the code in next ourselves:

12. In the **AddWorkItemController** controller, add the following code:

```
private readonly IWorkItemService _workItemService;

public AddWorkItemController(IWorkItemService workItemService)
{
    _workItemService = workItemService;
}

public ActionResult AddItem()
```

```
{
    return View();
}

[HttpPost]
public ActionResult CreateWorkItem(AddWorkItem addWorkItem)
{
    var workItem = new WorkItem(addWorkItem);
    _workItemService.InsertWorkItem(workItem);
    return RedirectToAction("Index", "Home");
}
```

You will notice that the HttpPost action is called CreateWorkItem. This is the reason that the AddItem.cshtml file had a form action called CreateWorkItem. It tells the view what action to call on the controller when the **Create** button is clicked.

Redirecting to the list of work items

Another interesting thing to note is that after we call the InsertWorkItem method on the WorkItemService, we redirect the view to the Index action on the HomeController. As we already know, this we know will take us to the list of work items:

1. Speaking of HomeController, modify the code there to add another action called AddWorkItem that calls the AddItem action on the AddWorkItemController class:

```
public ActionResult AddWorkItem()
{
    return RedirectToAction("AddItem", "AddWorkItem");
}
```
Your HomeController code will now look as follows:
```
private readonly IWorkItemService _workItemService;

public HomeController(IWorkItemService workItemService)
{
    _workItemService = workItemService;
}

public IActionResult Index()
{
    var workItems = _workItemService.GetAllWorkItems();
    return View(workItems);
}
```

```
public ActionResult AddWorkItem()
{
    return RedirectToAction("AddItem", "AddWorkItem");
}
```

2. Now, let's modify the `Index.cshtml` view slightly. To make the list on the Index view more intuitive, modify the `Index.cshtml` file.

3. Add an `if` statement to allow for the addition of new work items from the list if the list is empty.

4. Add an `ActionLink` to call the `AddWorkItem` action on the `HomeController` when clicked:

```
@if (Model.Count() == 0)
@if (Model.Count() == 0)
{
    <tr>
        <td colspan="6">There are no Work Items in BugTracker.
@Html.ActionLink("Add your first Work Item", "AddWorkItem")
now.</td>
    </tr>
}
else
{

    @foreach (var item in Model)
    {
        <tr>
            <td>
                @Html.DisplayFor(modelItem => item.Title)
            </td>
            <td>
                @Html.DisplayFor(modelItem => item.Description)
            </td>
            <td>
                @Html.DisplayFor(modelItem => item.Severity)
            </td>
            <td>
                @Html.DisplayFor(modelItem => item.WorkItemType)
            </td>
            <td>
                @Html.DisplayFor(modelItem => item.AssignedTo)
            </td>
            <td>
            @Html.ActionLink("Edit", "Edit", new { /*
             id=item.PrimaryKey */ }) |
            @Html.ActionLink("Details", "Details", new { /*
```

```
                 id=item.PrimaryKey */ }) |
             @Html.ActionLink("Delete", "Delete", new { /*
               id=item.PrimaryKey */ })
             </td>
         </tr>
      }
   }
```

5. For now, wrap the Create New `asp-action` in the following `if` statement:

```
@if (Model.Count() > 0)
{
<p>
    <a asp-action="Create">Create New</a>
</p>
}
```

We will be looking at this later on.

To take a look at the logic of the application at this point, we will see that the `HomeControllerIndex` action lists the work items. When we click on the **Add your first Work item** link, we call the `AddWorkItem` action on the `HomeController`.

The `AddWorkItem` action on the `HomeController` in turn calls the `AddItem` action on the `AddWorkItemController`. This simply returns the `AddItem` view where we enter the work item details and click on the **Create** button.

The **Create** button in turn does an `HttpPost`, and because the form action on the `AddItem` view points to the `CreateWorkItem` action on the `AddWorkItemController` class, we insert the work item into our MongoDB database and redirect back to the list of work items by performing a `RedirectToAction` call to the `Index` action on the `HomeController`.

Now at this point, if you are thinking that it this a long-winded way to redirect back to the `HomeController` just to redirect to the `AddItem` action on the `AddWorkItemController`, then you're 100% correct. I will show you a quick way to redirect directly to the `AddItem` action on the `AddWorkItemController` when the user clicks on the link to create a new work item. For now, just stick with me. I'm trying to show you how we can interact with controllers and actions.

Now, run your application again.

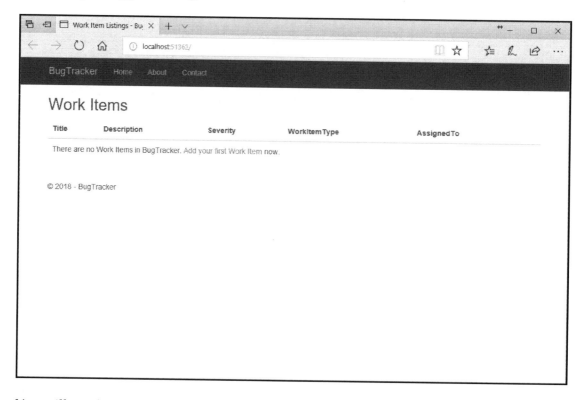

You will see that a link in the list allows you to add your first work item.

This is the link that redirects back to the `AddWorkItem` action on the `HomeController`. To run it, do the following:

1. Click on the link and you will see the output, as shown in the following screenshot:

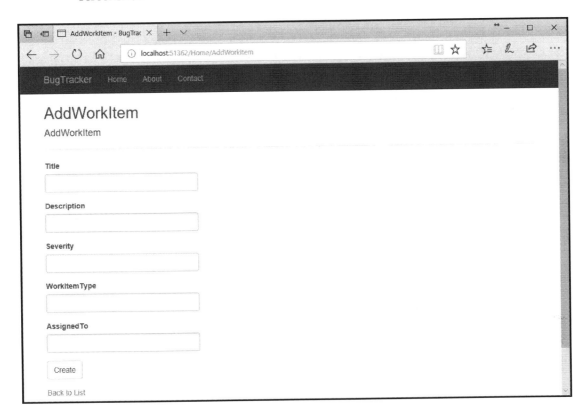

2. This will take you to the view to add a new work item. Enter in some information into the fields and click on the **Create** button.

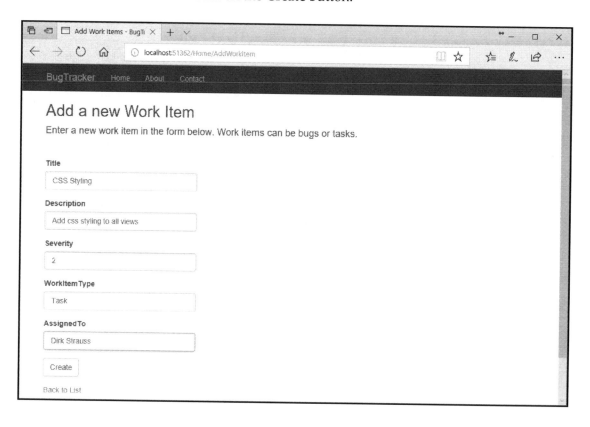

3. The **Create** button calls the `CreateWorkItem` action on the `AddWorkItemController` and redirects back to the work item list on the `Index` action of the `HomeController`.

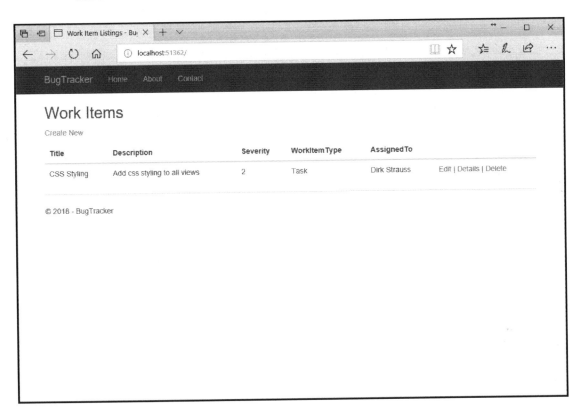

4. You can see that the **Create New** link is now displayed at the top of the list. Let's modify the **Index.cshtml** view to make that link redirect directly to the `AddItem` action on the `AddWorkItemController` class. Change the Razor as follows:

```
@if (Model.Count() > 0)
{
<p>
    @Html.ActionLink("Create New", "AddWorkItem/AddItem")
</p>
}
```

You can see that we can specify the route that the application must take to get to the correct action. In this instance, we are saying that we must call the `AddItem` action on the `AddWorkItemController` class when the **Create New** link is clicked.

Run your application again and click on the **Create New** link. You will see that you are redirected to the input form that we added the work item to earlier.

 The default styling of the views doesn't look too shabby, but they are definitely not the most beautiful designs out there. This, at least, gives you as a developer the ability to go back and style the screens with CSS, to "prettify" them according to your needs. For now, the dull screens are 100% functional and good enough for our purposes.

Open **MongoDB Compass** and you will see that there is a **workitem** document in there. View that document and you will see the information that we just added from our ASP.NET Core MVC application.

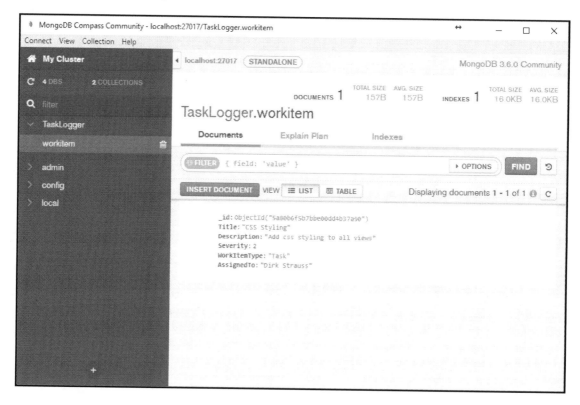

Summary

In this chapter, we had a look at:

- Setting up MongoDB on your local machine
- Using MongoDB Compass
- Creating an ASP.NET Core MVC application connected to MongoDB

We saw that MongoDB Compass gives developers a nice graphical view of their MongoDB data. Developers therefore don't need to know any MongoDB query syntax. If, however, you would like to take a look at the query syntax, head on over to, `https://docs.mongodb.com/manual/tutorial/query-documents/`.

There is still so much that you can learn when it comes to MongoDB and ASP.NET Core MVC. A single chapter is hardly enough to cover it all. What is certain though is that MongoDB is very powerful while remaining extremely simple to use in your applications. MongoDB is well-documented and there is a thriving community out there that can assist and guide you along the way.

In the next chapter, we will take a look at SignalR and how to create a real-time chat application.

5
ASP.NET SignalR Chat Application

Imagine having the ability to have your server-side code push data to your web page in real time, without the user needing to refresh the page. As they say, there are many ways to skin a cat, but the ASP.NET SignalR library provides developers with a simplified method to add real-time web functionality to applications.

To showcase the capabilities of SignalR, we'll build a simple ASP.NET Core SignalR chat application. This will include the use of NuGet and **Node Package Manager** (**npm**) to add the required package files to the project.

In this chapter, we will look into the following:

- Overall project layout
- Setting up the project
- Adding the SignalR libraries
- Building the server
- Creating a client
- Solution overview
- Running the application

Let's dive in.

Project layout

For this project, we'll need the following elements:

- **Chat Server**: This will be our server-side C# code that will process and direct the messages sent from the client(s)
- **Chat Client(s)**: A client will consist of JavaScript functions for sending messages to and receiving messages from the server, and HTML elements for display

We'll start with the server code and move over to the client, building a simple bootstrap layout and calling some JavaScript functions from there.

As a bonus, we'll include a method to archive our conversation history to a text file.

Setting up the project

Let's set up this project:

1. Using Visual Studio 2017, we will create an **ASP.NET Core Web Application**. You can call the application anything you like, but I called mine Chapter5:

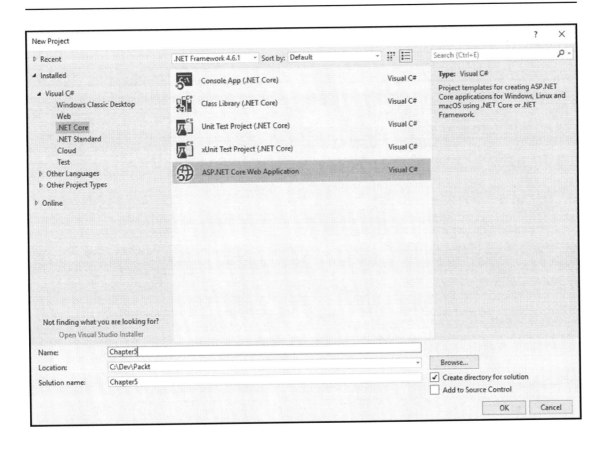

2. We'll go with an empty project template. Be sure to select **ASP.NET Core 2.0** from the dropdown:

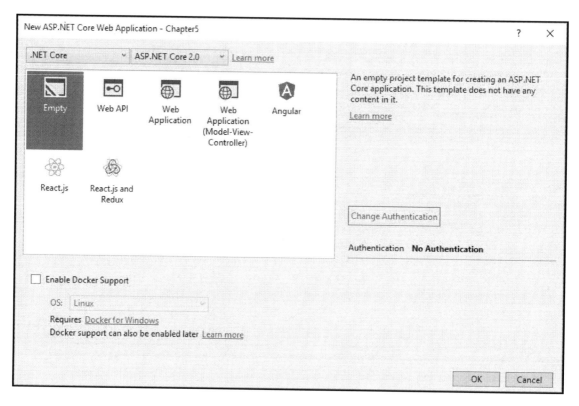

The project will be created and will look as follows:

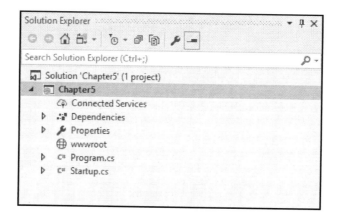

Adding the SignalR libraries

Next, we need to add the SignalR package files to our project.

At the time of writing, the package for **ASP.NET Core SignalR** could not be found when browsing in the **NuGet Package Manager**, so we'll use the **Package Manager Console** to add the packages needed.

1. Go to **Tools** | **NuGet Package Manager** | **Package Manager Console**:

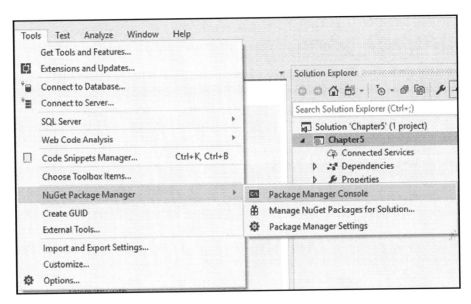

2. In the console window type the following command and hit enter:

```
Install-Package Microsoft.AspnetCore.SignalR -Version 1.0.0-
alpha2-final
```

You should see a few response lines showing the items that were **Successfully installed**.

We also need the SignalR client JavaScript library for our project. For this we'll use an npm command.

npm is a package manager, like NuGet, but for JavaScript. Feel free to check it out at https://www.npmjs.com.

3. In the console window type the following command and hit *enter*:

```
npm install @aspnet/signalr-client
```

This will download a host of js files to a `node_modules` folder within your project's root directory. The output may show some warnings, but fear not. You can confirm that the download was successful if the `node_modules` directory exists.

With our packages in place, we can (finally) start writing some code.

Building the server

We'll need to build a server for our chat program, which will contain the methods we want to call from our connected clients. We'll use the SignalR Hubs API, which provides the methods needed for connected clients to communicate with our chat server.

SignalR Hub subclass

We now need to create the SignalR Hub. To do this, perform the following steps:

1. Add a class to your project to handle the server-side of the chat. We'll call it `Chat`:

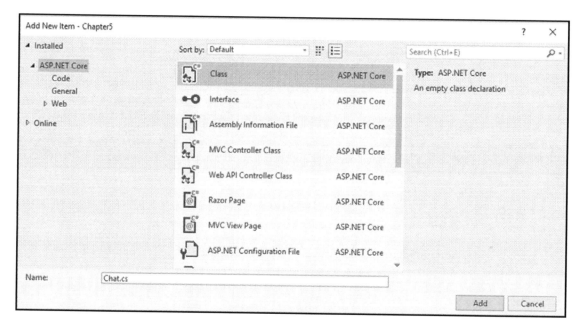

This will need to be a subclass of the SignalR Hub class. Make sure to add the using directive for `Micosoft.AspNetCore.SignalR`. Visual Studio's *Quick Actions* works well for this:

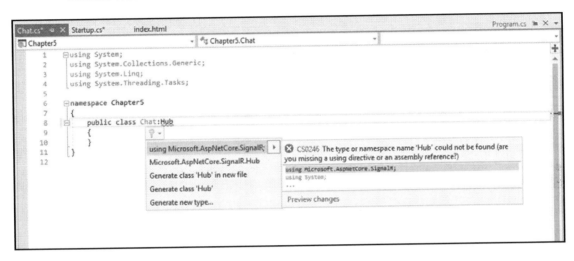

2. Now add a `Task` method to the class to handle the sending of the messages:

```
public Task Send(string sender, string message)
{
    return Clients.All.InvokeAsync("UpdateChat", sender,
    message);
}
```

This method will be called through any of the connected clients and will invoke all connected clients' `Send` function, passing through the sender and message parameters.

3. Now add a `Task` method to handle the archive functionality:

```
public Task ArchiveChat(string archivedBy, string path,
  string messages)
{
    string fileName = "ChatArchive" +
    DateTime.Now.ToString("yyyy_MM_dd_HH_mm") + ".txt";
    System.IO.File.WriteAllText(path + "\" + fileName,
    messages);
    return Clients.All.InvokeAsync("Archived", "Chat
    archived by "+ archivedBy);
}
```

As you can see, this method simply takes the value of the messages string parameter, writes it to a new text file named `ChatArchive_[date].txt`, which is saved to the given path, and invoke the client(s) `Archived` function.

For these two tasks to actually work we need to do some more scaffolding.

Configuration changes

In the `Startup.cs` file, we need to add the SignalR service to the container as well as configure the HTTP request pipeline.

1. In the `ConfigureServices` method, add the following code:

```
services.AddSignalR();
```

2. In the `Configure` method, add the following code:

```
app.UseSignalR(routes =>
    {
        routes.MapHub<Chat>("chat");
    });
```

Your code window will now look as follows:

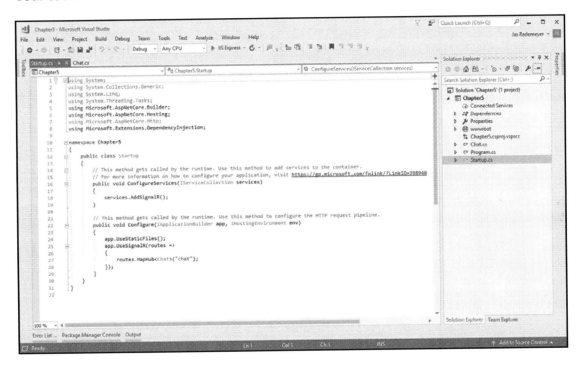

That's our server done.

You will note that I have added the following line of code, `app.UseStaticFiles()` to the `Configure` method. Static files are assets that an ASP.NET Core app serves directly to clients. Examples of static files are HTML, CSS, JavaScript, and images.

We can (and will) extend our server's functionality a bit later, but, for now, let's head over to our client.

Creating a client

As mentioned in our Project Layout, the client will consist of JavaScript functions for sending messages to and receiving message from the server, and HTML elements for display.

1. In your project, add a new folder under `wwwroot`, called `scripts`:

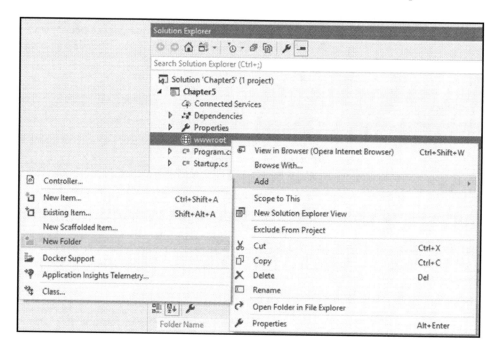

Remember that the `node_modules` directory that was created for us by our `npm` command earlier?

2. Navigate to the following path within the `node_modules` directory:

```
\@aspnet\signalr-client\dist\browser
```

Take a look at the following screenshot:

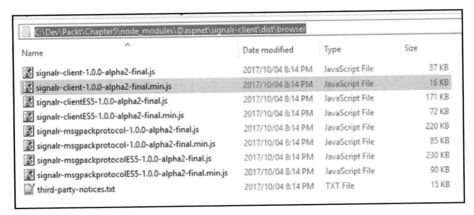

3. Copy the `signalr-client-1.0.0-alpha2-final.min.js` file to the scripts folder we just created in our project. We will be referencing this library within our HTML file, which we will create now.

4. Add an HTML page to the `wwwroot` folder. I've named mine `index.html`. I'll recommend naming yours the same. I'll explain later:

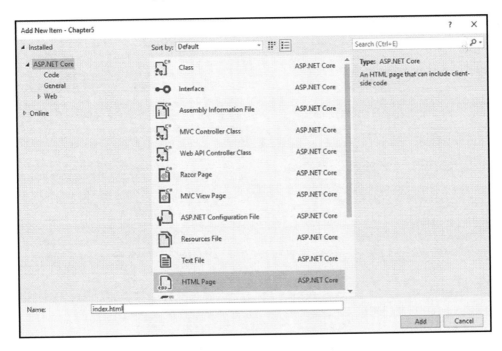

We'll keep the client page really simple. I'm using `div` tags as panels to show and hide the different sections on the page. I'm also using bootstrap to make it look nice, but you can design it whichever way you like. I'm also not going to bore you with the basics like where to specify your page title. We'll stick to the relevant elements.

Let me show you the entire HTML layout code as well as the JavaScript and we'll break it down from there:

```
<!DOCTYPE html>
<html>
<head>
    <title>Chapter 5- Signal R</title>
    <link rel="stylesheet"
href="https://maxcdn.bootstrapcdn.com/bootstrap/3.3.7/css/boots
trap.min.css">
    <script
src="https://ajax.googleapis.com/ajax/libs/jquery/3.2.1/jquery.
min.js"></script>
    <script
src="https://maxcdn.bootstrapcdn.com/bootstrap/3.3.7/js/bootstr
ap.min.js"></script>
    <script src="/Scripts/signalr-client-1.0.0-alpha2-
final.min.js"></script>

    <script type="text/javascript">
        let connection = new signalR.HubConnection('/chat');
        connection.start();

        connection.on('UpdateChat', (user, message) => {
            updateChat(user, message);
        });
        connection.on('Archived', (message) => {
            updateChat('system', message);
        });

        function enterChat() {
            $('#user').text($('#username').val());
            sendWelcomeMessage($('#username').val());
            $('#namePanel').hide();
            $('#chatPanel').show();
        };

        function sendMessage() {
            let message = $('#message').val();
            let user = $('#user').text();
            $('#message').val('');
            connection.invoke('Send', user, message);
```

```
        };

        function sendWelcomeMessage(user) {
            connection.invoke('Send','system',user+' joined the
            chat');
        };

        function updateChat(user, message) {
            let chat = '<b>' + user + ':</b> ' + message +
            '<br/>'
            $('#chat').append(chat);
            if ($('#chat')["0"].innerText.length > 0) {
                $('#historyPanel').show();
                $('#archivePanel').show();
            }
        };

        function archiveChat() {
            let message = $('#chat')["0"].innerText;
            let archivePath = $('#archivePath').val();
            let archivedBy = $('#username').val();
            connection.invoke('ArchiveChat', archivedBy,
             archivePath, message);
        };
    </script>

</head>
<body>
    <div class="container col-md-10">
        <h1>Welcome to Signal R <label id="user"></label></h1>
    </div>
    <hr />
    <div id="namePanel" class="container">
        <div class="row">
            <div class="col-md-2">
                <label for="username" class="form-
                    label">Username:</label>
            </div>
            <div class="col-md-4">
                <input id="username" type="text" class="form-
                    control" />
            </div>
            <div class="col-md-6">
                <button class="btn btn-default"
                    onclick="enterChat()">Enter</button>
            </div>
        </div>
    </div>
```

```
    <div id="chatPanel" class="container" style="display:
none">
        <div class="row">
            <div class="col-md-2">
                <label for="message" class="form-
label">Message:
                </label>
            </div>
            <div class="col-md-4">
                <input id="message" type="text" class="form-
                control" />
            </div>
            <div class="col-md-6">
                <button class="btn btn-info"
                onclick="sendMessage()">Send</button>
            </div>
        </div>
        <div id="historyPanel" style="display:none;">
            <h3>Chat History</h3>
            <div class="row">
                <div class="col-md-12">
                    <div id="chat" class="well well-lg"></div>
                </div>
            </div>
        </div>
    </div>
    <div id="archivePanel" class="container"
style="display:none;">
        <div class="row">
            <div class="col-md-2">
                <label for="archivePath" class="form-
                label">Archive Path:</label>
            </div>
            <div class="col-md-4">
                <input id="archivePath" type="text"
class="form-
                control" />
            </div>
            <div class="col-md-6">
                <button class="btn btn-success"
                onclick="archiveChat()">Archive Chat</button>
            </div>
        </div>
    </div>
</body></html>
```

Included libraries

Add `link` and `script` tags to include the required libraries:

```
<link rel="stylesheet"
href="https://maxcdn.bootstrapcdn.com/bootstrap/3.3.7/css/
bootstrap.min.css">
<script
src="https://ajax.googleapis.com/ajax/libs/jquery/3.2.1/jquery.min.
js">
</script>
<script
src="https://maxcdn.bootstrapcdn.com/bootstrap/3.3.7/js/bootstrap.m
in.js">
</script>
<script src="/Scripts/signalr-client-1.0.0-alpha2-final.min.js">
</script>
```

If you do not want to use bootstrap for the look and feel, you don't need the bootstrap JavaScript library or CSS, but note that we will be using jQuery in our scripts, so leave that one in.

Naming section

We'll need to know who our chatroom attendee is. Add an input element to capture the username and a button to call the `enterChat` function:

- `<input id="username" type="text" class="form-control" />`
- `<button class="btn btn-default"`
  `onclick="enterChat()">Enter</button>`

Chat input

Add the required elements to enable our user to type a message (input) and post it to the server (event button for `sendMessage`):

- `<input id="message" type="text" class="form-control" />`
- `<button class="btn btn-info"`
  `onclick="sendMessage()">Send</button>`

Conversation panel

Add a `div` tag with ID "`chat`". We will use this as a container for our conversation (chat history):

- `<div id="chat" class="well well-lg"></div>`

Archive function

Add the required elements to enable our user to specify a path where the archive file needs to be saved (input) and post the messages to the server (event button for `archiveChat`):

- `<input id="archivePath" type="text" class="form-control" />`
- `<button class="btn btn-info" onclick="archiveChat()">Archive Chat</button>`

JavaScript functions

Our client will need some code to send and consume messages to and from the server. I've tried to keep the JavaScript as simple as possible, opting for jQuery code for readability:

1. Create a variable (I've named mine `connection`) for our SignalR Hub Server and call its start function:

   ```
   let connection = new signalR.HubConnection('/chat');
   connection.start();
   ```

   The '`/chat`' parameter for `signalR.HubConnection` refers to our `Chat.cs` class, which inherits the Hub interface from SignalR.

2. Add the `UpdateChat` and `Archived` methods, which will be invoked by the server:

   ```
   connection.on('UpdateChat', (user, message) => {
   updateChat(user, message);
   });
   connection.on('Archived', (message) => {
   updateChat('system', message);
   });
   ```

We simply pass the parameters we get from the server onto our `updateChat` method. We'll define that method in a bit.

3. Define the `enterChat` function:

```
function enterChat() {
$('#user').text($('#username').val());
sendWelcomeMessage($('#username').val());
$('#namePanel').hide();
$('#chatPanel').show();
};
```

We set the text of our `user` label from the value of the username input element, pass it through to our `sendWelcomeMessage` method (which we'll define in a bit), and toggle the display of the relevant panels.

4. Define the `sendMessage` method:

```
function sendMessage() {
let message = $('#message').val();
$('#message').val('');
let user = $('#user').text();
connection.invoke('Send', user, message);
};
```

We set the `message` variable from the message input element, before clearing it for the next message, and the `user` variable from the user label. Then we call the `Send` method on our server by using the `connection.invoke` method and pass through our variables as parameters.

5. Define the `sendWelcomeMessage` function:

```
function sendWelcomeMessage(user) {
connection.invoke('Send','system',user+' joined the chat');
};
```

Just like the `sendMessage` function described in step 4, we will use the `connection.invoke` function to call the `Send` method on our server. This time though we pass through the string `'system'` as the user parameter and a little informational message about the user that just joined.

6. Define the `updateChat` method:

```
function updateChat(user, message) {
let chat = '<b>' + user + ':</b> ' + message + '<br/>'
```

```
$('#chat').append(chat);
if ($('#chat')["0"].innerText.length > 0) {
$('#historyPanel').show();
$('#archivePanel').show();
}
};
```

`updateChat` is just our custom function used to update the chat history panel. We could have done this inline in the two `connection.on` functions, but that means we would have repeated ourselves. As a general rule in any coding you should try not to repeat code.

In this function, we set the `chat` variable to however we want each chat history line to look in terms of styling. In this case, we simply style our user (with a colon) bold with the message un-styled afterwards and a line-break at the end. A few lines of chat will look something like this:

- **John**: Hello people
- **Sarah**: Hi John
- **server**: Peter joined the chat
- **John**: Hi Sarah, Hello Peter
- **Peter**: Hello Everyone

I also check the chat div `innerText` property to determine if the chat history and archive panels should be visible.

Define the `archiveChat` function:

```
function archiveChat() {
let message = $('#chat')["0"].innerText;
let archivePath = $('#archivePath').val();
connection.invoke('ArchiveChat', archivePath, message);
};
```

Like everything else, I've tried to keep this as simple as possible. We take the `innerText` of our chat panel (div) and the path specified in the `archivePath` input and pass it through to the server's `ArchiveChat` method.

Of course we have a small window for error here: if the user does not type in a valid path for the file to be saved, the code will throw an exception. I'll leave it to your own creativity to sort that one out. I'm just here for the SignalR functionality.

Solution overview

Now you should have a complete, buildable solution. Let's have a quick look at the solution in **Solution Explorer**:

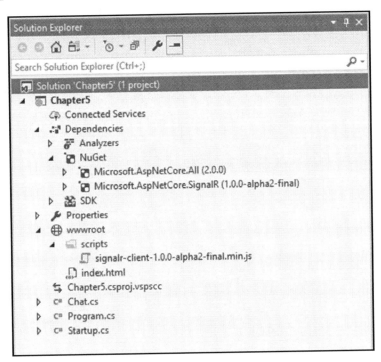

Starting at the top, let me list the changes we've made to our Chapter5 project:

1. The following is the SignalR Asp.NET Core library we added through NuGet:

   ```
   Dependencies/NuGet/Microsoft.AspNetCore.SignalR (1.0.0-
   alpha2-final)
   ```

2. We copied this JavaScript library manually from the node_modules folder after we downloaded it using npm:

   ```
   wwwroot/scripts/signalr-client-1.0.0-alpha2-final.min.js
   ```

3. Our client page with HTML markup, styling and JavaScript all in one: one.wwwroot/index.html

If you are going to use this application as a base and extend it, I recommend moving the JavaScript code to a separate `.js` file. It is easier to manage and is another good coding standard to follow.

1. `Chat.cs`: This is our chat server code—or rather any custom Task methods that we declared
2. `Startup.cs`: This file is standard in an Asp.NET Code web application, but we changed the configuration to make sure SignalR is added as a service

1. Let's build our project. On the top menu in Visual Studio, click the **Build menu** button:

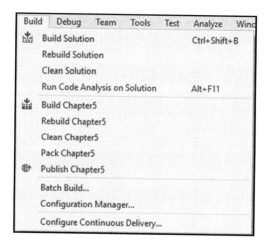

You can choose to either build the entire solution, or in individual project. Seeing that we only have one project in our solution, we can choose either. You can also use the keyboard shortcut *Ctrl + Shift + B*.

You should see some (hopefully successful) build messages in the **Output** window:

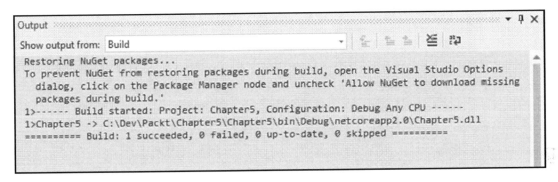

If you get any errors, go through the chapter again and see whether you have missed something. A small thorn can cause a lot of discomfort.

Showing and telling

It's time. You've created the project, added the libraries, and wrote the code. Now let's see this thing in action.

Running the application

To run the app, hit *F5* (or *Ctrl + F5* to start without debugging). The app will open in your default browser and you should see this:

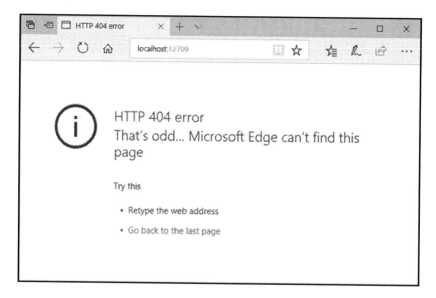

Wait. What? We must be missing something here.

Now we could just navigate to the index.html page by changing our URL to `localhost:12709/index.html` (just check your port number) and we'll be all good.

Instead, let's specify our `index.html` page as our default launch page.

In the `Startup.cs` class, in the `Configure` method, add this line at the top:

```
app.UseDefaultFiles();
```

With this little gem, any request to the `wwwroot` folder (which at any time navigates to your website) will search for one of the following:

- `default.htm`
- `default.html`
- `index.htm`
- `index.html`

The first file found will be the file served as your default page. Great!

Now let's run our app again:

Even though our URL still does not show the `/index.html` part, our web app now knows which page to serve. Now we can start chatting. Type a username and hit *Enter*:

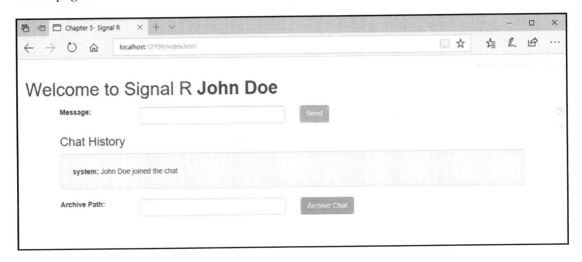

As you can see, our name panel is now hidden and our chat and archive panels are showing.

Our server was also kind enough to inform us that we joined the chat, thanks to our `sendWelcomeMessage(user)` function.

Every time we send a message, our **Chat History** will be updated:

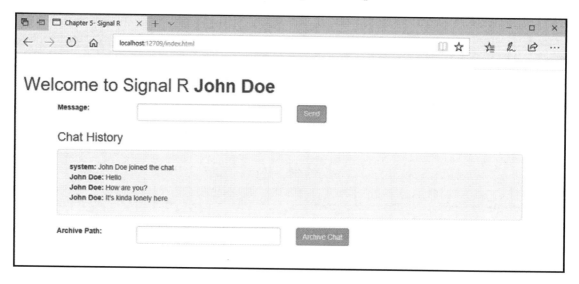

Getting the party started

A conversation is only a conversation if multiple parties are involved. So let's start a party.

If you publish the app on a network you can use actual network clients to chat with, but I'm not on a network (not in that sense), so we use another trick. We can use various browsers to represent our different party guests (network clients).

Copy your application URL (once again, check the port number) and paste it into a few other browsers.

For each new guest (browser) you will need to specify a username. To make it easier to follow, I'll call my additional guests the different browser names.

As each of them enter the chat and start sending messages, you'll see our **Chat History** grow:

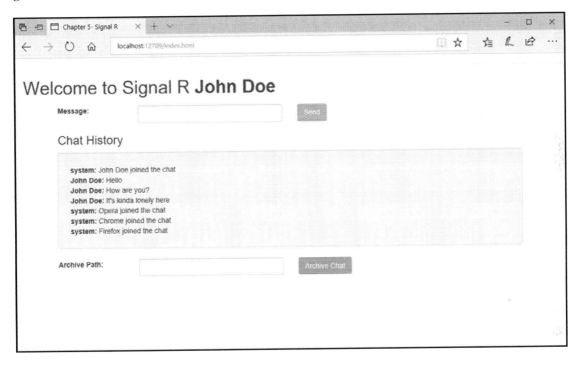

You can tile the browsers (or move them to other monitors if you have extra) to see how many message sent by one, gets delivered to all instantaneously, which is the whole point of SignalR.

We started with **John Doe** in Microsoft Edge, so we'll continue with him there:

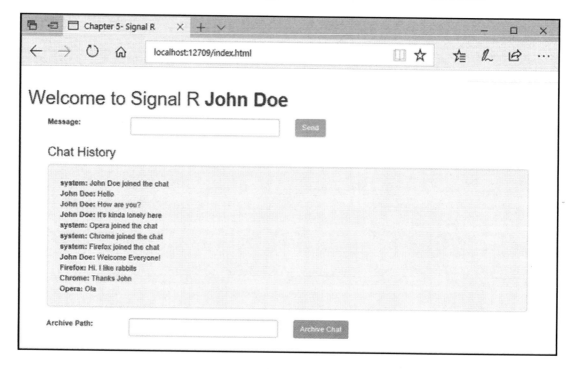

Opera was the first to join the party:

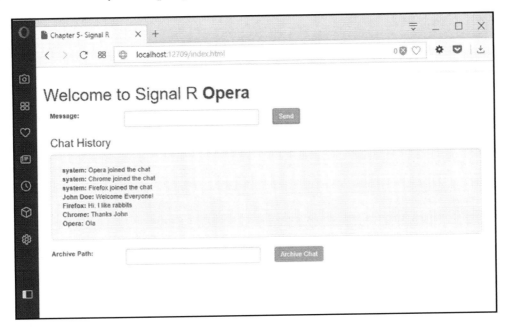

Then Chrome arrived:

And finally, Firefox joined as well:

You'll also notice that each guest's chat history only starts when they join the chat. This is by design. We don't send historical chats to clients when they join.

Archiving the chat

To save the chat history to a text file, enter a valid local folder path in the `archivePath` input element and hit the **Archive Chat** button:

As mentioned earlier, we haven't built in proper validation for our path, so make sure you test it using a valid path. If successful, you should see a message in the chat window like this:

> **system:** Chat archived by John Doe

You will also find the newly created text file in the specified path with the `ChatArchive_[date].txt` naming convention.

Summary

As shown in this chapter, SignalR is really easy to implement. We created a chat application, but there are a number of apps that can benefit from real-time experiences. These include stock exchange, social media, multiplayer games, auctions, e-commerce, financial reporting, and weather notifications

The list can go on. Even if the need for real-time data is not a requirement, SignalR can still be beneficial for any app to make communication between nodes seamless.

Glancing at the GitHub page for Asp.NET SignalR (`https://github.com/aspnet/SignalR`), it is obvious that the library is constantly being worked on and improved, which is great news.

With the need for quick, relevant, and accurate information becoming more critical, SignalR is a great player to have on your team.

6

Web Research Tool with Entity Framework Core

"The biggest lie I tell myself is that I don't need to write it down, I'll remember it."
— Unknown

So, you've got a few minutes to catch up on your feeds. As you scroll through, you come across a link to an article that someone shared about new ways to remember your guitar chords. You really want to read it, but you don't have enough time now. *"I'll read it later"*, you tell yourself, and later becomes never. Mainly because you did not write it down.

Now there are various applications out there that cater for your need to save links for later use. But we're developers. Let's just have some fun writing our own.

In this chapter, we will look at the following:

- **Entity Framework (EF)** Core history
- Code-First versus Model-First versus Database-First approach
- Developing a database design
- Setting up the project
- Installing EF Core
- Creating the models
- Configuring the services
- Creating the database
- Seeding the database with test data

- Creating the controller
- Running the application
- Deploying the application

That is quite a mouthful, but don't fret, we'll take it one step at a time. Let's take a walk.

Entity Framework (EF) Core history

One of the most frustrating parts of developing an application that needs to read data from and write data to some sort of database, is trying to get the communication layer between your code and the database established.

At least, it used to be.

Enter Entity Framework

Entity Framework is an **object-relational mapper (ORM)**. It maps your .NET code objects to relational database entities. As simple as that. Now, you don't have to concern yourself with scaffolding the required data-access code just to handle plain CRUD operations.

When the first version of Entity Framework was released with .NET 3.5 SP1 in August 2008, the initial response wasn't that great, so much so that a group of developers signed a *vote of no confidence* with regards to the framework. Thankfully, most of the raised concerns were addressed and the release of Entity Framework 4.0, together with .NET 4.0, put to bed a lot of the criticisms around the stability of the framework.

Microsoft then decided to take .NET cross-platform with .NET Core, which meant that Entity Framework Core was a complete rewrite. This obviously has its pros and cons as a comparison between EF Core and EF6 reveals that, while EF Core introduces new features and improvements, it remains a new code base and thus does not yet have all the features available in EF6.

Code-First versus Model-First versus Database-First approach

With Entity Framework, you can choose between three approaches of implementation, and it's always nice to have a choice. Let's have a quick look at the differences between them.

Code-First approach

The weapon of choice for hardcore programmers, this approach gives you full control over the database, from code. The database is seen a simple storage location and will most likely not contain any logic or business rules. Everything is driven from the code and thus any changes required need to be done in code as well:

Model-First approach

If you prefer painting over poetry, then you might prefer the Model-First approach. In this approach, you create or draw your model, and the workflow will generate a database script. You could also extend your model with partial classes, if there is a need to add specific logic or business rules, but it could become hairy and it might be better to consider the Code-First approach if there are too many specifics:

Database-First approach

The Database-First approach works well for large projects where you have a dedicated DBA designing and maintaining your database. Entity Framework will create your entities for you from the database design and you can run model updates whenever database changes are done:

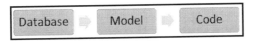

Developing a database design

We can't know what we're doing until we know what we're doing. Before we jump in and create a Solution with our database, models, and controllers, we need to first figure out how we want to design the database.

According to Microsoft's TechNet, there are five basic steps one could follow to plan a database:

1. Gather information
2. Identify the objects
3. Model the objects
4. Identify the types of information for each object
5. Identify the relationship between objects

Our requirement is pretty simple. We only need to save a web link to navigate to later, so we won't have multiple objects with relationships between them.

We do, however, need to clarify the types of information we'd like to save for our object (web link). Obviously, we need the URL, but what else do we need? Make sure you understand what information is required for your Solution and how it will be used.

Think about it in everyday terms—if you write an address for a friend's house, you might want something more that just a street, possibly your friend's name or a note of some kind.

In our Solution, we want to know what the URL is, but we also want to know when we saved it and have a place to capture a note so we can add more personal detail to an entry. Our model will thus contain the following:

- URL
- DateSaved
- Notes

We'll go into more detail when we start creating our models, but let's not jump the gun. We still need to create our project.

Setting up the project

Using Visual Studio 2017, create an **ASP.NET Core Web Application**. Please note that we are taking a Code-First approach to this project:

1. Let's call the application `WebResearch`. This is shown in the following screenshot:

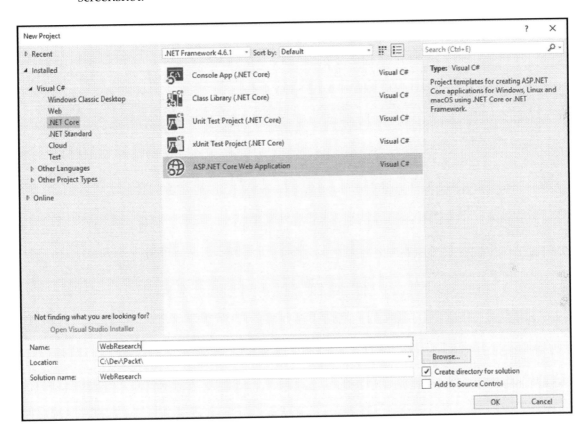

2. On the next screen, choose **Web Application (Model-View-Controller)** as a project template. To keep things simple, keep the authentication as **No Authentication**. Refer to the following screenshot:

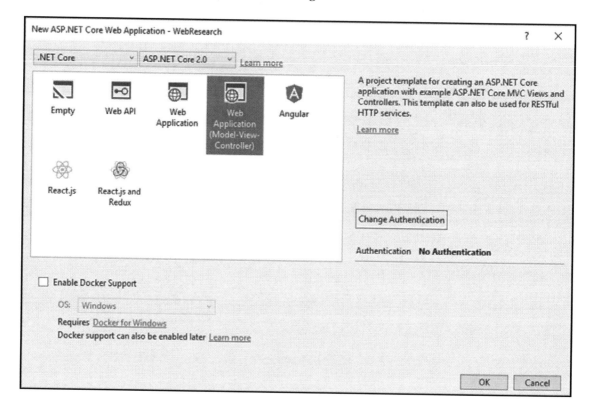

3. The created project will look as follows:

Installing the required packages

We need to install three NuGet packages to our Solution that will assist us in our quest. This is done through the **Package Manager Console**.

Go to **Tools** | **NuGet Package Manager** | **Package Manager Console**:

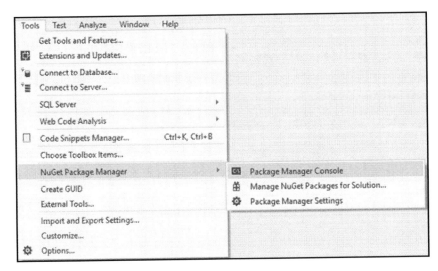

Entity Framework Core SQL Server

There are various database providers catered for by EF Core, including Microsoft SQL Server, PostgreSQL, SQLite, and MySQL. We will use SQL Server as a database provider.

 For a full list of database providers, have a look at the official Microsoft documentation

at: `https://docs.microsoft.com/en-us/ef/core/providers/index`.

In the console window, type the following command and hit *Enter*:

```
Install-Package Microsoft.EntityFrameworkCore.SqlServer
```

You should see a few response lines showing the items that were successfully installed.

Entity Framework Core tools

Next up, we'll install some Entity Framework Core tools that will assist us with creating our database from our models.

In the console window, type the following command and hit *Enter*:

```
Install-Package Microsoft.EntityFrameworkCore.Tools
```

Once again, you should see a few response lines showing the items that were successfully installed.

Code generation design

Instead of writing all the code ourselves, we can use some ASP.Net Core code generation tools to aid us with our scaffolding.

Next up in the console window, type the following command and hit *Enter*:

```
Install-Package Microsoft.VisualStudio.Web.CodeGeneration.Design
```

As usual, check to see that you get the `Successfully Installed` items.

> If you have problems installing any NuGet packages, it might point to an access control issue. As a general rule, I set up my Visual Studio to run as administrator, which sorts out most of those problems.

After installation, our Solution will reflect the added NuGet packages under the **Dependencies** section, shown as follows:

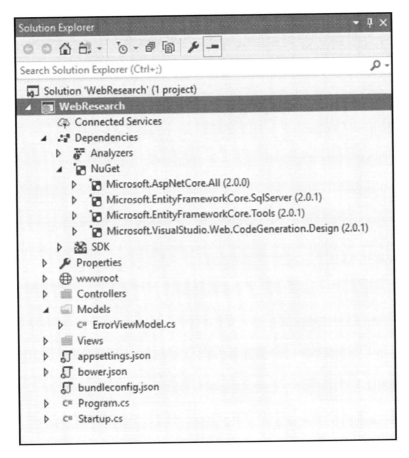

Creating the models

Right-click on the **Models** folder in your project and add a class called `ResearchModel.cs`:

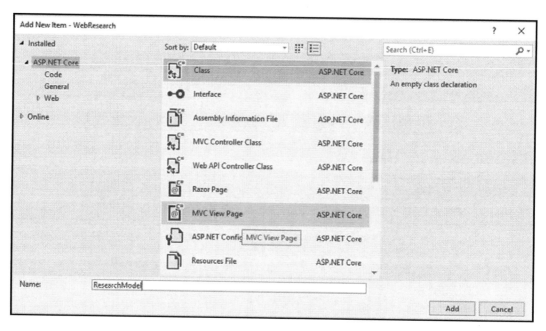

We actually need two classes—a `Research` class that is a representation of our `entity` object, and another, `ResearchContext`, which is a subclass of `DbContext`. To keep things simple, we can put both classes in our `ResearchModel` file.

Here's the code:

```
using Microsoft.EntityFrameworkCore;
using System;

namespace WebResearch.Models
{
    public class Research
    {
        public int Id { get; set; }
        public string Url { get; set; }
        public DateTime DateSaved { get; set; }
        public string Note { get; set; }
    }

    public class ResearchContext : DbContext
```

```
    {
        public ResearchContext(DbContextOptions<ResearchContext>
        options) : base(options)
        {
        }

        public DbSet<Research> ResearchLinks { get; set; }
    }
}
```

Let's break it down as follows:

Firstly, we have our `Research` class, which is our `entity` object representation. As covered in our *Developing a database design* section, as discussed earlier, for each link we will save the URL, the date, and a note. The ID field is standard practice for a database table that holds information.

Our second class, `ResearchContext`, is a subclass of `DbContext`. This class will have an empty constructor taking `DbContextOptions` as a parameter and a `DbSet<TEntity>` property for our data collection.

I could give you a brief overview here about `DbSet<Entity>`, but I'd rather let Visual Studio help us out. If you hover over `DbSet`, you'll get an informational pop-up with everything you need to know:

```
class Microsoft.EntityFrameworkCore.DbSet<TEntity> where TEntity : class
A DbSet<TEntity> can be used to query and save instances of TEntity. LINQ queries against a DbSet<TEntity> will be translated into queries against the database.

The results of a LINQ query against a DbSet<TEntity> will contain the results returned from the database and may not reflect changes made in the context that have not been persisted to the database. For example, the results will not contain newly added entities and may still contain entities that are marked for deletion.

Depending on the database being used, some parts of a LINQ query against a DbSet<TEntity> may be evaluated in memory rather than being translated into a database query.

DbSet<TEntity> objects are usually obtained from a DbSet<TEntity> property on a derived DbContext or from the DbContext.Set<TEntity>() method.

TEntity is Research
```

Configuring the services

In the `Startup.cs` class, in the `ConfigureServices` method, add the `DbContext` service with the following code:

```
string connection =
Configuration.GetConnectionString("LocalDBConnection");
services.AddDbContext<ResearchContext>(options =>
options.UseSqlServer(connection));
```

As you can see, we set a connection string variable from the configuration, and then pass that in as an options parameter for `SqlServer` for our `DbContext`.

But hold on. Where does `LocalDBConnection` come from? We haven't set anything in our configuration. Not yet, anyway. Let's get that done now.

Open the `appsettings.json` file in the root of the project:

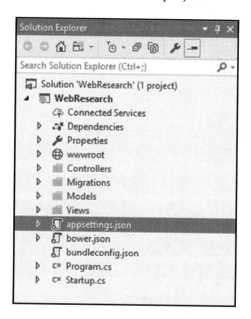

By default, you should see a logging entry. Add your `ConnectionStrings` section after the `Logging` section with a `LocalDBConnection` property.

The full file should look something like this:

```
{
  "Logging": {
    "IncludeScopes": false,
    "LogLevel": {
      "Default": "Warning"
    }
  },

  "ConnectionStrings": {
    "LocalDBConnection": "Server=(localdb)\mssqllocaldb;
    Database=WebResearch;
    Trusted_Connection=True"
```

```
        }
    }
```

Later on, we will look at how to connect to an existing database, but for now we are just connecting to a local db file.

Creating the database

During the development phase of any application, there is a fairly high probability that your data model can change. When that happens, your EF Core model differs from the database schema and you have to delete the outdated database and create a new one based on the updated model.

This is all fun and games until you've done your first live implementation and your application runs in a production environment. You cannot then go and drop a database just to change a few columns. You have to make sure the live data persists when you make any changes.

Entity Framework Core Migrations is a nifty feature that enables us to make changes to the database schema instead of recreating the database and losing production data. There is a lot of functionality and flexibility possible with `Migrations`, and it is a topic well worth spending time on, but we'll just cover some of the basics for now.

We can use EF Core Migration commands in the `Package Manager Console` to set up, create, and if needed, update our database.

In the `Package Manager Console`, we will execute the following two commands:

1. `Add-Migration InitialCreate`
2. `Update-Database`

The first command will generate the code in the `Migrations` folder of the project, which is used to create the database. The naming convention for these files is `<timestamp>_InitialCreate.cs`.

The second command will create the database and run the `Migrations`:

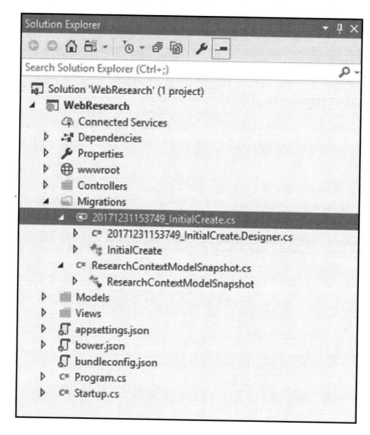

There are two methods of `Note` in the `InitialCreate` class, Up and `Down`. Simply put, the Up method code executes when you Up-grade the application and the `Down` method code is run when you Down-grade the application.

Let's say we want to add a Boolean property to our `Research` model called `Read`. To persist the value, we would obviously need to add that column to our table as well, but we don't want to drop the table just to add a field. With `Migrations` we can update the table rather than recreate it.

We'll start by altering our model. In the `Research` class, add the `Read` property. Our class will look as follows:

```
public class Research
{
    public int Id { get; set; }
    public string Url { get; set; }
    public DateTime DateSaved { get; set; }
    public string Note { get; set; }
    public bool Read { get; set; }
}
```

Next, we'll add a `Migration`. We'll use the `Migration` name as an indication of what we're doing. Execute the following command in your `Package Manager Console`:

Add-Migration AddReseachRead

You will notice we have a new class in our `Migrations` folder:

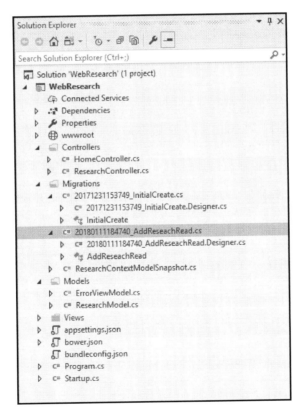

Let's have a look under the hood. You will see that our `Up` and `Down` methods aren't as empty as in the `InitialCreate` class:

```
20180111184740_AddReseachRead.cs  ⧵ X   ResearchModel.cs
WebResearch                                                    WebResearch.Migrations.Ad
  1     using Microsoft.EntityFrameworkCore.Migrations;
  2     using System;
  3     using System.Collections.Generic;
  4
  5     namespace WebResearch.Migrations
  6     {
  7         public partial class AddReseachRead : Migration
  8         {
  9             protected override void Up(MigrationBuilder migrationBuilder)
 10             {
 11                 migrationBuilder.AddColumn<bool>(
 12                     name: "Read",
 13                     table: "ResearchLinks",
 14                     nullable: false,
 15                     defaultValue: false);
 16             }
 17
 18             protected override void Down(MigrationBuilder migrationBuilder)
 19             {
 20                 migrationBuilder.DropColumn(
 21                     name: "Read",
 22                     table: "ResearchLinks");
 23             }
 24         }
 25     }
 26
```

As mentioned earlier, the `Up` method executes during an Up-grade and the `Down` method during a Down-grade. This concept is a lot clearer now that we can see the code. In the `Up` method, we are adding the `Read` column and in the `Down` method we are dropping the column.

We can make changes to this code if needed. We can, for example, change the `nullable` attribute of the `Read` column, but updating the code to look as follows:

```
protected override void Up(MigrationBuilder migrationBuilder)
{
    migrationBuilder.AddColumn<bool>(
        name: "Read",
        table: "ResearchLinks",
        nullable: true,
        defaultValue: false);
}
```

We can also add a custom SQL query that will update all existing entries to `Read`:

```
migrationBuilder.Sql(
    @"
```

```
UPDATE Research
SET Read = 'true';
");
```

I know this is not a great example, as you wouldn't want all your `Research` entries to be marked as `Read` every time you update the database, but hopefully you understand the concept.

This code has not yet been executed, though. So, at the current moment, our model and database schema are still out of sync.

Execute the following command again and we're all up to date:

```
Update-Database
```

Seeding the database with test data

Now that we have an empty database, let's fill it with some test data. To do this, we'll need to create a method that we will call after our database creation:

1. Create a folder in your project called `Data`. In the folder, add a class called `DbInitializer.cs`:

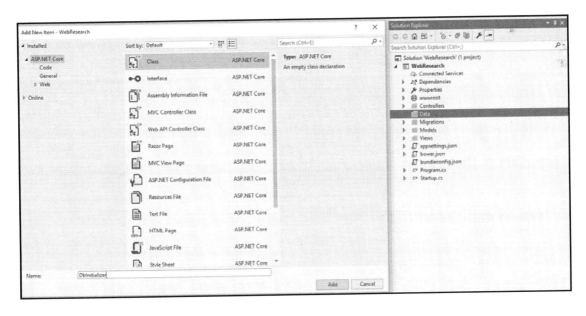

The class has an `Initialize` method that takes our `ResearchContext` as a parameter:

```
public static void Initialize(ResearchContext context)
```

2. In the `Initialize` method, we first call the `Database.EnsureCreated` method to make sure the database exists and creates it if not:

```
context.Database.EnsureCreated();
```

3. Next up, we do a quick `Linq` query to check if the `ResearchLinks` table has any records. The argument is that if the table is empty, we want to add some testing data:

```
if (!context.ResearchLinks.Any())
```

4. Then, we create an array of the `Research` model and add some test entries. The URLs can be anything you like. I just went with a few of the most common sites out there:

```
var researchLinks = new Research[]
{
 new Research{Url="www.google.com", DateSaved=DateTime.Now,
  Note="Generated Data", Read=false},
     new Research{Url="www.twitter.com", DateSaved=DateTime.Now,
  Note="Generated Data", Read=false},
     new Research{Url="www.facebook.com", DateSaved=DateTime.Now,
  Note="Generated Data", Read=false},
     new Research{Url="www.packtpub.com", DateSaved=DateTime.Now,
  Note="Generated Data", Read=false},
     new Research{Url="www.linkedin.com", DateSaved=DateTime.Now,
  Note="Generated Data", Read=false},
};
```

5. With our array populated, we loop through it and add the entries to our context, and finally call the `SaveChanges` method to persist the data to the database:

```
foreach (Research research in researchLinks)
{
 context.ResearchLinks.Add(research);
}
 context.SaveChanges();
```

6. Throwing it all together looks as follows:

```
using System;
using System.Linq;
using WebResearch.Models;

namespace WebResearch.Data
{
    public static class DbInitializer
    {
        public static void Initialize(ResearchContext context)
        {
            context.Database.EnsureCreated();

            if (!context.ResearchLinks.Any())
            {
                var researchLinks = new Research[]
                {
                    new Research{Url="www.google.com",
                     DateSaved=DateTime.Now, Note="Generated Data",
                     Read=false},
                    new Research{Url="www.twitter.com",
                     DateSaved=DateTime.Now, Note="Generated
                     Data",
                      Read=false},
                    new Research{Url="www.facebook.com",
                     DateSaved=DateTime.Now, Note="Generated Data",
                     Read=false},
                    new Research{Url="www.packtpub.com",
                     DateSaved=DateTime.Now, Note="Generated Data",
                     Read=false},
                    new Research{Url="www.linkedin.com",
                     DateSaved=DateTime.Now, Note="Generated Data",
                     Read=false},
                };
                foreach (Research research in researchLinks)
                {
                    context.ResearchLinks.Add(research);
                }
                context.SaveChanges();
            }
        }
    }
}
```

Creating the controller

Controllers are a fundamental building block of how ASP.NET Core MVC applications are built. The methods inside a controller are referred to as actions. Therefore, we can say that a controller defines a set of actions. The actions handle requests and these requests are mapped to the specific actions through routing.

To read more on the topic of controllers and actions see the Microsoft document at—`https://docs.microsoft.com/en-us/aspnet/core/mvc/controllers/actions`. To read more on routing, see the Microsoft document at—`https://docs.microsoft.com/en-us/aspnet/core/mvc/controllers/routing`. Follow these steps:

1. Right-click on the **Controllers** folder and choose **Add | Controller**.
2. On the scaffolding screen, choose **MVC Controller with views, using Entity Framework** and click **Add**:

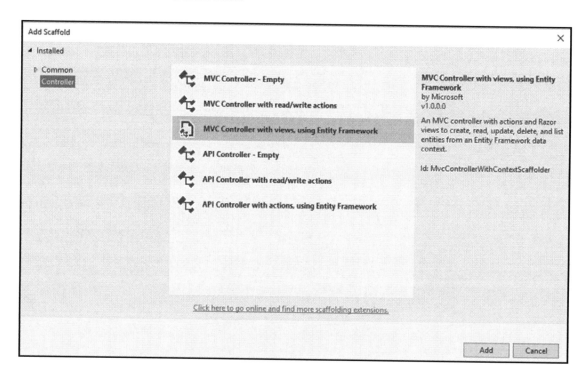

3. On the next screen, select our **Research** model for the **Model class**, and **ResearchContext** for the **Data context class**. You can leave the rest as is, unless you'd like to change the **Controller name**:

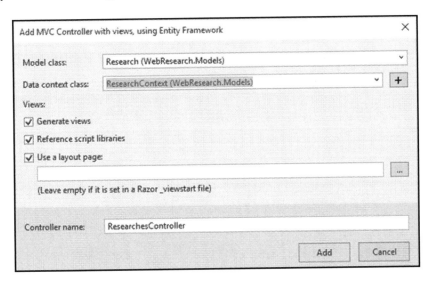

A brief look at the created controller shows us that we now have our basic **create, read, update, and delete (CRUD)** tasks in place. Now, it's time for the main event.

Running the application

Before we jump in and run the application, let's make sure our new page is easily accessible. The simplest way to do that is to just set it as the default home page:

1. Have a look at the `Configure` method in `Startup.cs`. You'll notice that the default route is specified as the `Home` controller.

2. Simply change the controller to your `Research` controller as follows:

```
app.UseMvc(routes =>
{
    routes.MapRoute(
        name: "default",
        template: "{controller=Researches}/{action=Index}/{id?}");
});
```

3. Lastly, make sure that your `Main` method looks as follows:

```
public static void Main(string[] args)
{
  var host = BuildWebHost(args);
  using (var scope = host.Services.CreateScope())
  {
    var services = scope.ServiceProvider;
    try
    {
      var context = services.GetRequiredService<ResearchContext>();
      DbInitializer.Initialize(context);
    }
    catch (Exception ex)
    {
      var logger = services.GetRequiredService<ILogger<Program>>
        ();logger.LogError(ex, "An error occurred while seeding the
        database.");
    }
  }host.Run();
}
```

4. Now, hit *Ctrl + F5* to run the application and see the fruits of your labor:

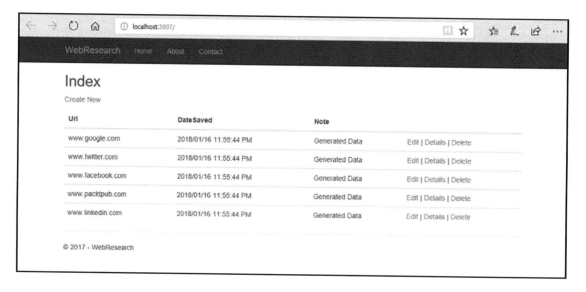

5. As you can see, our test entries are available for us to play with. Let's have a quick look at the available functionality:
  - Click on **Create New** to see the entry form for our links:

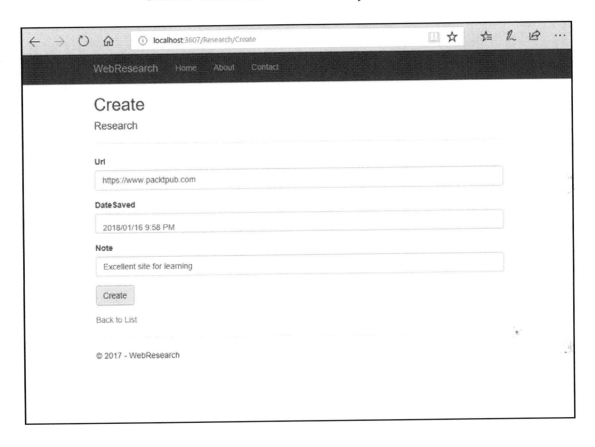

6. Enter some interesting data and hit the **Create** button. You'll be redirected back to the list view and see our new entry added to the bottom of the list:

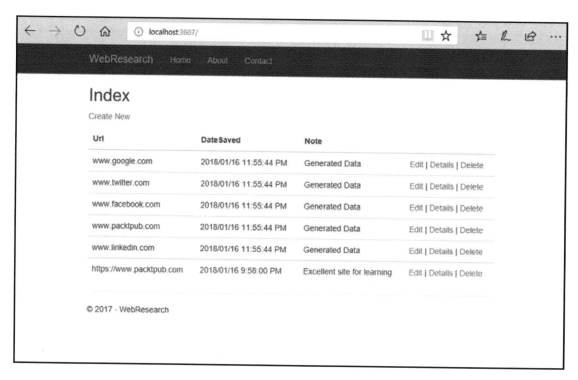

Next to each item, you have the option to **Edit, Details**, or **Delete**. Go ahead and play around with the functionality. There is quite a bit one could do to improve the user experience, such as filling in the date field automatically. I'll leave it to your own creativity to improve the user experience as you see fit.

Deploying the application

Once your application is ready for deployment, there are a few options available that you can use:

1. Microsoft Azure App Service
2. Custom targets (IIS, FTP)
3. File System
4. Import Profile

Under the **Build** menu item in Visual Studio, click on **Publish WebResearch** (or whatever you decided to name your project):

You should be presented with a screen showing you the available publishing options. Let's take a closer look.

Microsoft Azure App Service

Microsoft Azure takes care of all the infrastructure requirements needed to create and maintain a web application. This means that we developers don't need to worry about things such as server management, load balancing, or security. With the platform being improved and extended almost daily, we can also be fairly confident that we'll have the latest and greatest functionality available for us.

We're not going to go into too much detail about Azure App Services as it can turn into a whole book by itself, but we can surely have a look at the required steps to publish our web app to this cloud platform:

1. Select **Microsoft Azure App Service** as your publishing target. If you have an existing site that you want to publish to, you can choose **Select Existing**. For now, I'll assume you need to **Create New**:

2. After hitting the **OK** button, Visual Studio will contact Azure with your logged in Microsoft account, which in turn will check if you have an Azure account and will return the available service details.

   I created a trial account for this blueprint with no specific details set up beforehand, and as you can see from the following screenshot, Azure will recommend an available **App Name** and **App Service Plan** for you.

3. The **Resource Group** is optional and will get a unique group name if you do not specify anything:

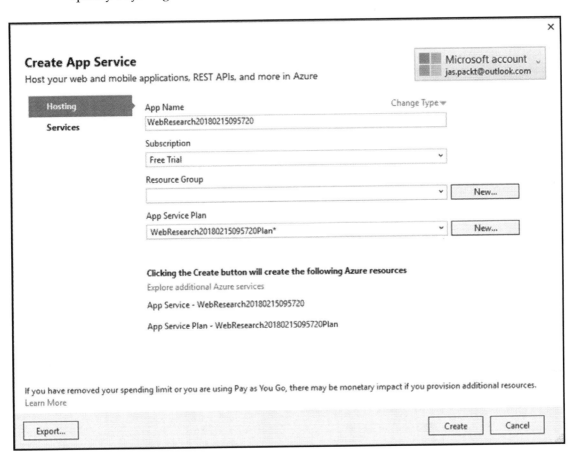

4. You can change the type of application you want to publish under the **Change Type** option. In our case, we'll obviously go with **Web App**:

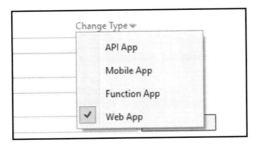

5. Click on **Services** on the left-hand side to see the services that will be set up with your publication.

The first box shows any **Recommended** resource types your application might benefit from. In our case, an **SQL Database** is recommended, and we do need it, so we'll simply add it by hitting the Add (**+**) button:

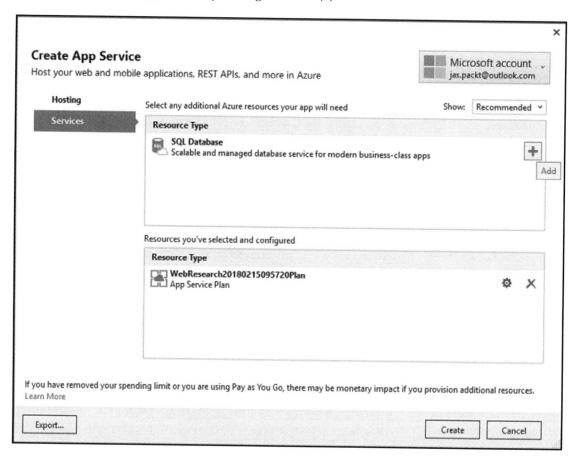

Azure will take care of the SQL installation, but we need to give it the required information, such as which server to use if you already have one on your profile, or to create a new one if you haven't.

6. We will configure a new SQL Server in this case. Click the **New** button next to the **SQL Server** drop-down to open the Configure SQL Server form. Azure will provide a recommended name for the server. Although you can provide your own, the chances are that the Server Name will most likely not be available, so I recommend that you just use what they recommend.

7. Provide an **Administrator Username** and **Administrator Password** for the server and hit **OK**:

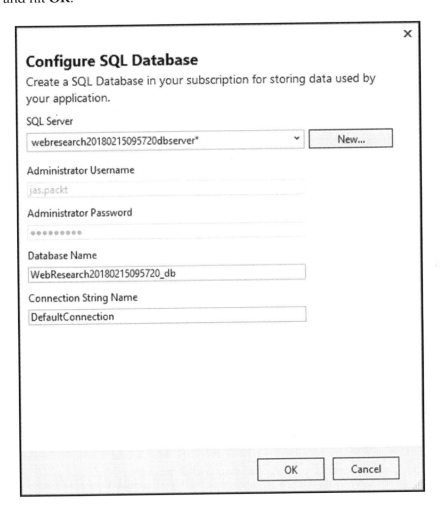

8. Doing this will bring you back to the **Configure SQL Database** form, where you need to specify the **Database Name** as well as the **Connection String Name**:

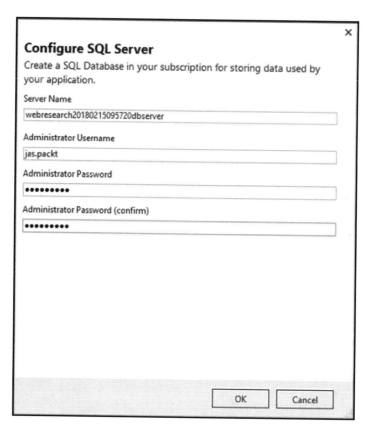

9. Take a look again at the **Create App Service** form. You will notice that the **SQL Database** has been added to the **Resources you've selected and configured** section:

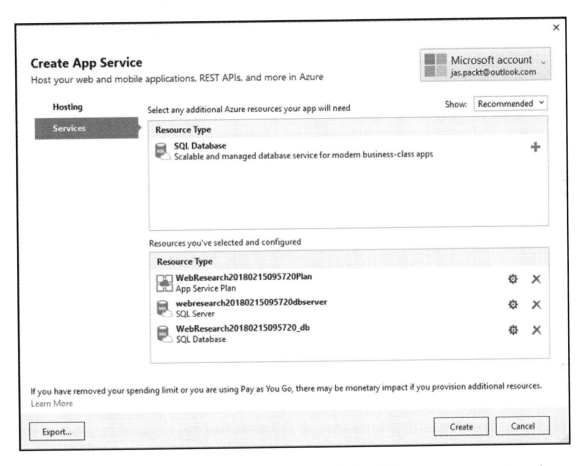

10. We can now go back to the **Hosting** tab, which will show you an overview of what will happen when you hit the **Create** button.

11. As shown in the following screenshot, the following three Azure resources will be created:
     1. **App Service**
     2. **App Service Plan**
     3. **SQL Server**

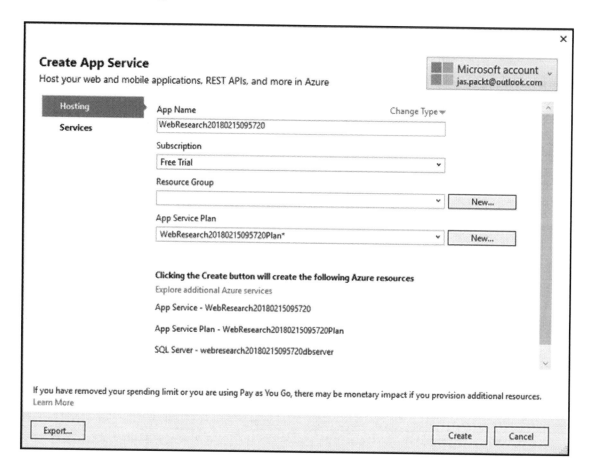

12. After creation, we can publish to our new Azure profile by hitting the **Publish** button.

13. You will see some **Build** messages in your output window and should end up with the following:

```
Publish Succeeded.
Web App was published successfully
http://webresearch20180215095720.azurewebsites.net/
========== Build: 1 succeeded, 0 failed, 0 up-to-date, 0 skipped
==========
========== Publish: 1 succeeded, 0 failed, 0 skipped ==========
```

14. You can have a look at your Dashboard on the Azure Portal (`portal.azure.com`), which will show you the resources enabled on your account due to our **Service** creation:

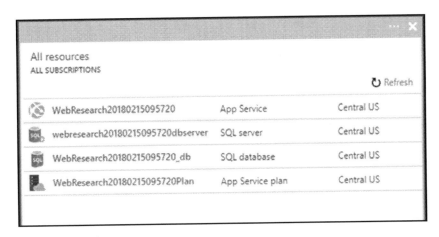

15. The published app will open up in your browser and you'll most likely see an error message. By default, you won't see much detail around the error, but at least Azure gives you some pointers to get the error details by setting your ASPNETCORE_ENVIRONMENT environment variable to Development and restarting the application:

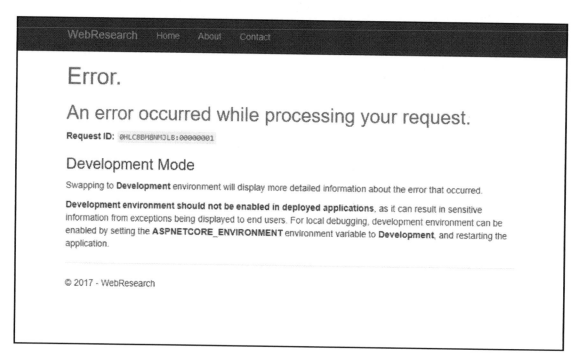

16. When you log in to your Azure portal, you can navigate to your **App Service** and then in the **Application settings**, add the **ASPNETCORE_ENVIRONMENT** setting with the value of Development and restart your app:

17. Now, we can refresh the site, and we should see a bit more detail about the underlying error:

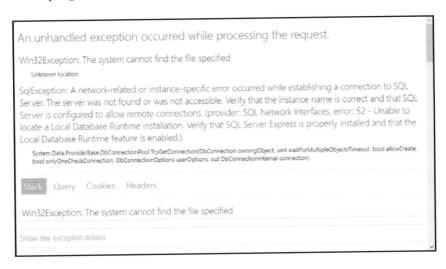

18. Ah, yes! We are still pointing to our local db, and we don't have access to that from the publish environment. Let's update our `appsettings.json` to point to our Azure db.

19. Navigate to the SQL Server from your Azure dashboard and then to **Properties**. On the right-hand pane, you should see an option to **Show database connection strings**:

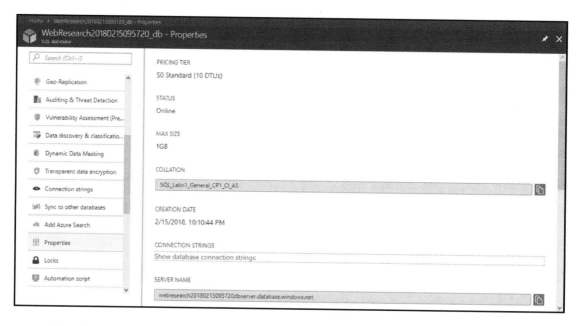

20. Copy the **ADO.NET connectionstring,** head back to your code, and update the **CONNECTION STRINGS** entry in the `appsettings.json` file.

21. Republish the app and you should be good to go.

Custom targets

The next publishing option is generally referred to as custom targets.

This option basically includes anything that is not Azure or a local filesystem. After hitting the **OK** button, you get to choose the publish method:

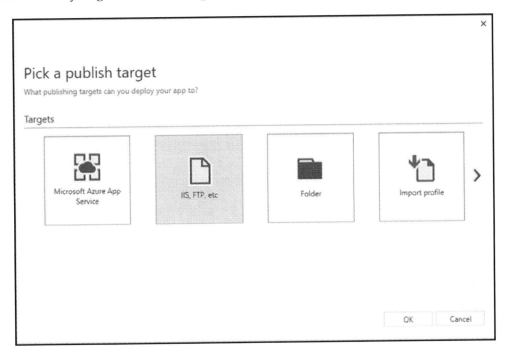

There are four publish methods, or custom targets, available with each having its own requirements:

1. FTP
2. Web Deploy
3. Web Deploy Package
4. File System

We also have a **Settings** tab, which is applicable to all four methods. Let's have a quick look at what our options are there:

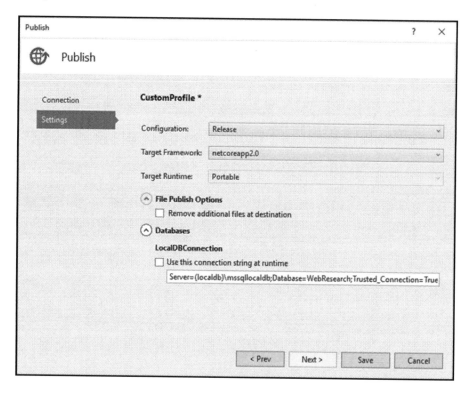

The **Configuration** option can be set to either **Debug** or **Release**.

With **Debug,** your generated files are debug-able, meaning that it is possible to hit specified break points. But it also means that there is a performance decrease.

With **Release**, you won't be able to debug on the fly, but will have an increase in performance as your application is fully optimized.

In our case, the only available target framework is **netcoreapp2.0**, but in standard .NET applications, this is where you could set the target to .NET 3.5 or .NET 4.5, or whichever is available.

You can then also specify the **Target Runtime**, choose to have Visual Studio clean up the destination folder, and specify a connection string specifically for runtime.

As mentioned previously, these settings are applicable to all four publishing methods, which we will have a look at now.

FTP

The FTP publish method enables you to publish to a hosted FTP location. For this option, you need to provide the following:

- **Server URL**
- **Site path**
- **User name**
- **Password**
- **Destination URL**

It also allows you to validate the connection from the entered details:

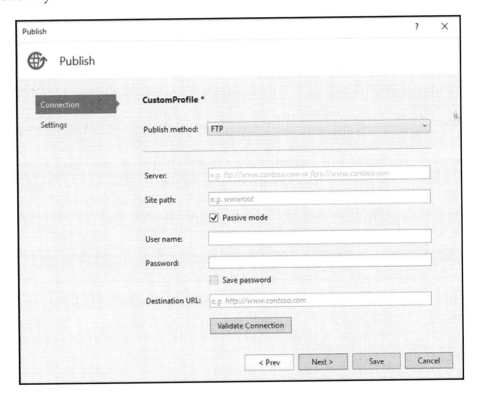

Web Deploy

Looking at the forms of both **Web Deploy** as well as **FTP**, you could be excused to believe they're the same thing. Well, both result in basically the same thing in that you publish directly to a hosted site, but with **Web Deploy** you get quite a few extra benefits, including the following:

- **Web Deploy** compares the source with the destination and only syncs required changes, resulting in a significant decrease in publish time compared to **FTP**
- Even though **FTP** also has its secure cousins SFTP and FTPS, **Web Deploy** always supports secure transfers
- Proper database support, which enables you to apply SQL scripts during the sync process

The **Publish** screen looks as follows:

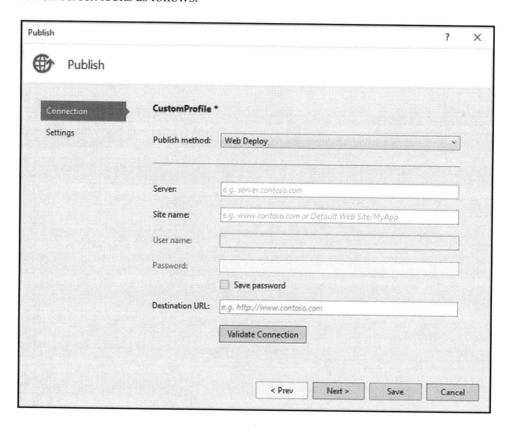

Web Deploy Package

The **Web Deploy Package** option is used to create a deployment package that you can use to install your application wherever you choose afterwards. Refer to the following screenshot:

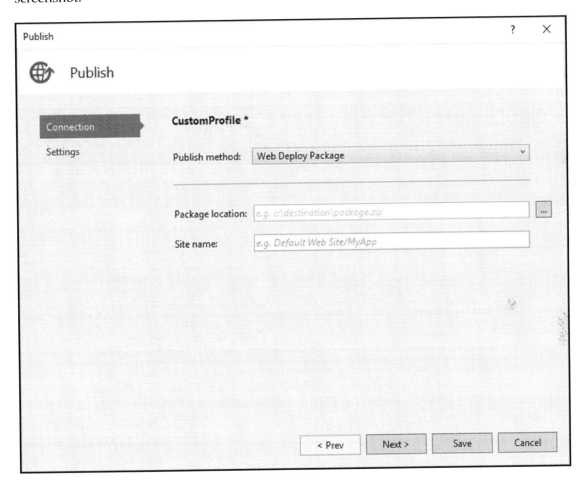

File System

Used by old school developers the world over, mainly due to the fact that we still don't really trust some of the available tools enough, this option allows you to publish to a folder location of your choice, and then go and copy it over to the publish environment manually:

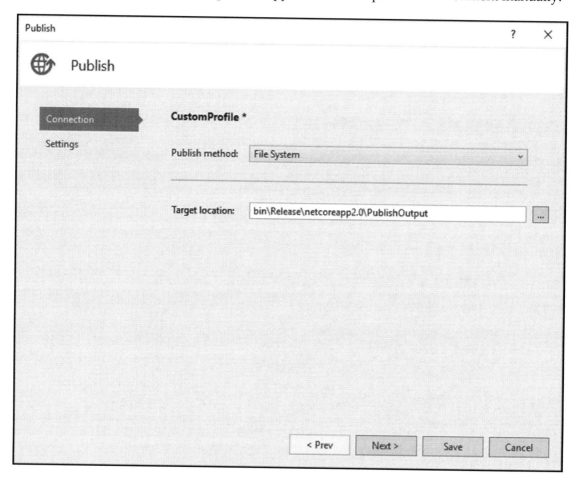

Folder

Just to show you how popular it is for developers to still have that control over the published code, we have two paths that end up with publishing to a folder location.

Once again, just specify the folder location, and hit **OK**:

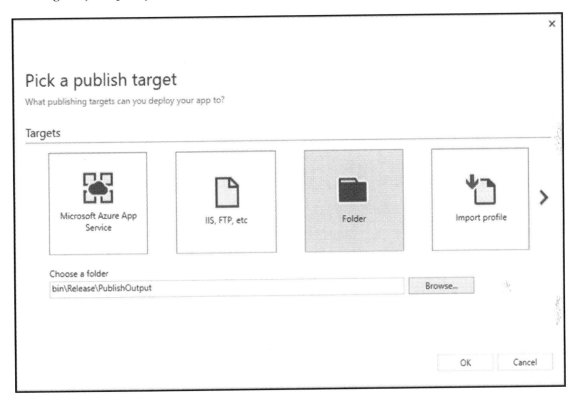

Import Profile

The **Import Profile** method is not an actual publishing method, but rather a simple option to import a previously saved profile, either from a backup or possibly used to share a publishing profile between a team of developers:

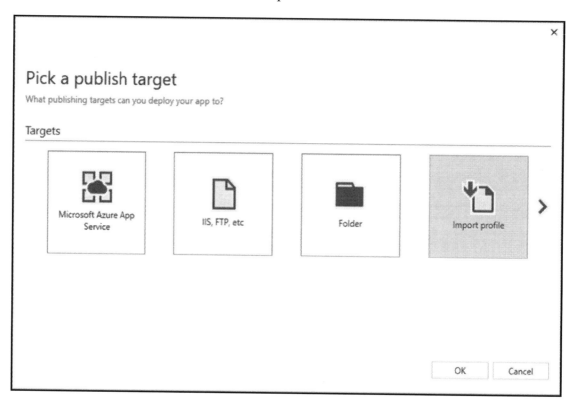

Summary

In this chapter, we've taken a bit of a guided tour around the Entity Framework Core neighborhood. We started off at the museum to look at the history of Entity Framework, before visiting the schools district to discuss some of the differences between the Code-First, Model-First, and Database-First implementation approaches. There was even a quick visit from TechNet, who offered some ideas around designing a database.

Afterwards, we spent some time building our own EF Core solution and looked at the various ways of deploying our application. We also had a look at populating our new building with some test data to see how it will hold up once opened up to the public.

The tour concluded with a visit to the distribution district to get an overview of the available deployment options.

The visit was far too brief to cover all that is available and possible in the world of Entity Framework Core as it is a framework with a large community constantly working on improving and extending its already extensive functionality.

It is great to know that the development community does not settle for any mediocrity and constantly works towards improving and extending functionality, such as Entity Framework, which might seem quite mature and extensive already.

7
A Serverless Email Validation Azure Function

This chapter will take us into the realm of serverless computing. Just what is serverless computing, I hear you ask? Well, the answer is really simple once you grasp the idea that the term *serverless computing* has nothing to do with the lack of a server. It is quite the opposite, in fact.

In this chapter, we will have a look at:

- Creating an Azure Function
- Testing your Azure Function in the browser
- Calling an Azure Function from an ASP.NET Core MVC application

We will be creating a simple Azure Function that uses regular expressions to validate an email address. You need to keep in mind that Azure Functions are small pieces of code in the cloud. Do not think of them as large sections of complicated code. The smaller the better.

Beginning with serverless computing

Traditionally, companies spend time and money managing a server's computing resources. These represent a fixed and recurring cost to the company. It doesn't matter if the server is idle or if it is performing some form of computing task. The bottom line is that it costs money just by being there.

With serverless computing, the computing resources are scalable cloud services. This means that it is an event-driven application design. Basically, with serverless computing, you only pay for what you use. This is true of Azure Functions.

Azure Functions are small bits of code that reside in the cloud. Your applications can simply just use these functions as needed, and you only pay for the computing power used. It does not matter if one or one million people access your application. Azure Functions will automatically scale to handle the additional load. When the usage of your application drops, the Azure Function scales back down.

Importance of serverless computing

Imagine that you saw frequent (but not constant) spikes in your application usage. Because the server that handles the requests from your application is not serverless, it needs to be upgraded (as a cost to you or your company) to be able to handle the additional load. In times of low usage, the server does not have less resources. You upgraded it to be able to handle a specific load of users. It will always be running at this level of performance, and as you know, performance comes at a cost.

With serverless computing, the resources are automatically scaled up and down as demand increases and decreases. This is a much more efficient way of using a server, because you are not paying for underutilized computing power.

Features of Azure Functions

Azure Functions offer developers a rich set of features. Refer to the Microsoft documentation to read up more on Azure Functions—https://docs.microsoft.com/en-us/azure/azure-functions/. For now, we will have a look at a few of those features.

Choice of languages

The great thing about Azure Functions is that you can create them in a language of your choice. For a list of supported languages, browse to the following URL: https://docs.microsoft.com/en-us/azure/azure-functions/supported-languages.

For this chapter, we will be using C# to write the Azure Function.

Pay-per-use pricing

As mentioned earlier, you will only pay for the actual time spent that your Azure Function runs. The consumption plan is billed per second. Microsoft have a great document on Azure Functions pricing at the following URL:

```
https://azure.microsoft.com/en-us/pricing/details/functions/.
```

Flexible development

You can create your Azure Functions directly in the Azure portal. You can also set up continuous integration with Visual Studio Team Services and GitHub.

What types of Azure Functions can I create?

You can use Azure Functions as a solution to integrate with your application, processing data, working with IoT, APIs, and microservices. Azure Functions also work well on a trigger, so you can even schedule tasks. These are some of the Azure Function templates available to you:

- HTTPTrigger
- TimerTrigger
- GitHub webhook
- Generic webhook
- BlobTrigger
- CosmosDBTrigger
- QueueTrigger
- EventHubTrigger
- ServiceBusQueueTrigger
- ServiceBusTopicTrigger

To read up more on these templates and Azure Functions in general, go through the Microsoft document, *An introduction to Azure Functions*, at the following URL:

```
https://docs.microsoft.com/en-us/azure/azure-functions/functions-overview.
```

Creating an Azure Function

Without further delay, let's create our own Azure Function. The function we are going to create is going to validate an email address using regular expressions. This is a very standard development task to code. It is also a function that will be widely used across many applications:

 You will need to have an Azure account. If you do not have one, you can set up a free trial account at—https://azure.microsoft.com/en-us/free/.

1. Point your browser at—https://portal.azure.com and log on to your Azure portal.
2. Once logged in, look for the **Create a resource** link. Click on the link and then look for the **Compute** link under the **Azure Marketplace** section. Refer to the following screenshot:

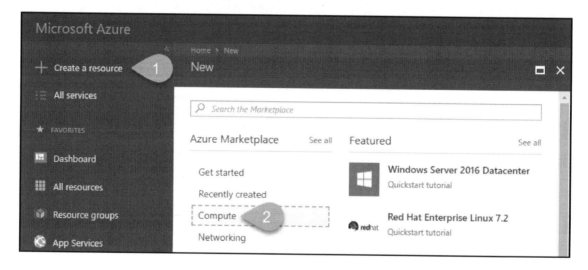

3. A little way down under the **Featured** section, you will see **Function App** as an option. Click on that link:

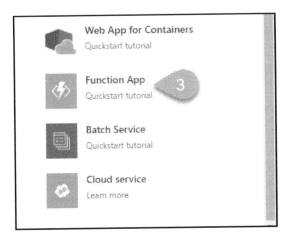

4. You will now be presented with the **Function App** settings screen. The following options need to be entered:
   - **App name**: This is the globally unique name of your Azure Function.
   - **Subscription**: This is the subscription under which your function will be created.
   - **Resource group**: Create a new resource group for your function.
   - **OS**: You have a choice of Windows or Linux. I chose Windows.
   - **Hosting plan**: This will define how resources are allocated to your function.
   - **Location**: It is a good idea to choose a location geographically closest to you.
   - **Storage**: Keep this as default.

5. You also have the option to switch **Application Insights** to **On** or **Off**. You can also select the **Pin to dashboard** option.

 We have called our Azure Function **core-mail-validation**.

6. Once you have added all the required settings, click on the **Create** button.

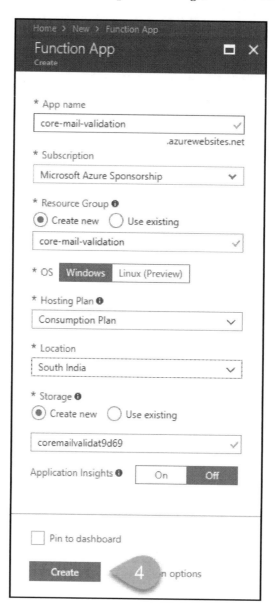

7. After you click on the **Create** button, you will see a **Validating...** message. This could take several seconds:

8. Keep your eye on the notifications section (the little bell icon) in the top right hand corner of the Azure portal. New notifications are displayed there and are indicated by a number representing the number of unread notifications:

9. If you click on the notifications, you will see that Azure is in the progress of deploying the Azure Function you created:

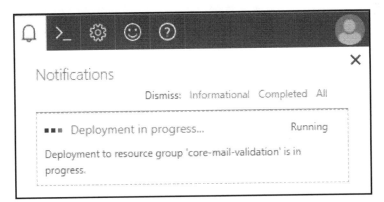

10. When your Azure Function is deployed, you will see a **Deployment succeeded** message appear in the **Notifications** section. From there, you can click on the **Pin to dashboard** to **Go to resource** buttons.

Pinning your function to the dashboard just makes it easier for you to access it again later on. It's a good idea to pin frequently used services to your dashboard.

11. To access your Azure Function, click on the **Go to resource** button:

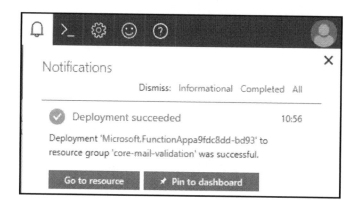

12. You will then be taken to the **Function Apps** section of your Azure portal. You will see the **core-mail-validation** function listed under the **Function Apps** section:

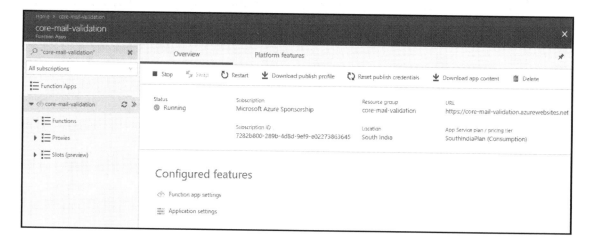

13. Under the **core-email-validation**, click on the **Functions** option. Then, click on the **New function** option in the panel on the right:

14. You are now presented with a series of templates that can get you started. Scroll down to see all the templates available (there are more than just the four shown in the following screenshot):

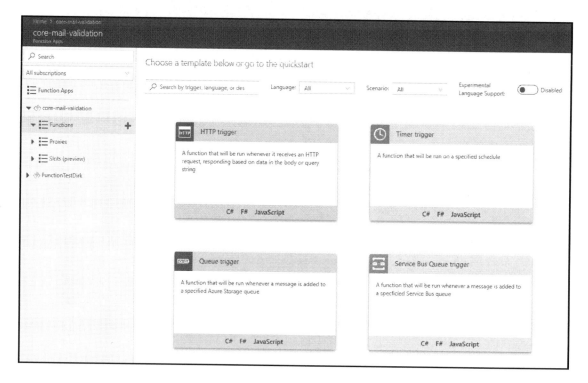

15. We are not going to go through all the templates available. We are going to keep things simple and just select the **go to the quickstart** option, as shown in the following screenshot:

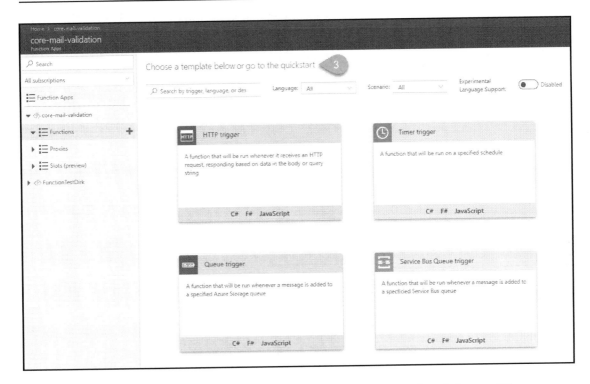

16. For our purposes, we will simply select **Webhook + API** and choose **C#** as our language. There are other languages available to choose from, so select the language you are most comfortable with.

17. To create the function, click on the **Create this function** button:

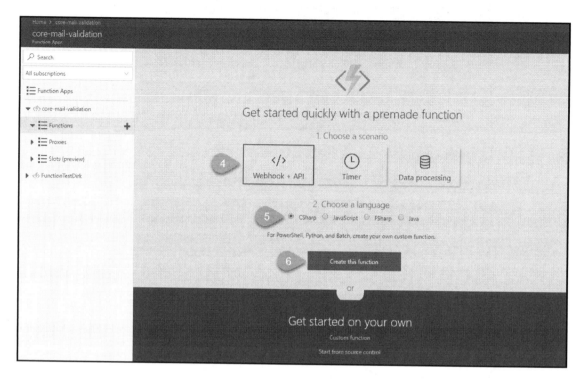

18. The Azure Function is created and some boilerplate code is automatically added for you so that you can get a feel for how the code needs to look inside the function. All this code does is it looks for a variable called name in the query string and displays that in the browser, if found:

```
using System.Net;
public static async Task<HttpResponseMessage>
 Run(HttpRequestMessage req, TraceWriter log)
{
   log.Info("C# HTTP trigger function processed a request.");

   // parse query parameter
   string name = req.GetQueryNameValuePairs()
   .FirstOrDefault(q => string.Compare(q.Key, "name", true) == 0)
   .Value;

   if (name == null)
   {
     // Get request body
```

```
dynamic data = await req.Content.ReadAsAsync<object>();
name = data?.name;
}

return name == null
? req.CreateResponse(HttpStatusCode.BadRequest,
"Please pass a name on the query string or in the request body")
: req.CreateResponse(HttpStatusCode.OK, "Hello " + name);
}
```

19. Have a look at the top-right corner of the screen. You will see a **</> Get function URL** link. Click on the following link:

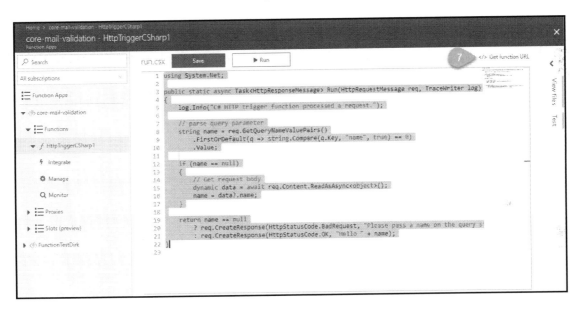

20. This will display a pop-up screen with the URL to access the Azure Function you just created. Click on the **Copy** button to copy the URL to your clipboard:

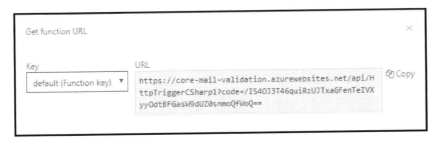

21. The URL that you copy will look something as follows:

    ```
    https://core-mail-validation.azurewebsites.net/api/HttpTriggerCShar
    p1?code=/IS4OJ3T46quiRzUJTxaGFenTeIVXyyOdtBFGasW9dUZ0snmoQfWoQ==
    ```

22. To run our function, we need to add a `name` parameter in the query string of the URL. Go ahead and add `&name==[YOUR_NAME]` where `[YOUR_NAME]` is your own name into the URL. In my case, I added `&name=Dirk` to the end of my URL:

    ```
    https://core-mail-validation.azurewebsites.net/api/HttpTriggerCShar
    p1?code=/IS4OJ3T46quiRzUJTxaGFenTeIVXyyOdtBFGasW9dUZ0snmoQfWoQ==&na
    me=Dirk
    ```

23. Paste this URL into the browser address bar and hit the return button. A message saying (in my case) **"Hello Dirk"** is displayed in the browser:

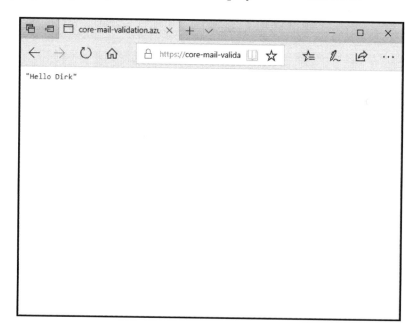

 Note that in Chrome and Firefox, you might see the message **This XML file does not appear to have any style information associated with it**. To see the output, use Microsoft Edge.

24. Back in the Azure portal, you will see the **Logs** window at the bottom of the Azure Function screen. If it isn't displayed, click on the Λ arrow to expand the panel. Here, you will see that the Azure Trigger was run successfully:

```
Logs                                          ❚❚ Pause  ▰ Clear  ▢ Copy logs  ⟋ Expand  ⌄
2018-03-03T09:20:04  No new trace in the past 5 min(s).
2018-03-03T09:20:55.318 [Info] Function started (Id=262ff967-99b7-4cef-9abe-05697cc3467f)
2018-03-03T09:20:55.395 [Info] C# HTTP trigger function processed a request.
2018-03-03T09:20:55.395 [Info] Function completed (Success, Id=262ff967-99b7-4cef-9abe-05697cc3467f, Duration=88ms)
2018-03-03T09:22:04  No new trace in the past 1 min(s).
2018-03-03T09:23:04  No new trace in the past 2 min(s).
2018-03-03T09:24:04  No new trace in the past 3 min(s).
```

Congratulations, you have just run your new Azure Function.

Modifying the Azure Function code

While this is all quite exciting (it should be, this is really cool tech), we need to make a few changes to the Azure Function to meet our requirements:

1. Identify the `return` statement in your Azure Function. It will look as follows:

```
return name == null
  ? req.CreateResponse(HttpStatusCode.BadRequest,
   "Please pass a name on the query string or in the request
   body")
  : req.CreateResponse(HttpStatusCode.OK, "Hello " + name);
```

Let's simplify the code a bit and just return `true` if the email address is not empty. Replace the `return` statement with the following code:

```
if (email == null)
{
   return req.CreateResponse(HttpStatusCode.BadRequest,
    "Please pass an email address on the query string or
    in the request body");
}
else
{
   bool blnValidEmail = false;
   if (email.Length > 0)
   {
       blnValidEmail = true;
```

```
      }

   return req.CreateResponse(HttpStatusCode.OK,
     "Email status: " + blnValidEmail);
   }
```

2. The code in your Azure Function should now look as follows:

```
using System.Net;

public static async Task<HttpResponseMessage>
 Run(HttpRequestMessage req, TraceWriter log)
{
   log.Info("C# HTTP trigger function processed a new email
    validation request.");

   // parse query parameter
   string email = req.GetQueryNameValuePairs()
     .FirstOrDefault(q => string.Compare(q.Key, "email", true) ==
     0)
     .Value;

   if (email == null)
   {
     // Get request body
     dynamic data = await req.Content.ReadAsAsync<object>();
     email = data?.email;
   }

   if (email == null)
   {
     return req.CreateResponse(HttpStatusCode.BadRequest,
       "Please pass an email address on the query string or
        in the request body");
   }
   else
   {
     bool blnValidEmail = false;
     if (email.Length > 0)
     {
       blnValidEmail = true;
     }

     return req.CreateResponse(HttpStatusCode.OK,
       "Email status: " + blnValidEmail);
   }
}
```

3. Be sure to click on the **Save** button to save the changes to your Azure Function. You will then see that the function is compiled and a **Compilation succeeded** message is displayed in the **Logs** window:

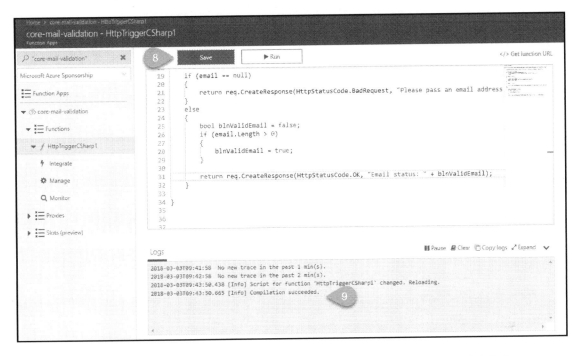

4. As previous, copy the URL by clicking on the **</> Get function URL** link:

```
https://core-mail-validation.azurewebsites.net/api/HttpTriggerCShar
p1?code=/IS4OJ3T46quiRzUJTxaGFenTeIVXyyOdtBFGasW9dUZ0snmoQfWoQ==
```

This time though, we want to pass it as an email address. You can see that the parameter name has changed to `email` and the value can be any email address you choose to enter. I therefore appended `&email=dirk@email.com` to the end of the URL:

```
https://core-mail-validation.azurewebsites.net/api/HttpTriggerCShar
p1?code=/IS4OJ3T46quiRzUJTxaGFenTeIVXyyOdtBFGasW9dUZ0snmoQfWoQ==&em
ail=dirk@email.com
```

5. Paste the URL into your browser and hit the **return** button to see the result displayed in the browser:

6. We are now confident that the Azure Function is performing a rudimentary validation of our email address (even if it is just checking to see if it exists). However, we need the function to do so much more. To validate the email address, we will be using regular expressions. To do this, add the following namespace to the Azure Function:

```
using System.Text.RegularExpressions;
```

In the section of code that does the validation, enter the code to match the email to the regex pattern.

There are a million different regular expression patterns on the internet. Regular expressions are a whole different topic altogether and beyond the scope of this book. If matching a pattern of text is required by your application, Google to see if there isn't a regex pattern available for it. If you are really brave, you can write your own.

7. Regular expressions have been baked into the .NET Framework, and the code is quite straightforward:

```
blnValidEmail = Regex.IsMatch(email,
                @"^(?("")("".+?(?<!\)""@)|(([0-9a-z]((.(?!.))|[-
!#$%&'*+/=?^`{}|~w])*)(?<=[0-9a-z])@))" +
                @"(?([)([(d{1,3}.){3}d{1,3}])|(([0-9a-z][-0-9a-
z]*[0-9a-z]*.)+[a-z0-9][-a-z0-9]{0,22}[a-z0-9]))$",
                RegexOptions.IgnoreCase,
TimeSpan.FromMilliseconds(250));
```

8. After you have added all the code, your Azure Function will look as follows:

```
using System.Net;
using System.Text.RegularExpressions;

public static async Task<HttpResponseMessage>
 Run(HttpRequestMessage req, TraceWriter log)
{
   log.Info("C# HTTP trigger function processed a new email
    validation request.");

   // parse query parameter
   string email = req.GetQueryNameValuePairs()
      .FirstOrDefault(q => string.Compare(q.Key, "email", true) ==
      0)
      .Value;

   if (email == null)
   {
      // Get request body
      dynamic data = await req.Content.ReadAsAsync<object>();
      email = data?.email;
   }

   if (email == null)
   {
```

```
       return req.CreateResponse(HttpStatusCode.BadRequest,
         "Please pass an email address on the query string or in
          the request body");
     }
    else
     {
       bool blnValidEmail = false;
       blnValidEmail = Regex.IsMatch(email,
          @"^(?("")("".+?(?<!\)""@)|(([0-9a-z]((.(?!.))|
          [-!#$%&'*+/=?^`{}|~w])*)(?<=[0-9a-z])@))" +
          @"(?([)([(d{1,3}.){3}d{1,3}])|(([0-9a-z][-0-9a-z]*
          [0-9a-z]*.)+[a-z0-9][-a-z0-9]{0,22}[a-z0-9]))$",
          RegexOptions.IgnoreCase,
          TimeSpan.FromMilliseconds(250));

       return req.CreateResponse(HttpStatusCode.OK,
         "Email status: " + blnValidEmail);
     }
   }
```

9. Use the same URL you copied earlier and paste it into the browser window and hit the *Return* or *Enter* key:

   ```
   https://core-mail-validation.azurewebsites.net/api/HttpTriggerCShar
   p1?code=/IS4OJ3T46quiRzUJTxaGFenTeIVXyyOdtBFGasW9dUZ0snmoQfWoQ==&em
   ail=dirk@email.com
   ```

10. The email address `dirk@email.com` is validated and the message "**Email status: True**" is displayed in the browser. What has happened here is that the email address was passed to the Azure Function. The function then read the value of the `email` parameter from the query string and passed that to the regular expression.

The email address is matched against the regular expression pattern, and if a match is found, then the email address is considered a valid email:

11. Let's enter the same URL into the browser, only this time enter an email address you know will be invalid. For example, an email address can only contain a single @ sign. The parameter I then added to the URL is as follows:

```
https://core-mail-validation.azurewebsites.net/api/HttpTriggerCShar
p1?code=/IS4OJ3T46quiRzUJTxaGFenTeIVXyyOdtBFGasW9dUZ0snmoQfWoQ==&em
ail=dirk@@email.com
```

You can then see that when we hit the *Return* or *Enter* key, the invalid email address `dirk@@email.com` is validated and found not to match the regular expression. The text **"Email status: False"** is therefore displayed in the browser:

This is fantastic! We have seen that the Azure Function we created uses the regular expression we added to validate the email address it receives. Based on the result of the regex validation, the function returns either true or false.

Lastly, before we carry on, we want the Azure Function to return a single `True` or `False` value to the calling application. Modify the `return` statement of your function to do just that:

```
return req.CreateResponse(HttpStatusCode.OK, blnValidEmail);
```

We have seen how this function works, by modifying the code step-by-step and running it directly from the browser window. However, this does not do us any good unless we can call this Azure Function from an application.

Let's have a look at how to create an ASP.NET Core MVC application that calls our Azure Function to validate an email address entered on a login screen.

Calling an Azure Function from an ASP.NET Core MVC application

In the previous section, we had a look at how our Azure Function worked. Now, we want to create an ASP.NET Core MVC application that will call our Azure Function to validate an email address entered into a login screen of the application:

 This application does no authentication at all. All it is doing is validating the email address entered. ASP.NET Core MVC authentication is a totally different topic and not the focus of this chapter.

1. In Visual Studio 2017, create a new project and select **ASP.NET Core Web Application** from the project templates. Click on the **OK** button to create the project. This is shown in the following screenshot:

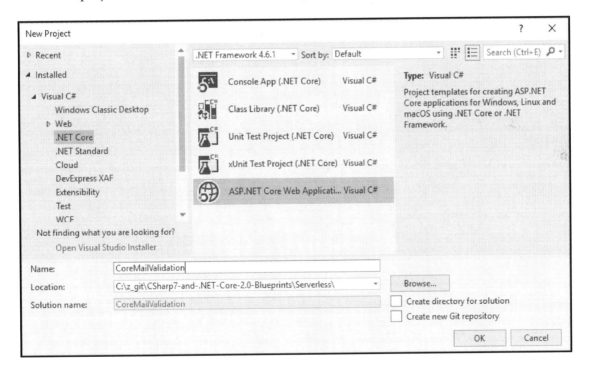

2. On the next screen, ensure that **.NET Core** and **ASP.NET Core 2.0** is selected from the drop-down options on the form. Select **Web Application (Model-View-Controller)** as the type of application to create.

Don't bother with any kind of authentication or enabling Docker support. Just click on the **OK** button to create your project:

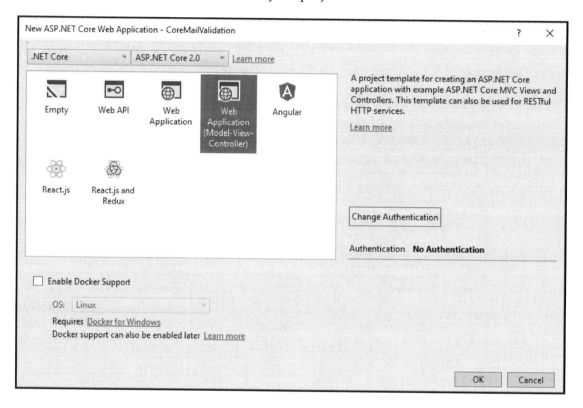

3. After your project is created, you will see the familiar project structure in the **Solution Explorer** of Visual Studio:

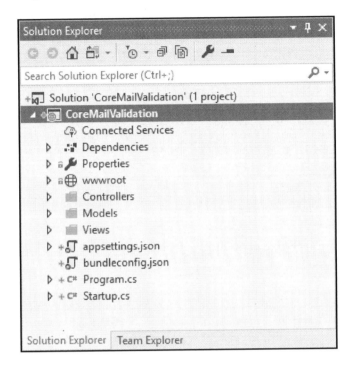

Creating the login form

For this next part, we can create a plain and simple vanilla login form. For a little bit of fun, let's spice things up a bit. Have a look on the internet for some free login form templates:

1. I decided to use a site called **colorlib** that provided 50 free HTML5 and CSS3 login forms in one of their recent blog posts. The URL to the article is:
   `https://colorlib.com/wp/html5-and-css3-login-forms/`.

2. I decided to use **Login Form 1 by Colorlib** from their site. Download the template to your computer and extract the ZIP file. Inside the extracted ZIP file, you will see that we have several folders. Copy all the folders in this extracted ZIP file (leave the `index.html` file as we will use this in a minute):

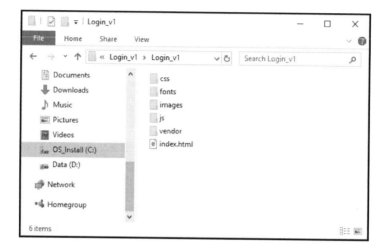

3. Next, go to the solution for your Visual Studio application. In the `wwwroot` folder, move or delete the contents and paste the folders from the extracted ZIP file into the `wwwroot` folder of your ASP.NET Core MVC application. Your `wwwroot` folder should now look as follows:

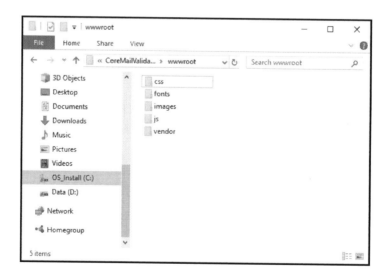

4. Back in Visual Studio, you will see the folders when you expand the **wwwroot** node in the **CoreMailValidation** project.

5. I also want to focus your attention to the `Index.cshtml` and `_Layout.cshtml` files. We will be modifying these files next:

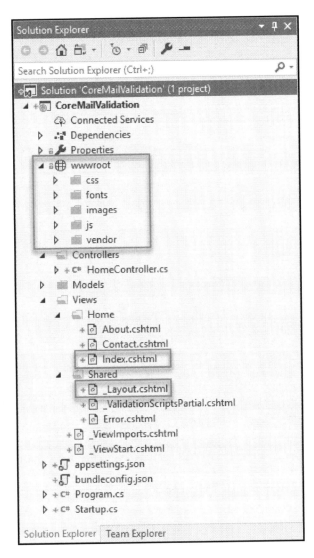

6. Open the `Index.cshtml` file and remove all the markup (except the section in the curly brackets) from this file. Paste the HTML markup from the `index.html` file from the ZIP file we extracted earlier.

Do not copy the all the markup from the `index.html` file. Only copy the markup inside the `<body></body>` tags.

7. Your `Index.cshtml` file should now look as follows:

```
@{
    ViewData["Title"] = "Login Page";
}

<div class="limiter">
    <div class="container-login100">
        <div class="wrap-login100">
            <div class="login100-pic js-tilt" data-tilt>
                <img src="images/img-01.png" alt="IMG">
            </div>

            <form class="login100-form validate-form">
                <span class="login100-form-title">
                    Member Login
                </span>

                <div class="wrap-input100 validate-input"
                 data-validate="Valid email is required:
                  ex@abc.xyz">
                    <input class="input100" type="text"
                     name="email" placeholder="Email">
                    <span class="focus-input100"></span>
                    <span class="symbol-input100">
                        <i class="fa fa-envelope"
                         aria-hidden="true"></i>
                    </span>
                </div>

                <div class="wrap-input100 validate-input"
                 data-validate="Password is required">
                    <input class="input100" type="password"
                     name="pass"
                     placeholder="Password">
                    <span class="focus-input100"></span>
                    <span class="symbol-input100">
```

```
                <i class="fa fa-lock"
                    aria-hidden="true"></i>
            </span>
        </div>

        <div class="container-login100-form-btn">
            <button class="login100-form-btn">
                Login
            </button>
        </div>

        <div class="text-center p-t-12">
            <span class="txt1">
                Forgot
            </span>
            <a class="txt2" href="#">
                Username / Password?
            </a>
        </div>

        <div class="text-center p-t-136">
            <a class="txt2" href="#">
                Create your Account
                <i class="fa fa-long-arrow-right m-l-5"
                    aria-hidden="true"></i>
            </a>
        </div>
    </form>
  </div>
 </div>
</div>
```

The code for this chapter is available on GitHub at the following link:
https://github.com/PacktPublishing/CSharp7-and-.NET-Core-2.0-Blueprints/tree/master/Serverless.

8. Next, open the `Layout.cshtml` file and add all the links to the folders and files we copied into the `wwwroot` folder earlier. Use the `index.html` file for reference. You will notice that the _Layout.cshtml file contains the following piece of code—`@RenderBody()`. This is a placeholder that specifies where the `Index.cshtml` file content should be injected. If you are coming from ASP.NET Web Forms, think of the _Layout.cshtml page as a master page. Your `Layout.cshtml` markup should look as follows:

```
<!DOCTYPE html>
<html>

<head>
    <meta charset="utf-8" />
    <meta name="viewport" content="width=device-width, initial-
scale=1.0" />
    <title>@ViewData["Title"] - CoreMailValidation</title>
    <link rel="icon" type="image/png"
href="~/images/icons/favicon.ico" />
    <link rel="stylesheet" type="text/css"
href="~/vendor/bootstrap/css/bootstrap.min.css">
    <link rel="stylesheet" type="text/css" href="~/fonts/font-
awesome-4.7.0/css/font-awesome.min.css">
    <link rel="stylesheet" type="text/css"
href="~/vendor/animate/animate.css">
    <link rel="stylesheet" type="text/css" href="~/vendor/css-
hamburgers/hamburgers.min.css">
    <link rel="stylesheet" type="text/css"
href="~/vendor/select2/select2.min.css">
    <link rel="stylesheet" type="text/css" href="~/css/util.css">
    <link rel="stylesheet" type="text/css" href="~/css/main.css">
</head>

<body>
    <div class="container body-content">
        @RenderBody()
        <hr />
        <footer>
            <p>&copy; 2018 - CoreMailValidation</p>
        </footer>
    </div>
    <script src="~/vendor/jquery/jquery-3.2.1.min.js"></script>
    <script src="~/vendor/bootstrap/js/popper.js"></script>
    <script src="~/vendor/bootstrap/js/bootstrap.min.js"></script>
    <script src="~/vendor/select2/select2.min.js"></script>
    <script src="~/vendor/tilt/tilt.jquery.min.js"></script>
    <script>
```

```
        $('.js-tilt').tilt({
            scale: 1.1
        })
    </script>
    <script src="~/js/main.js"></script>
    @RenderSection("Scripts", required: false)
</body>

</html>
```

9. If everything worked out right, you will see the following page when you run your ASP.NET Core MVC application. The login form is obviously totally non-functional:

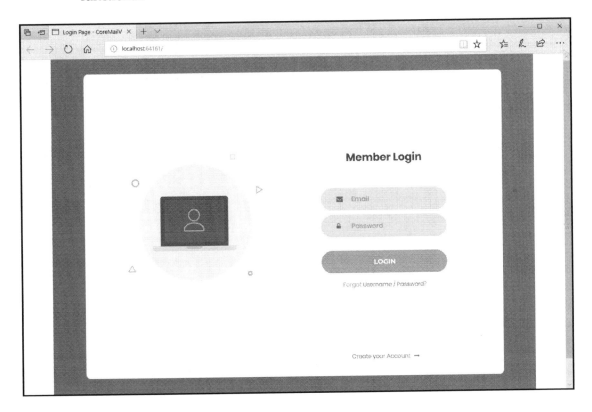

However, the login form is totally responsive. If you had to reduce the size of your browser window, you will see the form scale as your browser size reduces. This is what you want. If you want to explore the responsive design offered by Bootstrap, head on over to `https://getbootstrap.com/` and go through the examples in the documentation:

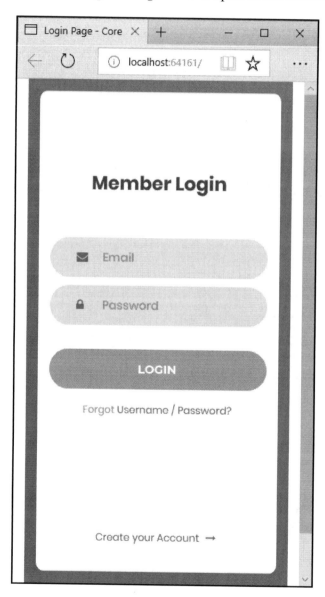

The next thing we want to do is hook this login form up to our controller and call the Azure Function we created to validate the email address we entered.

Let's look at doing that next.

Hooking it all up

To simplify things, we will be creating a model to pass to our controller:

1. Create a new class in the `Models` folder of your application called `LoginModel` and click on the **Add** button:

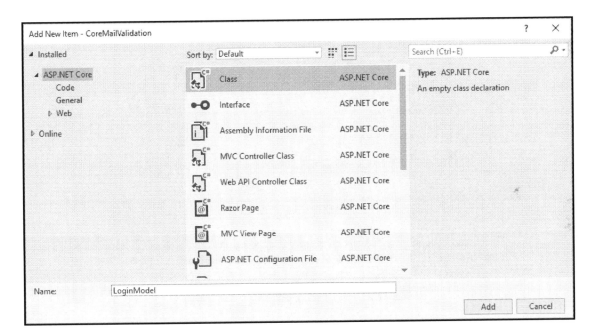

2. Your project should now look as follows. You will see the `model` added to the `Models` folder:

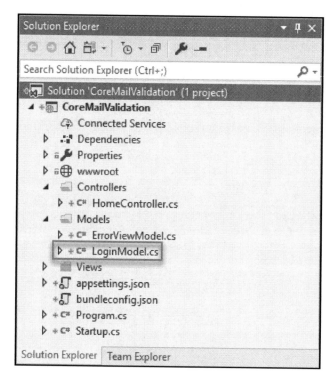

3. The next thing we want to do is add some code to our `model` to represent the fields on our login form. Add two properties called `Email` and `Password`:

```
namespace CoreMailValidation.Models
{
  public class LoginModel
  {
    public string Email { get; set; }
    public string Password { get; set; }
  }
}
```

4. Back in the `Index.cshtml` view, add the `model` declaration to the top of the page. This makes the `model` available for use in our view. Take care to specify the correct namespace where the `model` exists:

```
@model CoreMailValidation.Models.LoginModel
@{
    ViewData["Title"] = "Login Page";
}
```

5. The next portion of code needs to be written in the `HomeController.cs` file. Currently, it should only have an action called `Index()`:

```
public IActionResult Index()
{
    return View();
}
```

6. Add a new `async` function called `ValidateEmail` that will use the base URL and parameter string of the Azure Function URL we copied earlier and call it using an HTTP request. I will not go into much detail here, as I believe the code to be pretty straightforward. All we are doing is calling the Azure Function using the URL we copied earlier and reading the return data:

```
private async Task<string> ValidateEmail(string emailToValidate)
{
    string azureBaseUrl = "https://core-mail-
    validation.azurewebsites.net/api/HttpTriggerCSharp1";
    string urlQueryStringParams = $"?
    code=/IS4OJ3T46quiRzUJTxaGFenTeIVXyyOdtBFGasW9dUZ0snmoQfWoQ
    ==&email={emailToValidate}";

    using (HttpClient client = new HttpClient())
    {
        using (HttpResponseMessage res = await client.GetAsync(
        $"{azureBaseUrl}{urlQueryStringParams}"))
        {
            using (HttpContent content = res.Content)
            {
                string data = await content.ReadAsStringAsync();
                if (data != null)
                {
                    return data;
                }
                else
                    return "";
            }
```

```
        }
      }
    }
```

7. Create another `public async` action called `ValidateLogin`. Inside the action, check to see if the `ModelState` is valid before continuing.

For a nice explanation of what `ModelState` is, have a look at the following article—`https://www.exceptionnotfound.net/asp-net-mvc-demystified-modelstate/`.

8. We then do an `await` on the `ValidateEmail` function, and if the return data contains the word `false`, we know that the email validation failed. A failure message is then passed to the `TempData` property on the controller.

The `TempData` property is a place to store data until it is read. It is exposed on the controller by ASP.NET Core MVC. The `TempData` property uses a cookie-based provider by default in ASP.NET Core 2.0 to store the data. To examine data inside the `TempData` property without deleting it, you can use the `Keep` and `Peek` methods. To read more on `TempData`, see the Microsoft documentation here: `https://docs.microsoft.com/en-us/aspnet/core/fundamentals/app-state?tabs=aspnetcore2x`.

If the email validation passed, then we know that the email address is valid and we can do something else. Here, we are simply just saying that the user is logged in. In reality, we will perform some sort of authentication here and then route to the correct controller.

Another interesting thing to note is the inclusion of the `ValidateAntiForgeryToken` attribute on the `ValidateLogin` action on the controller. This ensures that the form has been posted from our site and prevents our site from being fooled by a cross site request forgery attack.

If we had to inspect the rendered markup of our page when we run the application, we will see that ASP.NET Core has automatically generated the anti-forgery token for us.

Inspect the markup via the browser's developer tools. Access it in Chrome by pressing *Ctrl + Shift + I* or *F12* if you are using Edge.

1. You will see the **__RequestVerificationToken** and the generated value as follows:

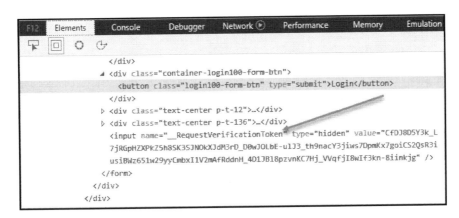

2. The complete `ValidateLogin` action on the `HomeController` should look as follows:

```
[HttpPost, ValidateAntiForgeryToken]
public async Task<IActionResult> ValidateLogin(LoginModel model)
{
  if (ModelState.IsValid)
  {
    var email = model.Email;
    string azFuncReturn = await ValidateEmail(model.Email);

    if (azFuncReturn.Contains("false"))
    {
      TempData["message"] = "The email address entered is
        incorrect. Please enter again.";
      return RedirectToAction("Index", "Home");
    }
    else
    {
      return Content("You are logged in now.");
    }
  }
  else
  {
    return View();
  }
}
```

Swing back to our `Index.cshtml` view and have a closer look at the `form` tag. We have explicitly defined which controller and action to call using `asp-action` (that specifies the action to call) and `asp-controller` (that specifies in which controller to go and look for the specified action):

```
<form class="login100-form validate-form" asp-
action="ValidateLogin" asp-controller="Home">
```

This maps the action `ValidateLogin` on the `HomeController` class that the `Index.cshtml` form will post back to:

3. Then, a little further down, ensure that your button has the `type` specified to submit:

```
<div class="container-login100-form-btn">
  <button class="login100-form-btn" type="submit">
    Login
  </button>
</div>
```

We are almost done with our `Index.cshtml` view. We want some sort of notification when the email entered is invalid. This is where Bootstrap comes in handy. Add the following markup for a `modal` dialog that will be displayed, notifying the user that the entered email address is invalid.

You will notice the inclusion of the @section Scripts block at the end of the page. What we are basically saying is that if the TempData property is not null, then we want to display the modal dialog via the jQuery script:

```
<div id="myModal" class="modal" role="dialog">
    <div class="modal-dialog">

        <!-- Modal content-->
        <div class="modal-content">
            <div class="modal-header alert alert-danger">
                <button type="button" class="close"
                 data-dismiss="modal">&times;</button>
                <h4 class="modal-title">Invalid Email</h4>
            </div>
            <div class="modal-body">
                <p>@TempData["message"].</p>
            </div>
            <div class="modal-footer">
                <button type="button" class="btn btn-default"
                 data-dismiss="modal">Close</button>
            </div>
        </div>

    </div>
</div>

@section Scripts
    {
    @if (TempData["message"] != null)
    {
        <script>
            $('#myModal').modal();
        </script>
    }
}
```

Run your application and enter an invalid email address on the login page. In my example, I simply added an email address containing two @ signs:

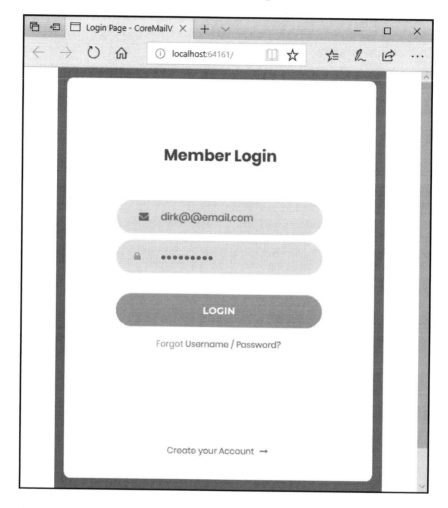

When the **LOGIN** button is pressed, the form posts back to the controller that in turn calls the Azure Function, which performs validation on the entered email address.

The result is a rather bland looking modal dialog notification popping up, notifying the user that the email address is incorrect:

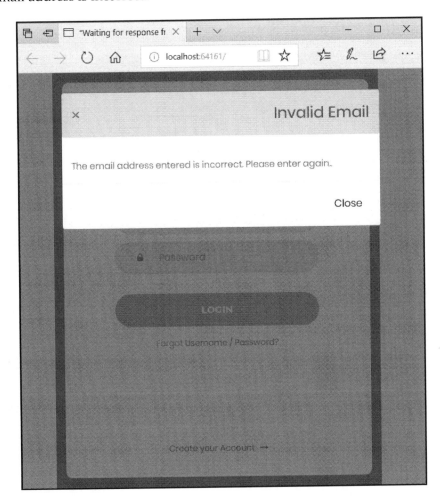

Entering a valid email address and clicking on the **LOGIN** button results in a successful validation on the entered email:

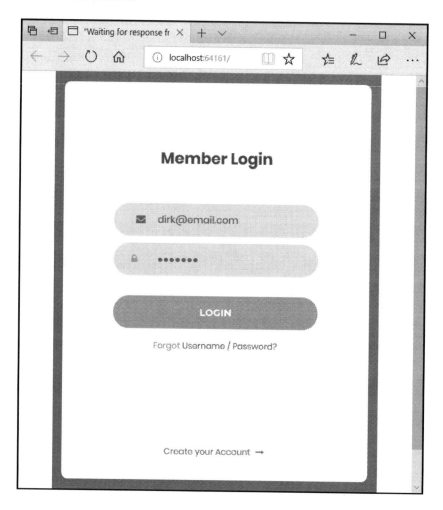

As mentioned previously, the email validation is not the same as authentication. If the email is validated, then the authentication process can take place. If this authentication process successfully authenticates the user logging in, only then will they be redirected to the logged in page:

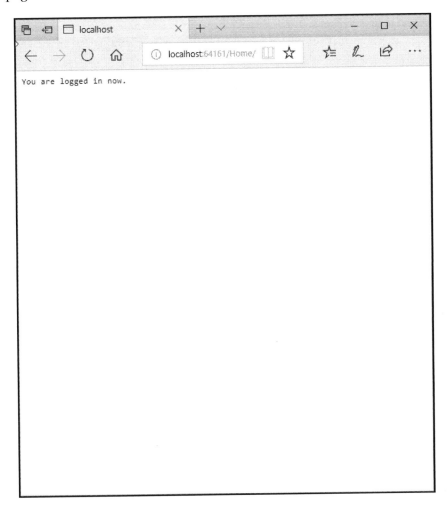

Summary

In this chapter, we saw how to create an Azure Function on the Azure portal. We learned that Azure Functions are small bits of code in the cloud that are used by applications when needed. Because they are priced on a pay-as-you-use model, you only pay for the actual computing power user. When the user load is high on your web application, the function automatically scales as required to meet the demands of the application accessing it.

We took a look at the process of getting to know the code in our Azure Function by posting the URL into the browser manually. Then, we created an ASP.NET Core MVC application that consisted of a single login page. We then had a look at how to use the Azure Function to validate the email address entered on the login screen. Azure Functions are an exciting technology to start using. There is still a lot to learn, and not enough left of the chapter to discuss this serverless technology. If this technology interests you, explore some of the other Azure Service templates available.

In the next chapter, we will be looking at creating a Twitter clone using an ASP.NET Core MVC application and a C# library called `Tweetinvi`. Stick around, there is still a lot of exciting content for you.

8
Twitter Clone Using OAuth

In this chapter, we will have a look at how easy it is to create a basic Twitter clone using ASP.NET Core MVC. We will be performing the following tasks:

- Creating your application on Twitter using Twitter's Application Management
- Creating an ASP.NET Core MVC application
- Reading your Home Timeline
- Posting a tweet

As you can imagine, Twitter functionality does not come as standard in .NET (let alone in .NET Core).

 Please be aware that you will need to create a Twitter account in order to perform the tasks in this chapter. You can do this by going to `https://twitter.com/` and registering.

Luckily for us, there are many dedicated and passionate developers out there who give their code away for free. You will usually find their code hosted on GitHub, and that is just the place that we will be looking at for a bit of code to integrate into our ASP.NET Core MVC application in order to give it that Twitter functionality. This chapter is by no means an endorsement of the particular Twitter library we're going to use. However, this library is by far one of the best I have used. It is also (at the time of writing) constantly being updated.

Let's have a look at Tweetinvi.

Using Tweetinvi

Point your browser to `https://github.com/linvi/tweetinvi`. The description of this library says it all:

> *Tweetinvi, the best Twitter C# library for the REST and Stream API. It supports .NET, .NETCore, UAP and Portable Class Libraries (Xamarin)...*

In other words, this library is exactly what we need to create our Twitter clone application. Tweetinvi is really well documented and has an active community that supports it.

The ASP.NET Core MVC Twitter clone application

Creating a fully-fledged Twitter clone application is a lot of work—more work than this chapter would allow me, I'm afraid. I will therefore just illustrate how to read the tweets in your main feed (the tweets of the people you follow on Twitter). I will also show you how to post a tweet from the application.

I will be dispensing with all the fancy UI elements in this application, and instead will give you a fantastic basis to carry on developing a fully-fledged Twitter clone. You can consider adding the following functionality:

- Deleting tweets
- Retweeting
- Following someone
- Unfollowing someone
- Sending private messages
- Searching
- Viewing profile information

There is a lot of additional functionality you can add; feel free to build in any missing functionality you would like to see. I for one would like a better way to curate and save tweets that I find interesting.

I know that some of you might wonder why liking a tweet won't suffice, and here is my reason why. Liking tweets has lately become a shorthand way for someone to let another person know that they have seen their tweet. This is especially true when you are mentioned in a tweet. Instead of just replying (especially to rhetorical questions), Twitter users simply like the tweet.

Liking a tweet is also not a curation tool. Everything you like is found under your likes. There is no way to differentiate. Aha! I hear some of you say, *What about moments?* Again, moments live on Twitter.

Think moments, but moments that come to you. Anyway, there are a lot of improvements that one can make to a custom Twitter clone such as this to truly make it your own. For now, let's start with the basics.

Creating your application on Twitter

Before we can begin creating our Twitter clone, we need to register it on the Twitter Application Management console.

To access the Application Management console, point your browser to `https://apps.twitter.com`:

1. Click on the **Sign in** link, as shown in the following screenshot:

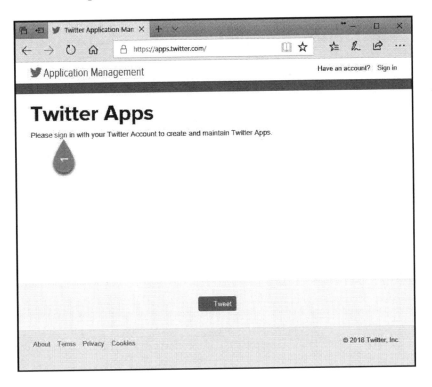

2. Sign in with your Twitter credentials on the login screen:

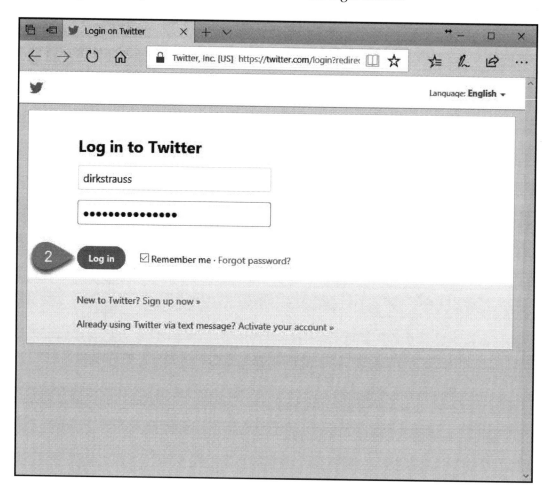

3. If you have created any applications before, you will see them listed. All the apps that you create are listed under your **Twitter Apps** section. Click on the **Create New App** button:

4. You will now see the **Create an application** form. Give your application a suitable **Name** and **Description**. Provide a **Website** for your application, and lastly, supply a **Callback URL** value. I have simply used `http://localhost:50000/` and I will show you how to configure this in your application later. This is shown in the following screenshot:

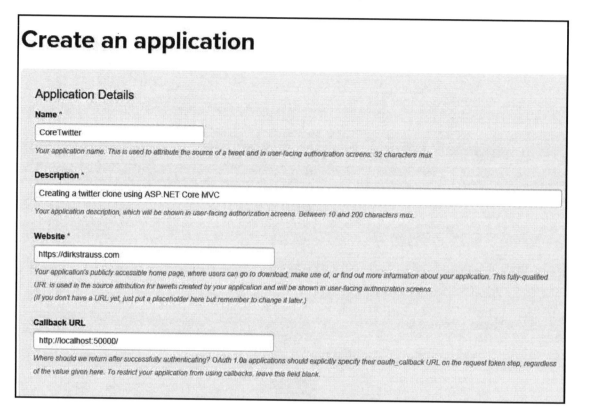

Create an application

Application Details

Name *

> CoreTwitter

Your application name. This is used to attribute the source of a tweet and in user-facing authorization screens. 32 characters max.

Description *

> Creating a twitter clone using ASP.NET Core MVC

Your application description, which will be shown in user-facing authorization screens. Between 10 and 200 characters max.

Website *

> https://dirkstrauss.com

Your application's publicly accessible home page, where users can go to download, make use of, or find out more information about your application. This fully-qualified URL is used in the source attribution for tweets created by your application and will be shown in user-facing authorization screens.

(If you don't have a URL yet, just put a placeholder here but remember to change it later.)

Callback URL

> http://localhost:50000/

Where should we return after successfully authenticating? OAuth 1.0a applications should explicitly specify their oauth_callback URL on the request token step, regardless of the value given here. To restrict your application from using callbacks, leave this field blank.

 If localhost gives you problems during the callback, try using `127.0.0.1` instead.

5. Check the option that you understand the **Twitter Developer Agreement** and then click on **Create your Twitter application**:

6. Next, you will see a summary of the **Application Settings** you just created. At the top of the screen, click on the **Keys and Access Tokens** tab:

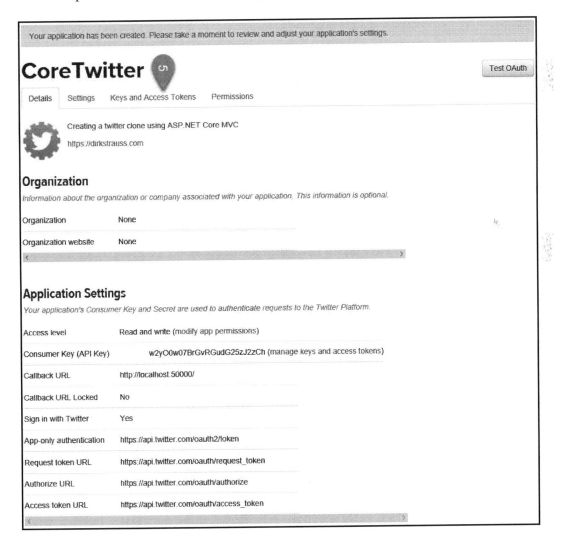

7. This will take you to your **Application Settings,** where the **Consumer Key** and **Consumer Secret** is provided. Be sure to make a note of these keys:

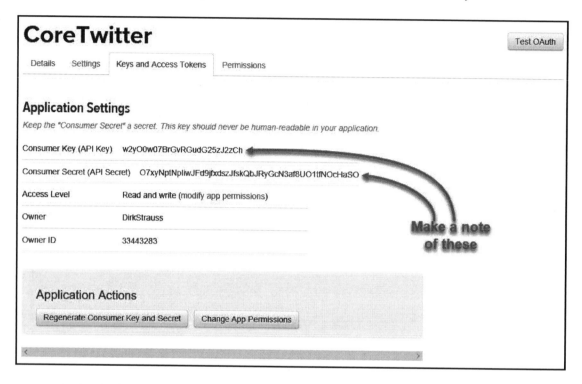

8. At the bottom of the page, you will see a button called **Create my access token**. Click on this button. This creates the token that will allow you to make API calls:

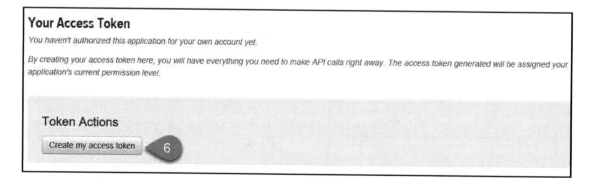

9. After the token is generated, the **Access Token** and **Access Token Secret** are displayed for you. Make a note of these too:

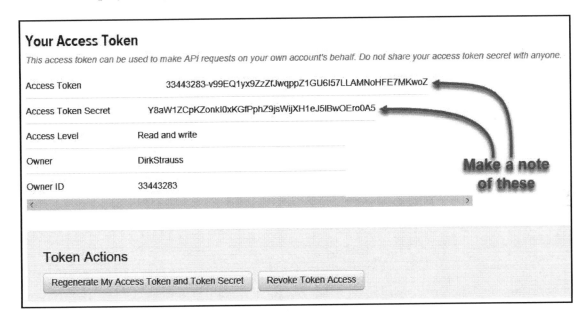

That is all there is to registering your application on Twitter's Application Management console. The next thing we need to do is create our ASP.NET Core MVC Application.

Creating the ASP.NET Core MVC Application and adding the NuGet package

Let's now begin to create the ASP.NET Core MVC application and add Twitter functionality to it:

1. In Visual Studio 2017, create a new **ASP.NET Core Web Application**. I just called my application the same as what I called it when I registered it on Twitter. Click on the **OK** button:

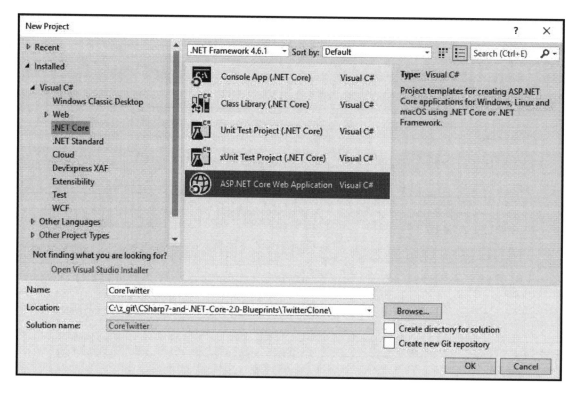

2. On the next screen, ensure that you have the **Web Application (Model-View-Controller)** template selected and that you have selected **ASP.NET Core 2.0** from the dropdown. I mention this explicitly, because I get feedback from readers where it turns out that they never selected ASP.NET Core 2.0. Click on the **OK** button:

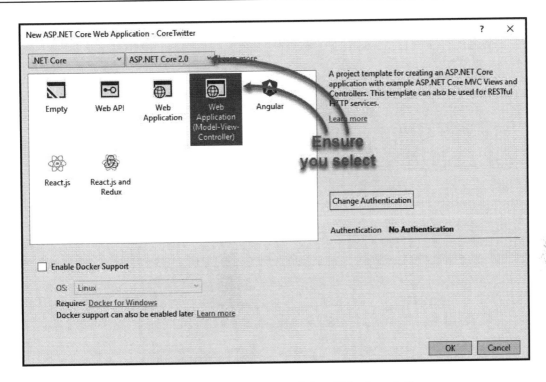

When your project has been created, it will look as follows:

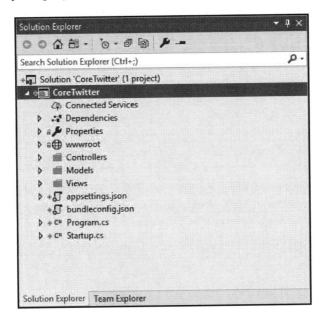

3. We now want to go and grab the Tweetinvi NuGet package, so right-click on the project and select **Manage NuGet Packages** from the context menu, shown as follows:

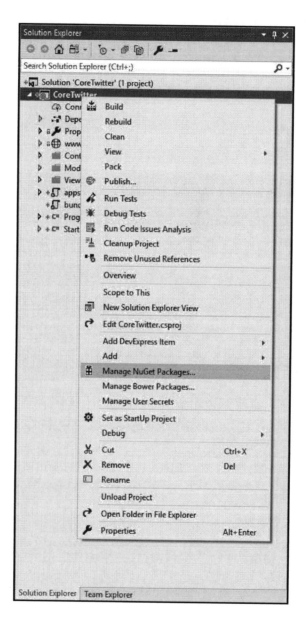

4. In the **Browse** tab, search for `tweetinvi` and select the project by the developer called **Linvi**. Click on the **Install** button to add it to your application:

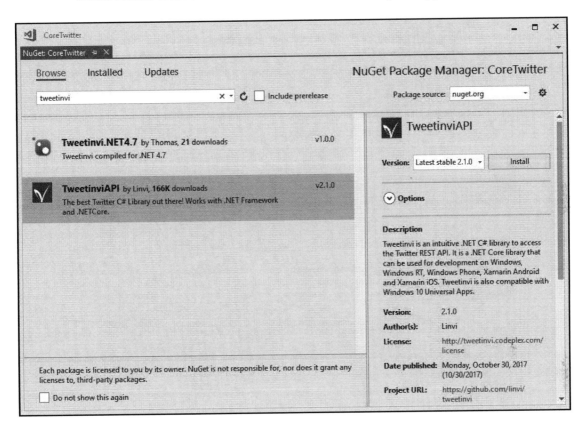

5. After a short while, the progress will display finished in the **Output** window of Visual Studio:

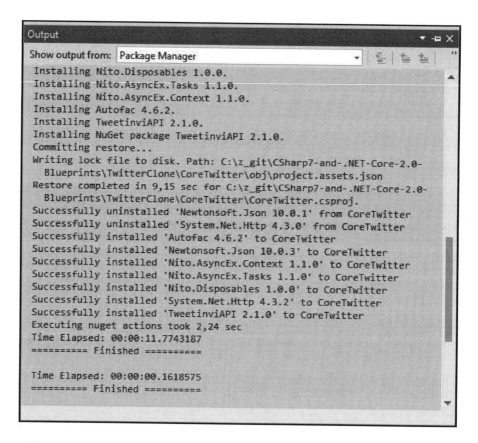

6. The next thing we want to do is set our URL to the callback URL set in the Twitter Application Management console earlier. To do this, right-click your project and click on **Properties** from the context menu:

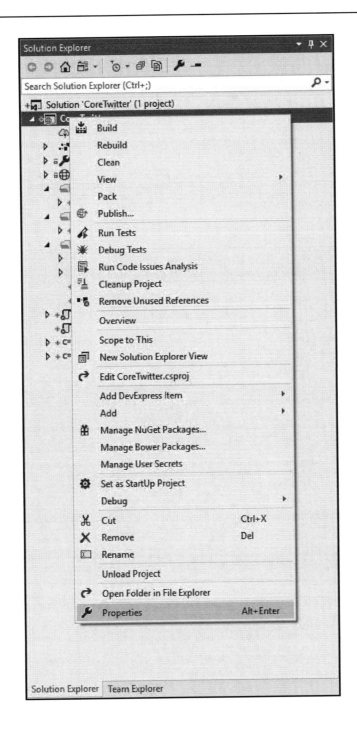

7. Select the **Debug** tab and then enter the callback URL in the **App URL** field:

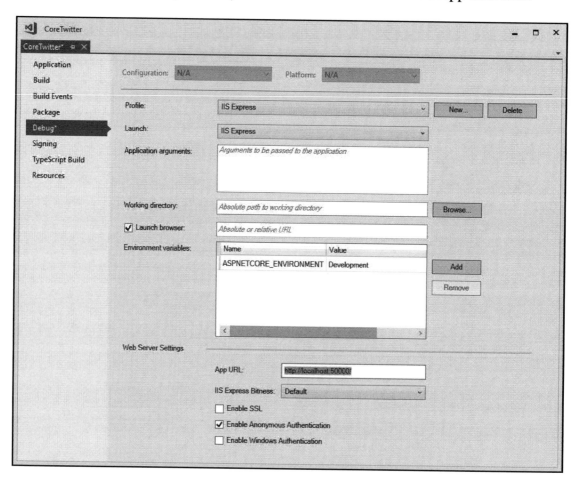

 If you set the `localhost` portion of the callback URL to `127.0.0.1` in the Application Management console, you need to set it here to `127.0.0.1` too.

8. Save your settings and return to your code window.

From a setup perspective, this should be all you need in order to start writing your code and wiring everything up. Let's start doing that next.

Let's code

All the code for this project will be available on GitHub. Point your browser to `https://github.com/PacktPublishing/CSharp7-and-.NET-Core-2.0-Blueprints` and grab the code to work through it as you read through the rest of this chapter.

Setting up the classes and settings

The first thing I want to do is create a class that will store my settings. For this, perform the following steps:

1. Create a folder called `Classes` and, in this folder, create a class called `CoreTwitterSettings`. Then, add a second class called `TweetItem` to the `Classes` folder (we will be using this class later). While you are at it, create another folder called `css`, which we will be using in a minute.

2. When you have done this, your project will look as follows:

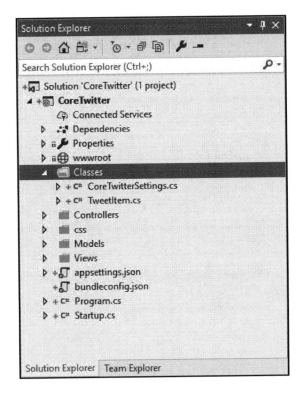

3. Open the `CoreTwitterSettings` class and add the following code to it:

```
public class CoreTwitterConfiguration
{
    public string ApplicationName { get; set; }
    public int TweetFeedLimit { get; set; } = 1;

    public TwitterSettings TwitterConfiguration { get; set; } = new
    TwitterSettings();
}

public class TwitterSettings
{
    public string Consumer_Key { get; set; }
    public string Consumer_Secret { get; set; }
    public string Access_Token { get; set; }
    public string Access_Secret { get; set; }
}
```

4. The next thing we want to do is locate our `appsettings.json` file. This file will be in the root of your project, as shown in the following screenshot:

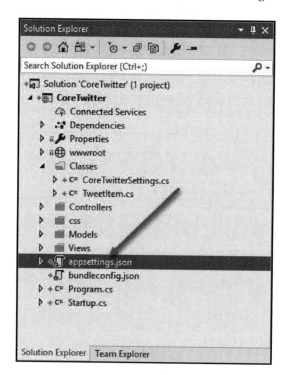

5. Double-click on the `appsettings.json` file to open it for editing. The default content of the file should look as follows:

```
{
  "Logging": {
    "IncludeScopes": false,
    "LogLevel": {
      "Default": "Warning"
    }
  }
}
```

6. Modify the file to include the settings you want to store. The `appsettings.json` file's purpose is to store all of your application's settings.

7. Add your **Consumer Key** and your **Consumer Secret** keys to the file. Also, note that I have used a setting for the base URL, which is the **Callback URL** set earlier. This is sometimes handy to have around in a setting. I have also created a setting called `TweetFeedLimit` to limit the tweets returned to the home timeline.

Your **Consumer Key** and **Consumer Secret** will definitely differ to the values in my example. So, be sure to change these accordingly in your application.

8. When you have modified your `appsettings.json` file, it will look as follows:

```
{
  "Logging": {
    "IncludeScopes": false,
    "LogLevel": {
      "Default": "Warning"
    }
  },

  "CoreTwitter": {
    "ApplicationName": "Twitter Core Clone (local)",
    "TweetFeedLimit": 10,
    "BaseUrl": "http://localhost:50000/",
    "TwitterConfiguration": {
      "Consumer_Key": "[YOUR_CONSSUMER_KEY]",
      "Consumer_Secret": "[YOUR_CONSUMER_SECRET]",
      "Access_Token": "",
      "Access_Secret": ""
    }
  }
}
```

```
     }
```

9. If you have a look at the `CoreTwitterSettings` class, you will see that it slightly resembles the JSON in the `appsettings.json` file.

10. In your Visual Studio solution, locate the `Startup.cs` file and open that for editing. You will see that Visual Studio 2017 has already added a lot of boilerplate code to this class for you already. Take special note of the `ConfigureServices` method. It should look something like this:

```
public void ConfigureServices(IServiceCollection services)
{
    services.AddMvc();
}
```

11. Since ASP.NET Core 1.1, we have been able to use `Get<T>`, which worked with entire sections. To make the settings available in our ASP.NET Core MVC application, change the code in this method as follows:

```
public void ConfigureServices(IServiceCollection services)
{
    services.AddMvc();
    var section = Configuration.GetSection("CoreTwitter");
    services.Configure<CoreTwitterConfiguration>(section);
}
```

You will notice that we are getting the `CoreTwitter` section defined in the `appsettings.json` file.

Creating the TweetItem class

The `TweetItem` class is simply going to contain the URL to a particular tweet. It isn't a very complex class at all, but its usefulness will become clear later on in the chapter. For now, just add the following code to it:

```
public class TweetItem
{
    public string Url { get; set; }
}
```

The URL it will store will be the URL to a particular tweet.

Setting up the CSS

In order to use the `<blockquote>` HTML tag for a tweet, you will want to add a CSS file to your CSS folder. In our example, we will not be using it, but as you build out your application even further, you would want to use this CSS to style your `<blockquote>` tweets.

If you are just playing around for now, and don't intend on building this application any further after completing this chapter, you can skip this section on adding the CSS file. If you want to go further with this application, then read on:

1. Right-click the css folder in your solution and add a new item to it. Call the file `site.css` and click on the **Add** button, as shown in the following screenshot:

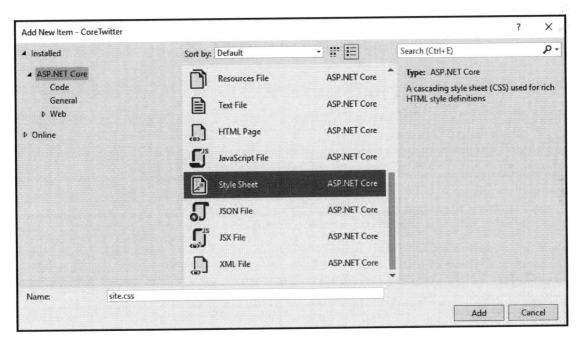

2. Delete the contents of the `site.css` file and add the following css to it:

```
blockquote.twitter-tweet {
    display: inline-block;
    font-family: "Helvetica Neue", Roboto, "Segoe UI", Calibri,
    sans-serif;
    font-size: 12px;
    font-weight: bold;
```

```
        line-height: 16px;
        border-color: #eee #ddd #bbb;
        border-radius: 5px;
        border-style: solid;
        border-width: 1px;
        box-shadow: 0 1px 3px rgba(0, 0, 0, 0.15);
        margin: 10px 5px;
        padding: 0 16px 16px 16px;
        max-width: 468px;
    }

blockquote.twitter-tweet p {
        font-size: 16px;
        font-weight: normal;
        line-height: 20px;
    }

blockquote.twitter-tweet a {
        color: inherit;
        font-weight: normal;
        text-decoration: none;
        outline: 0 none;
    }

blockquote.twitter-tweet a:hover,
blockquote.twitter-tweet a:focus {
        text-decoration: underline;
    }
```

To complement this section, you can read through the Twitter Developer Documentation at `https://dev.twitter.com/web/overview/css` and have a look at the CSS overview.

Adding the controllers

We now need to start adding our controllers. Controllers are responsible for responding to requests made to your application:

1. To the `Controllers` folder, add another controller called `TwitterController`. This controller will be responsible for composing a new tweet and for publishing a new tweet. We will get back to this controller later on. For now, just create the class. After you have added it, your solution should look as follows:

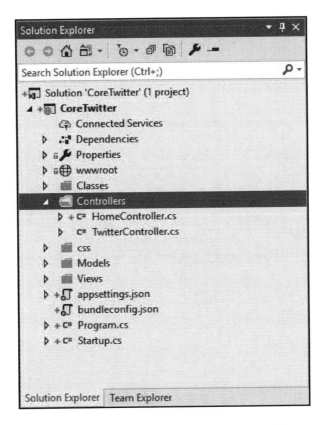

2. By default, Visual Studio has HomeController added for you when you created your ASP.NET Core MVC application. Open HomeController and look at the contents of the class. Be sure to add the following using statements to your HomeController class:

```
using Tweetinvi;
using Tweetinvi.Models;
```

3. The first thing I want to do is make my application settings stored in the appsettings.json file available in my class. You will remember that we modified the Startup.cs file to inject the settings at startup.

4. At the top of the HomeController class, add the following line of code:

```
CoreTwitterConfiguration config;
```

5. Directly underneath that line, add a constructor that brings the
   `CoreTwitterConfiguration` class into scope for our controller:

```
public HomeController(IOptions<CoreTwitterConfiguration> options)
{
    config = options.Value;
}
```

6. We will now modify the `Index` action of the `HomeController` class to check
   whether we have an access token or an access secret. You will remember seeing
   that we left these blank in the `appsettings.json` file earlier. If these are empty,
   then the user has not been authenticated and we then redirect the user to the
   `AuthenticateTwitter` action on `HomeController`:

```
public IActionResult Index()
{
    try
    {
        if
(String.IsNullOrWhiteSpace(config.TwitterConfiguration.Access_Token
)) throw new
Tweetinvi.Exceptions.TwitterNullCredentialsException();
        if
(String.IsNullOrWhiteSpace(config.TwitterConfiguration.Access_Secre
t)) throw new
Tweetinvi.Exceptions.TwitterNullCredentialsException();
    }
    catch (Tweetinvi.Exceptions.TwitterNullCredentialsException ex)
    {
        return RedirectToAction("AuthenticateTwitter");
    }
    catch (Exception ex)
    {
        // Redirect to your error page here
    }
    return View();
}
```

7. Let's now go and create the `AuthenticateTwitter` action. For this, we need the
   consumer credentials, which we copied from our Twitter Application
   Management console earlier and added to our `appsettings.json` file. We then
   made these settings available throughout our application; now we can see the
   benefit of having our settings stored in the `appsettings.json` file.

8. Inside the `AuthenticateTwitter` action, we simply pass the `ConsumerCredentials` object the consumer key and consumer secret. When we are validated, we are routed to the `ValidateOAuth` action, which we will create next:

```
public IActionResult AuthenticateTwitter()
{
    var coreTwitterCredentials = new ConsumerCredentials(
        config.TwitterConfiguration.Consumer_Key
        , config.TwitterConfiguration.Consumer_Secret);
        var callbackURL = "http://" + Request.Host.Value +
        "/Home/ValidateOAuth";
    var authenticationContext =
    AuthFlow.InitAuthentication(coreTwitterCredentials,
    callbackURL);

    return new
    RedirectResult(authenticationContext.AuthorizationURL);
}
```

9. At this point, we have been redirected to Twitter to authenticate the user via OAuth and have been redirected back to our ASP.NET Core application via the **Callback URL**. The code is really straightforward. One thing to note though is that `userCredentials.AccessToken` and `userCredentials.AccessTokenSecret` are returned from the `userCredentials` object. I just added these to the configuration settings for the application, but in reality, you might want to store these elsewhere (such as encrypted in a database). This will then allow you to use the application without having to authenticate yourself every time:

```
public ActionResult ValidateOAuth()
{
    if (Request.Query.ContainsKey("oauth_verifier") &&
    Request.Query.ContainsKey("authorization_id"))
    {
        var oauthVerifier = Request.Query["oauth_verifier"];
        var authId = Request.Query["authorization_id"];

        var userCredentials =
        AuthFlow.CreateCredentialsFromVerifierCode(oauthVerifier,
        authId);
        var twitterUser =
        Tweetinvi.User.GetAuthenticatedUser(userCredentials);

        config.TwitterConfiguration.Access_Token =
```

```
                    userCredentials.AccessToken;
                    config.TwitterConfiguration.Access_Secret =
                    userCredentials.AccessTokenSecret;
                    ViewBag.User = twitterUser;
            }

            return View();
    }
```

Seeing as this controller action is called `ValidateOAuth`, let's go and create a view with the same name so that we can route to a page that informs the user that they have been authenticated successfully.

Creating views

Views and traditional HTML pages are not the same thing. The pages of the ASP.NET Core MVC application are represented by views. As I pointed out earlier, controllers receive a request and handle that request. The controller can redirect you to another controller action, but it can also return a view:

1. We will now go ahead and create the views for our application. Expand the Home folder and add a new view called `ValidateOAuth` to the Home folder. Just create these views without models:

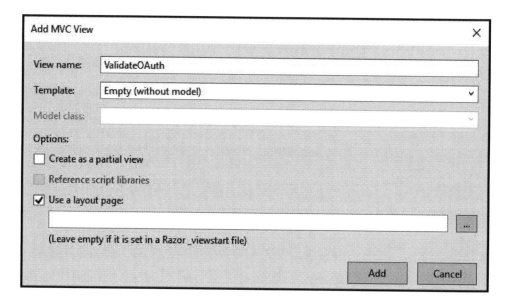

2. Add another folder to the `Views` folder called `Twitter` and add two views to that folder called `ComposeTweet` and `HomeTimeline`. After you have done that, your application will look as follows:

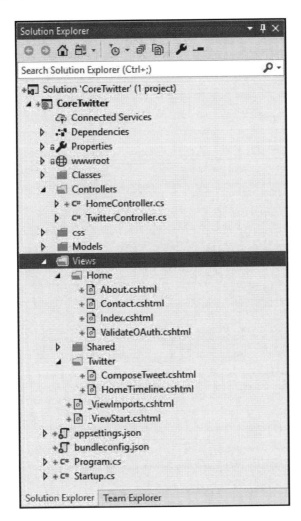

3. Open the `ValidateOAuth` view and add the following markup to it:

```
@if (@ViewBag.User != null)
{
    <h2>OAuth Authentication Succeeded!</h2>
    <p>Welcome to the CoreTwitter Demo Application
<b>@ViewBag.User.Name</b>. You have been successfully authenticated
```

```
        via Twitter.</p>

        <div class="row">
            <div class="col-md-4">
                <h2>Go to your home feed</h2>
                <p>
                    See what's new on your home feed.
                </p>
                <p>
                    <a class="btn btn-default"
                        href="/Home/GetHomeTimeline">Home &raquo;</a>
                </p>
            </div>
        </div>
    }
    else
    {
        <h2>OAuth Authentication failed!</h2>
        <p>An error occurred during authentication. Try <a
        href="/Home/TwitterAuth">authenticating</a> again.</p>
    }
```

Having a look at the markup, you will notice that all it does is notify the user of the authentication status. If authenticated, the user can check out their home feed, which is all the tweets of the people they follow on Twitter.

I want to call your attention here to the way I call the GetHomeTimeline action on the Home controller. You will see in the button link, the following href exists:

```
href="/Home/GetHomeTimeline"
```

This is one way to route the user to an action on a controller. A little later, I will show you another nicer method to do this.

So, we are allowing a successfully authenticated user to view the tweets of the people they follow by clicking on the Home link. This calls an action called GetHomeTimeline. Let's go and modify HomeController to add this action.

Modifying HomeController

Swing back to `HomeController` and add another action called `GetHomeTimeline`. This then takes the user credentials to find the home timeline tweets of the authenticated user. The user credentials consist of the following:

- Consumer key
- Consumer secret
- Access token
- Access secret

You will notice that these are all coming from the `CoreTwitterConfiguration` object. The twitter feed only consists of the limit set in the settings. I set mine to `10`, so this should only contain 10 tweets. For every tweet in the feed, I extract the URL of the tweet and add it to a list of type `TweetItem` (the class we created earlier). If everything runs smoothly, I route to the `HomeTimeline` view.

Add the following code to your `GetHomeTimeline` action.

 You should be getting an error on the code that references the `TwitterViewModel` instance called `homeView`. We will rectify this next.

Your action should look as follows:

```
public IActionResult GetHomeTimeline()
{
    TwitterViewModel homeView = new TwitterViewModel();

    try
    {
        if (config.TwitterConfiguration.Access_Token == null) throw new
        Tweetinvi.Exceptions.TwitterNullCredentialsException();
        if (config.TwitterConfiguration.Access_Secret == null) throw
        new Tweetinvi.Exceptions.TwitterNullCredentialsException();

        var userCredentials = Auth.CreateCredentials(
            config.TwitterConfiguration.Consumer_Key
            , config.TwitterConfiguration.Consumer_Secret
            , config.TwitterConfiguration.Access_Token
            , config.TwitterConfiguration.Access_Secret);

        var authenticatedUser =
```

```
        Tweetinvi.User.GetAuthenticatedUser(userCredentials);

        IEnumerable<ITweet> twitterFeed =
        authenticatedUser.GetHomeTimeline(config.TweetFeedLimit);

        List<TweetItem> tweets = new List<TweetItem>();
        foreach(ITweet tweet in twitterFeed)
        {
            TweetItem tweetItem = new TweetItem();

            tweetItem.Url = tweet.Url;
            tweets.Add(tweetItem);
        }

        homeView.HomeTimelineTweets = tweets;
    }
    catch (Tweetinvi.Exceptions.TwitterNullCredentialsException ex)
    {
        return RedirectToAction("AuthenticateTwitter");
    }
    catch (Exception ex)
    {
    }

    return View("Views/Twitter/HomeTimeline.cshtml", homeView);
}
```

As mentioned earlier, you will see some errors. This is because we don't yet have a model called `TwitterViewModel`. Let's create that next.

Creating the TwitterViewModel class

The `TwitterViewModel` class is just a really simple class that takes a collection of `TweetItem` as a property called `HomeTimelineTweets`.

Let's start by adding a model to our project:

1. Right-click your `Models` folder and add a class called `TwitterViewModel` to the folder. Then, add the following code to that class:

```
public class TwitterViewModel
{
    public List<TweetItem> HomeTimelineTweets { get; set; }
}
```

2. Also, add the using statement using `CoreTwitter.Classes;` to the class.

This is all that is needed. As you expand the `TweetItem` class later on (if you decide to add functionality to this app), this model will be responsible for passing that information through to our view for use in the Razor.

Creating the HomeTimeline view

Thinking back to the `HomeController` action we created earlier called `GetHomeTimeline`, you will remember that we routed to a view called `HomeTimeline`. We have already created this view, but now we need to add some logic to it to render the tweets in our home timeline.

We, therefore, need to add a view for our home timeline, which we will add next:

1. Open the `HomeTimeline.cshtml` file and add the following markup to the view:

```
@model TwitterViewModel
@{
    ViewBag.Title = "What's happening?";
}

<h2>Home - Timeline</h2>

<div class="row">
    <div class="col-md-8">

        @foreach (var tweet in Model.HomeTimelineTweets)
        {
            <blockquote class="twitter-tweet">
                <p lang="en" dir="ltr">
                    <a href="@Html.DisplayFor(m => tweet.Url)"></a>
            </blockquote>
            <script async
              src="https://platform.twitter.com/widgets.js"
              charset="utf-8"></script>

        }
    </div>

    <div class="col-md-4">
        <h2>Tweet</h2>
        <p>What's happening?</p>
        <a class="btn btn-default" asp-controller="Twitter" asp-
          action="ComposeTweet">Tweet &raquo; </a>
```

```
        </div>

    </div>
```

The first thing you need to notice is the `@model TwitterViewModel` statement at the top of the file. This allows us to use the values stored inside that model in our view. What our view does is loop through the collection of tweets contained in the `HomeTimelineTweets` property of the model and build up a list of tweets to display on the page.

Another thing I want to draw your attention to is the tag helpers `asp-controller` and `asp-action` on the Tweet link. This is a cleaner way of routing to a specific action on a specific controller (as opposed to doing it in the `href` as we saw in the `ValidateOAuth` view earlier).

Lastly, you might be wondering what the `widgets.js` reference is doing there. Well, I didn't want to style my tweets myself, so I decided to use Twitter to do it for me:

2. To get the markup, head over to `https://publish.twitter.com/#`:

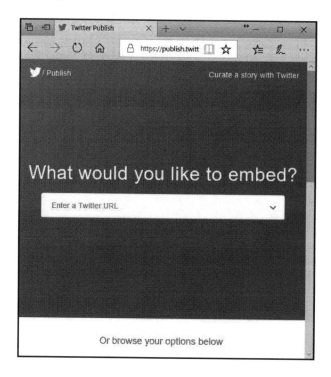

3. From the dropdown, select **A Tweet** as the option of the thing you are trying to embed, shown as follows:

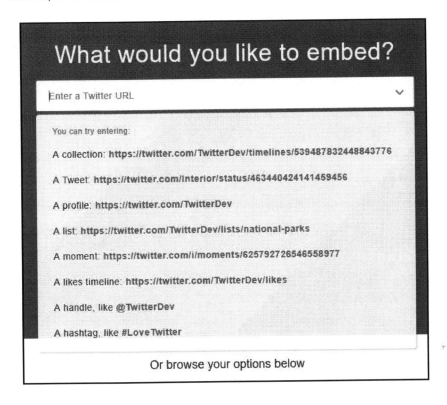

4. You will then be given some sample code to use. You can just click on the **Copy Code** button. This is just the way I did it, but you are welcome to go your own way without going through this step:

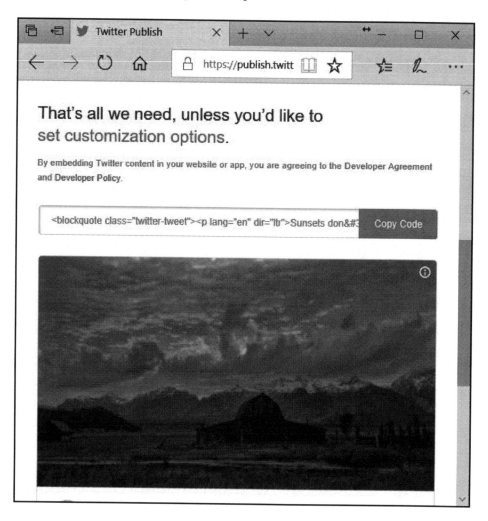

5. The code that you copied might look something like the following:

```
<blockquote class="twitter-tweet">
        <p lang="en" dir="ltr">Sunsets don't get much better than
        this one over <a href="https://twitter.com/GrandTetonNPS?
        ref_src=twsrc%5Etfw">@GrandTetonNPS</a>.
        <a href="https://twitter.com/hashtag/nature?
```

```
            src=hash&amp;ref_src=twsrc%5Etfw">#nature</a>
         <a href="https://twitter.com/hashtag/sunset?
            src=hash&amp;ref_src=twsrc%5Etfw">#sunset</a>
      <a href="http://t.co/YuKy2rcjyU">pic.twitter.com/YuKy2rcjyU</a>
            </p>&mdash; US Department of the Interior (@Interior)
      <a
   href="https://twitter.com/Interior/status/463440424141459456?
      ref_src=twsrc%5Etfw">May 5, 2014</a>
      </blockquote>
      <script async src="https://platform.twitter.com/widgets.js"
         charset="utf-8"></script>
```

6. Take that and modify it to be styled according to your page. Do this in a loop so that you can output all the tweets individually below each other. The code you should end up with is just:

```
<blockquote class="twitter-tweet">
    <p lang="en" dir="ltr">
        <a href="@Html.DisplayFor(m => tweet.Url)"></a>
</blockquote>
<script async src="https://platform.twitter.com/widgets.js"
charset="utf-8"></script>
```

It just contains the link to the Twitter URL.

Modifying the TwitterController class

Now we come to the part where we allow the user to send a tweet.

Open up the `TwitterController` class and add two actions called `ComposeTweet` and `PublishTweet`. The `TwitterController` class is really simple. It just contains the following code:

```
public class TwitterController : Controller
{
    public IActionResult ComposeTweet()
    {
        return View();
    }
    public IActionResult PublishTweet(string tweetText)
    {
        var firstTweet = Tweet.PublishTweet(tweetText);
        return RedirectToAction("GetHomeTimeline", "Home");
    }
}
```

The `ComposeTweet` action simply returns the user to a view where they can compose a tweet. You will remember that we created the `ComposeTweet` view earlier. The `PublishTweet` action is just as simple. It takes the text of what I am tweeting and passes it to the `PublishTweet` method of the `Tweetinvi.Tweet` class. After that, it makes sense to redirect back to the home timeline where we will expect to see the tweet we just created.

The last task we need to complete is to modify the `ComposeTweet` view. Let's do that next.

Finishing up—the ComposeTweet view

To finish up, we use the `ComposeTweet` view.

Open up the `ComposeTweet` view and add the following markup to the view:

```
@{
    ViewData["Title"] = "Tweet";
}

<h2>Tweet</h2>

<form method="post" asp-controller="Twitter" asp-action="PublishTweet">

    <div class="form-group">
        <label for="tweet">Tweet : </label>
        <input type="text" class="form-control" name="tweetText"
         id="tweetText" value="What's happening?" />
    </div>
    <div class="form-group">
        <input type="submit" class="btn btn-success" />
    </div>
</form>
```

You will notice that once again, I am making use of Tag Helpers to define the controller and action to call. Only this time, I am doing it on the `<form>` tag. At this point, you are ready to run your application for the first time. Let's have a look at how it performs.

Running the CoreTwitter application

Perform a build of your project to make sure everything builds correctly. Then, start debugging your application. Because you have not been authenticated, you will be redirected to Twitter to be authenticated.

This is a page that I am sure you are used to seeing:

1. Many web applications use OAuth for authentication. To continue, click on the **Authorize app** button, as follows:

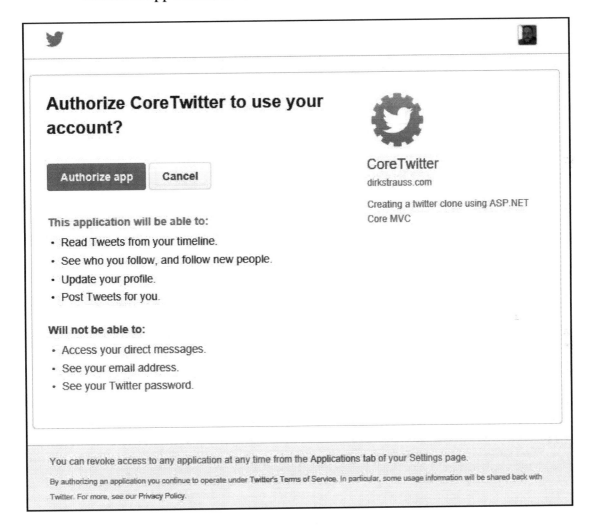

2. You will then see a redirection notice. This could take a few moments to redirect you. It all depends on your internet connection speed:

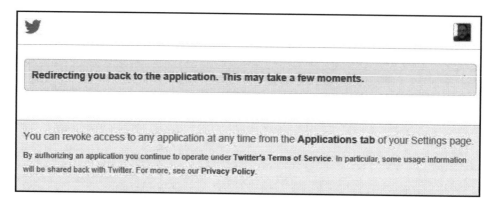

Redirecting you back to the application. This may take a few moments.

You can revoke access to any application at any time from the **Applications tab** of your Settings page.

By authorizing an application you continue to operate under **Twitter's Terms of Service**. In particular, some usage information will be shared back with Twitter. For more, see our **Privacy Policy**.

3. Once you have been redirected to your **CoreTwitter** application, you will see the **OAuth Authentication Succeeded** message displayed. Following that, click on the **Home** button to go to `HomeTimeline`:

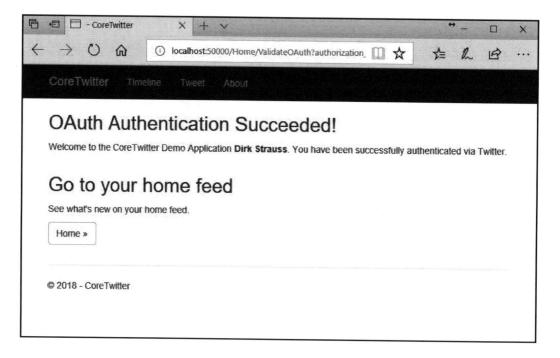

4. `HomeController` jumps into action as the `GetHomeTimeline` action is called and redirects you to the `HomeTimeline` view. You will see your tweets loaded in the page:

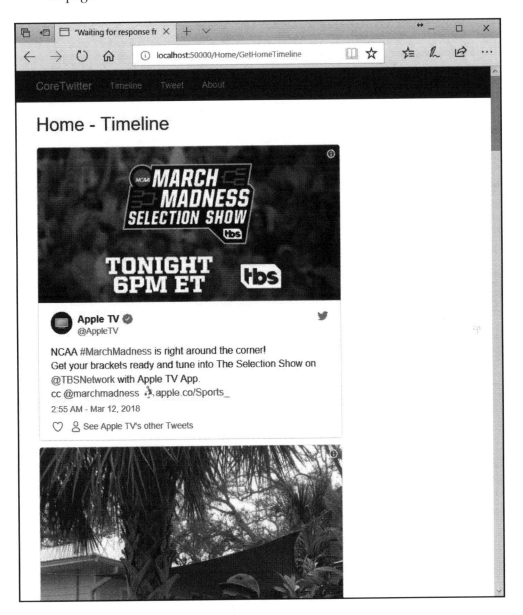

5. As you scroll through the tweets (remember, I only returned 10), you will see that there are videos included that will play when you click on the play button:

6. Media-rich tweets give you previews on articles too, and you will also see the plain old text tweets in your timeline. All the links are fully active and you can click on them to view the article:

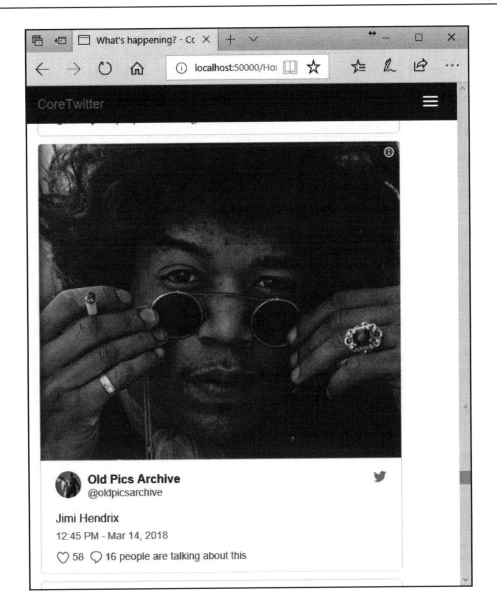

7. If you scroll right to the bottom of the timeline (this should have been at the top, but I told you that I wasn't going to do much around the UI), you will see the **Tweet** button. Click on that to compose a new tweet:

8. On the `ComposeTweet` view, you can enter anything into the tweet field and click on the **Submit Query** button:

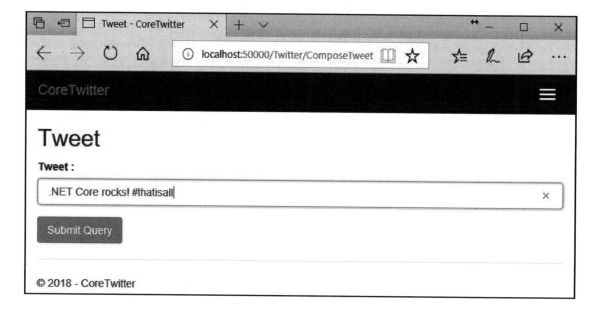

9. Your tweet is then posted on Twitter and you are redirected to the home timeline again, where you will see your newly posted tweet:

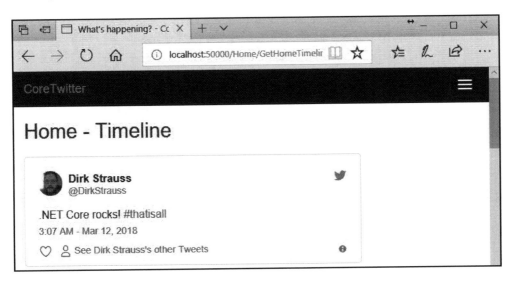

And, just for the sake of it, you can view that specific tweet by going to the following URL: `https://twitter.com/DirkStrauss/status/973002561979547650`.

Yes, it really is 3:07 AM right now. `#thatisall`.

Summary

Looking back at the chapter, we really did a lot. I encourage you to go through the code on GitHub as well as the Tweetinvi documentation available at `https://github.com/linvi/tweetinvi`. In this chapter, we saw how to register our application on Twitter's Application Management console. We saw that we could easily add Twitter functionality to our ASP.NET Core MVC app by using a NuGet package called Tweetinvi. We had a look at routing as well as controllers, models, views, and storing the settings in the `appsetting.json` file.

We were able to authenticate ourselves with OAuth and read the last 10 tweets from our home timeline. Lastly, we were able to post a tweet and view it in our home timeline.

There is still a lot of work that can be done inside of our Twitter Clone application. I hope that you have found it an interesting chapter and hope that you continue to work on it to improve it for your specific workflow and make it your own.

In the next chapter, we will be taking a look at Docker and what it means to you as a software developer. We will also see how to run our ASP.NET Core MVC application inside a Docker container.

9
Using Docker and ASP.NET Core

In this chapter, we will be looking at how Docker works. You may have heard about Docker before but have not had the opportunity to play around with it yet. In particular, we will be looking at the following:

- What Docker is
- Images and containers
- How Docker benefits web developers
- Installing Docker on Windows 10 Pro
- Running Docker and selecting some shared drives
- Troubleshooting shared drives when Windows Firewall seems to be the issue
- How Visual Studio 2017 integrates with Docker
- Creating an ASP.NET Core MVC application and running it inside a container
- Using Docker Hub with GitHub and setting up automated builds

Docker will open up a whole new world for you.

What is Docker?

Before we begin to work with Docker, let's have a look at exactly what Docker is. If you head on over to `https://www.docker.com` and look at the **What is Docker?** page, you will see that they say that Docker is a containerization platform. From a first-look perspective, this does not make much sense. Digging a little deeper though, you will see that Docker simplifies the application-building process and allows you to ship and run those applications in different environments. The different environments may be development, testing, user acceptance testing, and production environments.

Docker makes use of images and containers, and if you look at the Docker logo, you will see this idea of containers represented in their logo:

Cargo planners often have to be very careful how they stack the containers on a cargo ship. They need to keep the container destinations in mind when planning the location of the container on the ship.

For example, a container bound for the Middle East could not be loaded under a container bound for Tokyo, Japan. This would mean that they had to remove the top containers just to offload the bottom container and then load the top containers back again. The position of the containers has to be planned very carefully to optimize the efficiency of the freight logistics.

Docker is similar in its approach to using containers. So, let's clarify the terms **containers** and **images** a bit further.

Images and containers

A Docker image is just a file used to create a Docker container. Think of it as a blueprint that Docker needs to create a running container. Images are read-only templates, if you like, that are created as a layered filesystem which shares common files used to create container instances.

Containers, on the other hand, are instances created from these images. Containers are isolated and secure, and can be started, stopped, moved, or deleted.

Where does Docker run?

As mentioned earlier, using the analogy of the cargo ship, the cargo ship represents your development environment, test environment, or production environment.

Docker can run natively on the following:

- Linux
- Windows Server 2016
- Windows 10

Docker also runs in the cloud on the following:

- Amazon EC2
- Google Compute Engine
- Azure
- Rackspace

From the preceding points, you can see that Docker is extremely flexible and that using Docker can provide a huge benefit to developers. Let's have a look at how Docker can benefit web developers in particular.

How Docker benefits web developers

Docker provides several benefits to web developers. If you work in a mixed environment of developers, testers, designers, and so on, you probably want them to work with the actual application rather than with a prototype. You could set the application up on a server and hook it up to a SQL database and then manage the permissions needed for each user accessing the site from the server. Docker, on the other hand, allows us to make containers that can run on the individual developer or designer machines easily.

I previously mentioned that Docker containers are isolated and secure. Well, for this reason, containers eliminate application conflicts. I'm sure that if you have been developing for a while, you are bound to have run into a situation where the application is deployed on a production server. If you wanted (or needed) to upgrade the framework (for example) of the application, you might run into other application conflicts as a result of the upgrade. With Docker, the isolated containers can be upgraded without affecting other systems in the environment.

How many times have you heard a developer say, *But the application works fine on my system* when a deployed application fails? This is because there may be differences in the way a developer machine, staging server, or production server has been set up. With Docker, you simply move the image from one environment to another and get the containers up and running. This means that if your application runs fine inside its container on a dev machine, it definitely should run fine on a staging or production machine too.

Because of the predictability and stability of Docker containers, you are able to ship code much faster than before. This leads to increased productivity.

Installing Docker on Windows 10 Pro

For Windows 10 Pro and Windows 10 Enterprise, Docker **Community Edition (CE)** is available for free.

You can download Docker CE from
`https://www.docker.com/docker-windows`.

Docker CE requires Hyper-V and, for this reason, you need to be running Windows 10 Pro or higher. To see what version of Windows you have, open Command Prompt as Administrator and type in the following command at the prompt:

```
systeminfo
```

You will see the following information displayed:

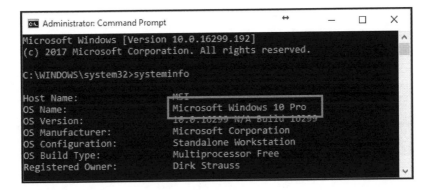

To check whether Hyper-V is enabled, scroll a little way down:

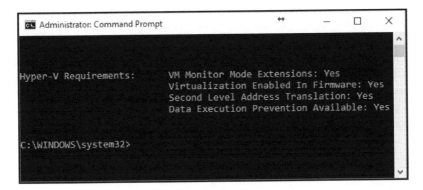

Earlier versions of Windows don't have Hyper-V, so Docker CE will not run. From the Docker documentation (`https://docs.docker.com/v17.09/docker-for-windows/faqs/#questions-about-stable-and-edge-channels`), Windows 10 Home is also not supported.

For older Mac and Windows systems, Docker Toolbox can be installed. This uses the free Oracle VM VirtualBox. For more information on this, have a look at `https://docs.docker.com/toolbox/toolbox_install_windows/`.

As mentioned earlier, Docker CE can be downloaded for Windows 10 Pro and Windows 10 Enterprise machines. You can get the installer from the Docker Store at `https://store.docker.com/editions/community/docker-ce-desktop-windows`.

At the time of writing, the download page on the store looks as follows:

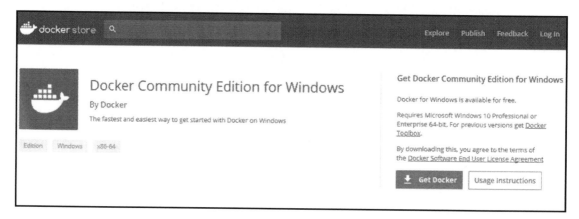

Click on the **Get Docker** button to download the Docker installer to your computer.

 The installer will require you to log out of Windows to complete the installation. It will not do this automatically but, before performing the installation, it's a good idea to close any other running applications.

The installer is actually one of the friendliest installers I have seen in recent years. It is also a breeze to install:

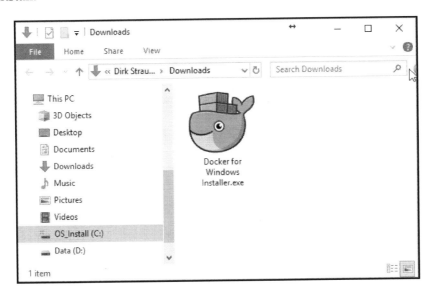

As a rule, I always run installers as Administrator. The installation process for Docker is really straightforward. After it has installed, it will prompt you to log out of Windows:

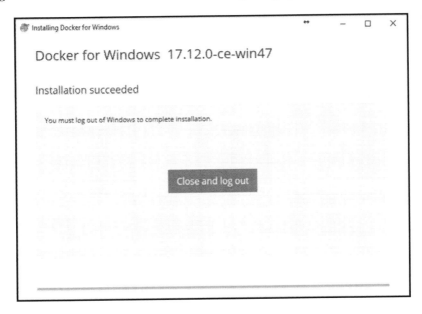

After you have logged back into Windows, you may see a message asking you to turn on Hyper-V to use Docker containers. Choose the option to turn on Hyper-V. At this point, your computer may restart again. After your computer has restarted, you will see a notification that Docker is running:

You have successfully installed Docker. I told you it was really easy.

Understanding Docker

To start using Docker, look for the Docker for Windows desktop application:

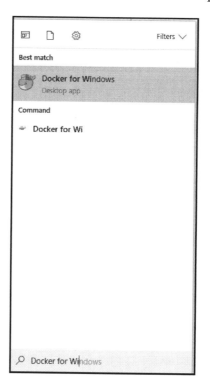

This will start Docker on your machine. When Docker is running, you will see it in your taskbar:

By default, Docker should be started after installation, so just check to see whether it's running from the taskbar first. Let's have a look at the various settings available to us with Docker. Right-click the Docker icon in the taskbar and select **Settings** from the context menu. When the screen opens, click on the **Shared Drives** tab:

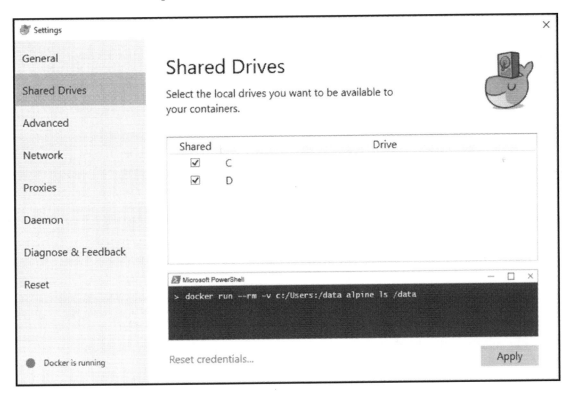

It is important that you select the local drives you want to be available to your containers. Checking the shared drives allows support for volumes. Volumes are the mechanism by which data that is generated by Docker containers is persisted. You can read more about volumes in the official Docker documentation at `https://docs.docker.com/engine/admin/volumes/volumes/`.

I do, however, want to point out the following bullet points from the documentation:

- Volumes can easily be backed up
- Volumes work on Linux and Windows containers
- You can share volumes between multiple containers
- You can use volume drivers to store volumes on remote machines or in the cloud
- You are able to encrypt the contents of volumes

Because a volume exists outside of a container, it is the preferred choice for persisting data. Docker also needs port 445 to be open to share drives between the host machine and the containers. If Docker detects that port 445 is closed, you will see the following screen:

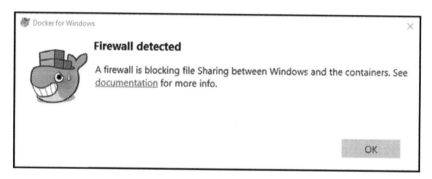

You can click on the link to read the documentation on this error.

 For more information on shared drives, see the Docker documentation at `https://docs.docker.com/docker-for-windows/#shared-drives`.

There are a few recommended ways online to resolve this issue. The first is to uninstall and re-install File and Printer Sharing for Microsoft Networks.

1. To do this, open the **Network and Sharing Center** from Windows settings. Then click on the **vEthernet (DockerNAT)** connection:

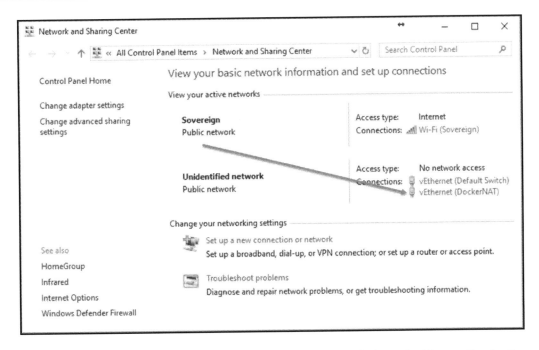

2. On the **vEthernet (DocketNAT) Status** window, click on the **Properties** button:

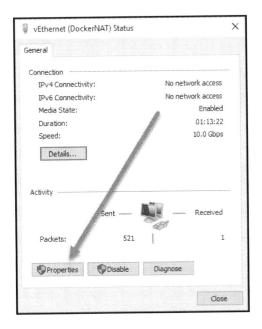

3. Here you will see **File and Printer Sharing for Microsoft Networks**. Your first step is to click on the **Uninstall** button. This will remove the entry from the list. Next you need to click on the **Install** button:

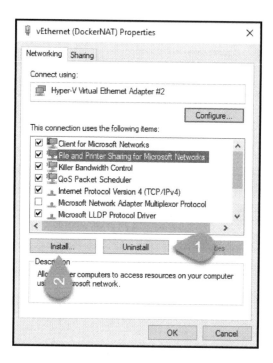

4. In the **Select Network Feature Type** screen, click on the **Service** feature and click on the **Add** button:

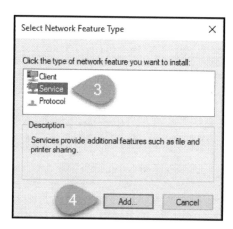

5. In the **Select Network Service** screen, select **Microsoft** as the manufacturer and click on the **File and Printer Sharing for Microsoft Networks** service:

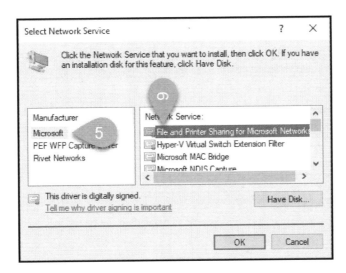

6. After clicking **OK** and closing all the screens, stop Docker by right-clicking the icon in the taskbar and click on **Quit Docker**. You can then restart Docker by clicking on the Docker for Windows application again.

At this point, you should be able to select the shared drives to use with Docker from the settings screen. If you still see the **Firewall detected** message, the chances are that your antivirus is blocking it.

In my case, it was ESET Endpoint Security that was blocking the communication. You may be using a different antivirus, so have a look at the particular list of applications it has recently blocked. In my case, I started ESET Endpoint Security and selected SETUP and then **Network**:

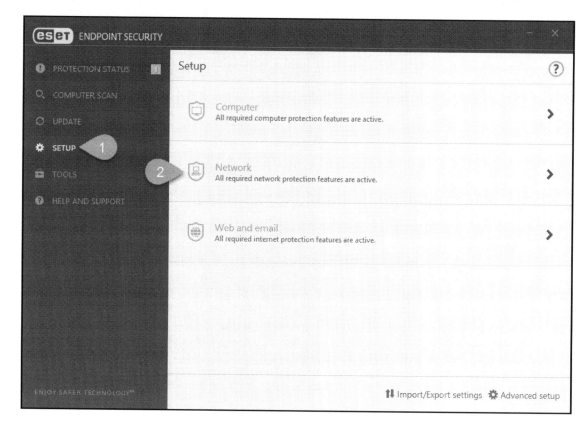

7. Next, I selected the **Recently blocked applications or devices** list:

Scrolling through the list, I saw that 10.0.75.2 was blocked by ESET. According to the Docker documentation, this is the IP to allow through the firewall:

"To share the drive, allow connections between the Windows host machine and the virtual machine in Windows Firewall or your third-party firewall software. You do not need to open port 445 on any other network. By default, allow connections to 10.0.75.1 port 445 (the Windows host) from 10.0.75.2 (the virtual machine). If the firewall rules appear to be open, consider reinstalling the File and Print Sharing service on the virtual network adapter."

8. Clicking on the **Unblock** button displays a confirmation screen:

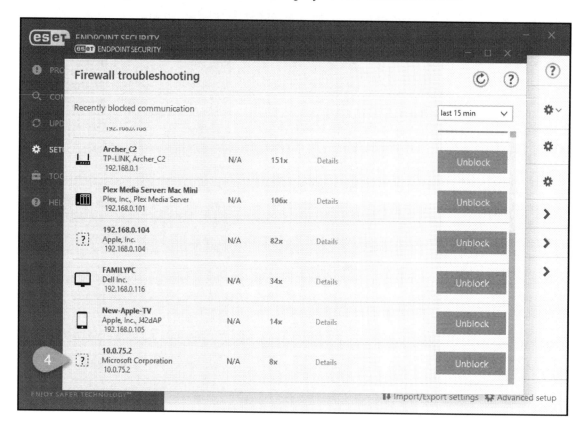

When you have done this, you have unblocked `10.0.75.2`:

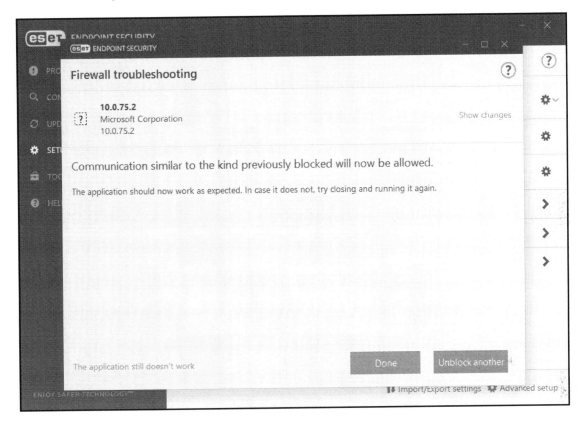

9. To finish, click **Done**, head on back to the Docker settings, and select the drives you want to share.

You should now be able to select the shared drives for Docker to use. If you are still not able to share drives, have a look at the following Stack Overflow article for additional troubleshooting tips: `https://stackoverflow.com/questions/42203488/settings-to-windows-firewall-to-allow-docker-for-windows-to-share-drive/43904051#43904051`.

Next, we will have a look at how Docker integrates into Visual Studio 2017, and what you can do to enable Docker support for your ASP.NET Core applications. We will also have a look at how to add Docker support (or Dockerize) existing ASP.NET Core applications.

Docker has a healthy community of developers and it also has a lot of help documentation available. Take the time to browse through this and research any issues you may come across.

Running an ASP.NET Core application from Visual Studio 2017 inside Docker

So where does this all leave us? We have had a look at how to set up Docker on Windows 10, as well as how to resolve a few issues surrounding this setup. Let us now have a look at how to create an ASP.NET Core application and add Docker support to the new application.

1. Create a new ASP.NET Core Web Application in Visual Studio 2017 and click **OK**:

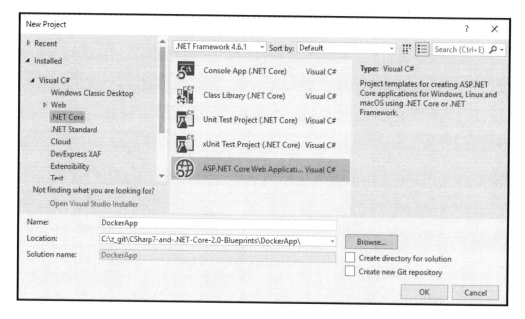

2. On the next screen, select **Web Application (Model-View-Controller)** or any type you like, while ensuring that **ASP.NET Core 2.0** is selected from the drop-down list. Then check the **Enable Docker Support** checkbox. This will enable the **OS** drop-down list. Select **Windows** here and then click on the **OK** button:

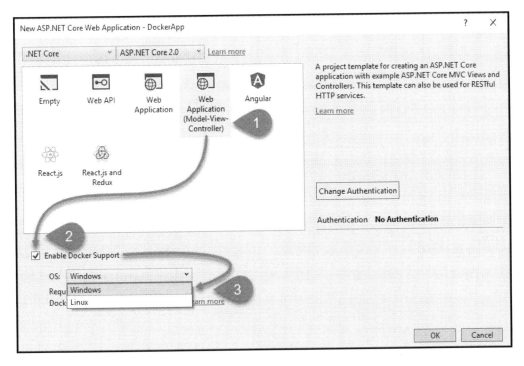

If you see the following message, you need to switch to Windows containers. This is because you have probably kept the default container setting for Docker as Linux:

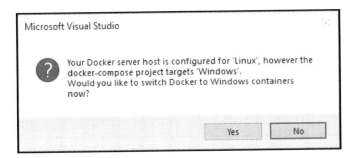

If you right-click on the Docker icon in the taskbar, you will see that you have an option to enable Windows containers there too. You can switch to Windows containers from the Docker icon in the taskbar by clicking on the **Switch to Windows containers** option:

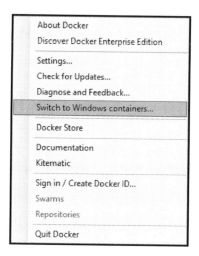

 Switching to Windows containers may take several minutes to complete, depending on your line speed and the hardware configuration of your PC.

If, however, you don't click on this option, Visual Studio will ask you to change to Windows containers when selecting the OS platform as Windows.

 There is a good reason that I am choosing Windows containers as the target OS. This reason will become clear later on in the chapter when working with Docker Hub and automated builds.

After your ASP.NET Core application is created, you will see the following project setup in Solution Explorer:

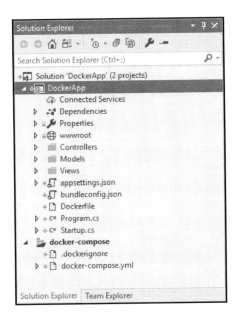

The Docker support that is added to Visual Studio comes not only in the form of the Dockerfile, but also in the form of the Docker configuration information. This information is contained in the global `docker-compose.yml` file at the solution level:

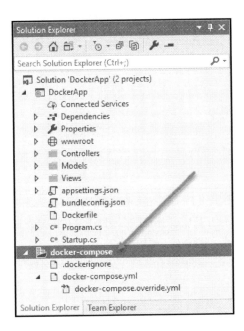

3. Clicking on the Dockerfile in Solution Explorer, you will see that it doesn't look complicated at all. Remember, the Dockerfile is the file that creates your image. The image is a read-only template that outlines how to create a Docker container. The Dockerfile, therefore, contains the steps needed to generate the image and run it. The instructions in the Dockerfile create layers in the image. This means that if anything changes in the Dockerfile, only the layers that have changed will be rebuilt when the image is rebuilt. The Dockerfile looks as follows:

```
FROM microsoft/aspnetcore:2.0-nanoserver-1709 AS base
WORKDIR /app
EXPOSE 80

FROM microsoft/aspnetcore-build:2.0-nanoserver-1709 AS build
WORKDIR /src
COPY *.sln ./
COPY DockerApp/DockerApp.csproj DockerApp/
RUN dotnet restore
COPY . .
WORKDIR /src/DockerApp
RUN dotnet build -c Release -o /app

FROM build AS publish
RUN dotnet publish -c Release -o /app

FROM base AS final
WORKDIR /app
COPY --from=publish /app .
ENTRYPOINT ["dotnet", "DockerApp.dll"]
```

When you have a look at the menu in Visual Studio 2017, you will notice that the **Run** button has been changed to **Docker**:

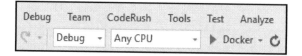

4. Clicking on the **Docker** button to debug your ASP.NET Core application, you will notice that there are a few things popping up in the **Output** window. Of particular interest is the IP address at the end. In my case, it reads **Launching http://172.24.12.112** (yours will differ):

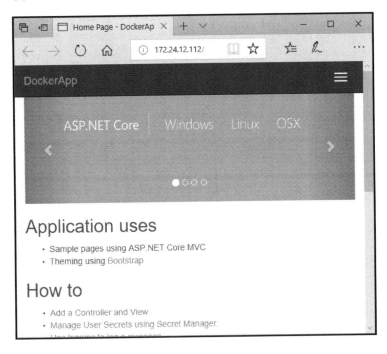

When the browser is launched, you will see that the ASP.NET Core application is running at the IP address listed previously in the **Output** window. Your ASP.NET Core application is now running inside of a Windows Docker container:

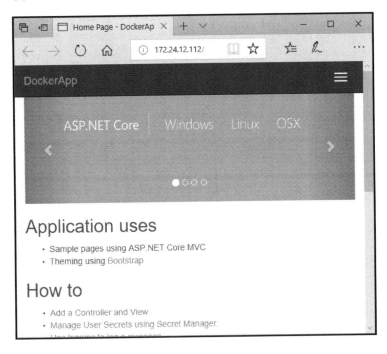

This is great and really easy to get started with. But what do you need to do to Dockerize an existing ASP.NET Core application? As it turns out, this isn't as difficult as you may think.

Adding Docker support to an existing ASP.NET Core application

Imagine that you have an ASP.NET Core application without Docker support. To add Docker support to this existing application, simply add it from the context menu:

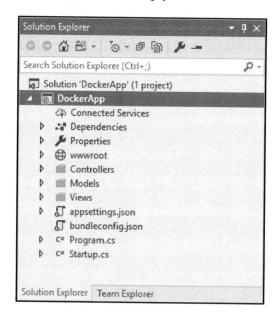

To add Docker support to an existing ASP.NET Core application, you need to do the following:

1. Right-click on your project in Solution Explorer
2. Click on the **Add** menu item
3. Click on **Docker Support** in the fly-out menu:

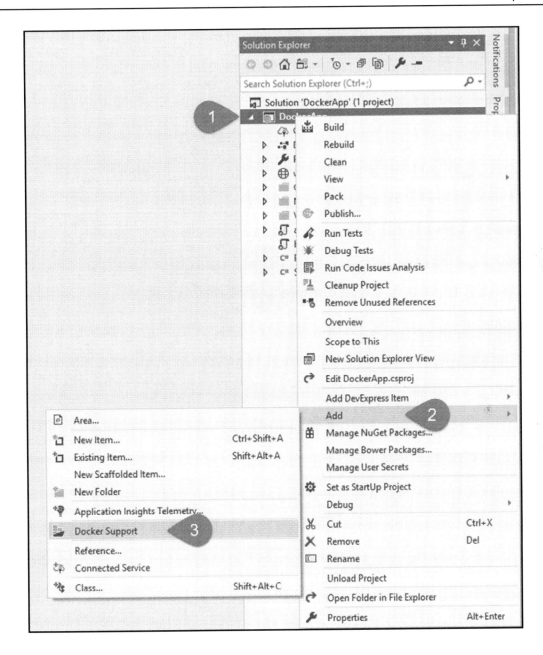

4. Visual Studio 2017 now asks you what the target OS is going to be. In our case, we are going to target Windows:

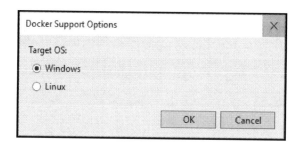

5. After clicking on the **OK** button, Visual Studio 2017 will begin to add the Docker support to your project:

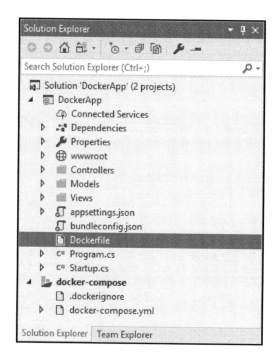

It is extremely easy to create ASP.NET Core applications that have Docker support baked in, and even easier to add Docker support to existing ASP.NET Core applications.

Lastly, if you experience any issues, such as file access issues, ensure that your antivirus software has excluded your Dockerfile from scanning. Also, make sure that you run Visual Studio as Administrator.

Using Docker Hub with GitHub

The following section will illustrate how to set Docker Hub up to do automated builds from your project in a GitHub repository.

 For this example, I will not be going through how to check your code into GitHub.

1. Using the DockerApp project created in the previous sections, check that into a new GitHub repository. Once you have checked in your code, swing on over to Docker Hub at `https://hub.docker.com/` and log in, or create an account if you haven't got one already:

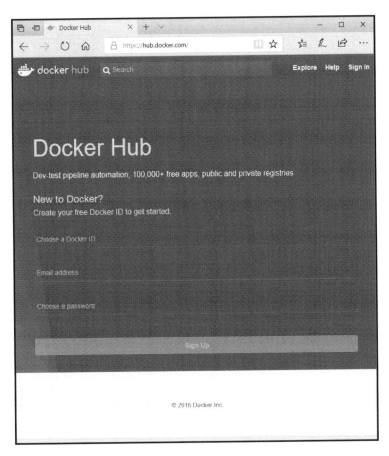

2. The sign-up process is really quick and easy. All you need to do is confirm your email address and you're in. After confirming your email address, you will be prompted to log in again. This will take you to your Docker Hub dashboard.

On this page, you have several options available to you. You can create repositories and organizations, and explore repositories:

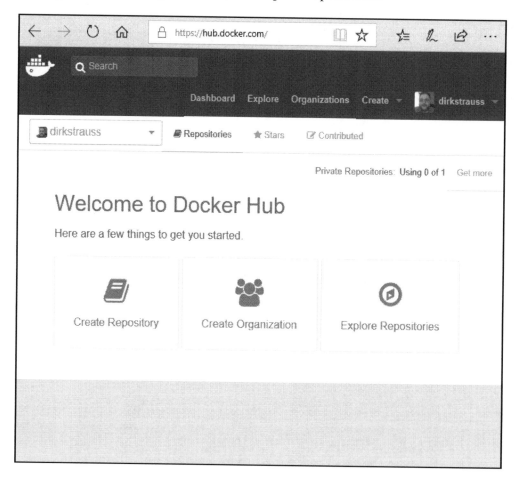

3. To start working with GitHub, we need to link Docker Hub with GitHub first. Click on the username you selected in the top right of the page. Then click on the **Settings** menu option:

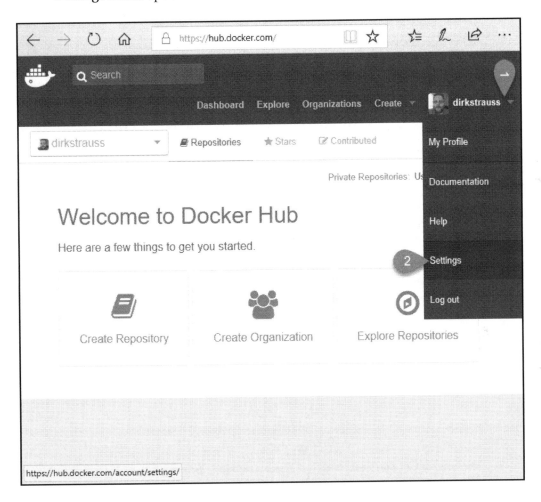

4. Under **Settings**, look for the **Linked Accounts & Services** tab and click on that. You will now need to click on the **Link Github** option to continue:

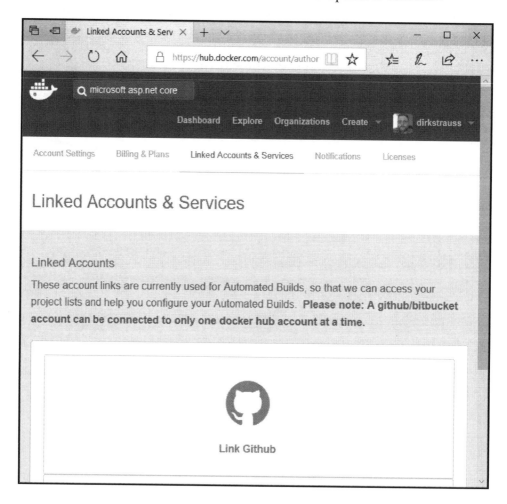

5. For simplicity's sake (and because it is recommended), I just went ahead and clicked on the **Public and Private** access setting:

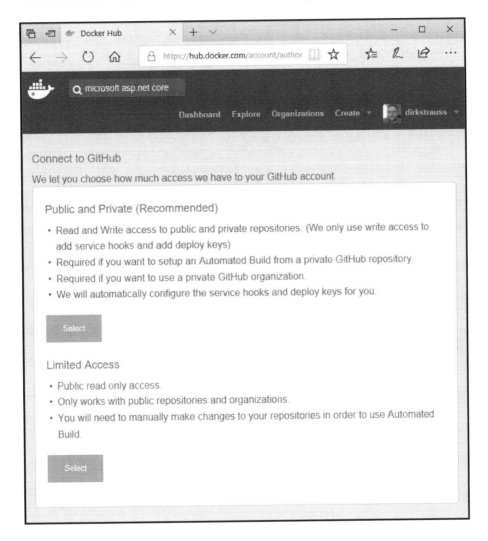

6. Docker Hub now redirects you to the authorization page to allow Docker Hub to access your GitHub repository. Here you need to sign in with your GitHub credentials:

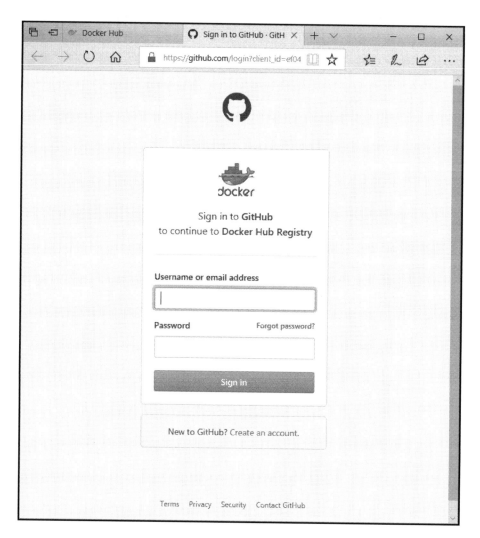

 Note that if you have two-factor authentication enabled, you will need to type in the authentication code generated by your smartphone app. So keep your mobile close by.

7. To authorize Docker Hub, click on the **Authorize docker** button:

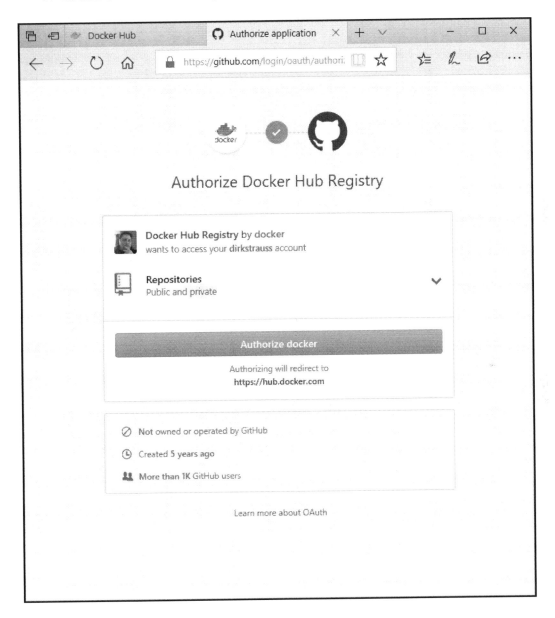

You are now taken back to the **Linked Accounts & Services** page, where you will see the linked accounts on your Docker Hub profile:

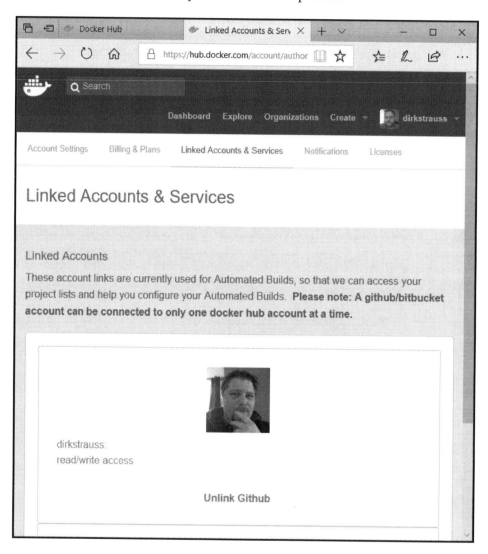

8. Next, we need to go and create an automated build. From the menu, click on the **Create** menu item and select **Create Automated Build** from the options below that:

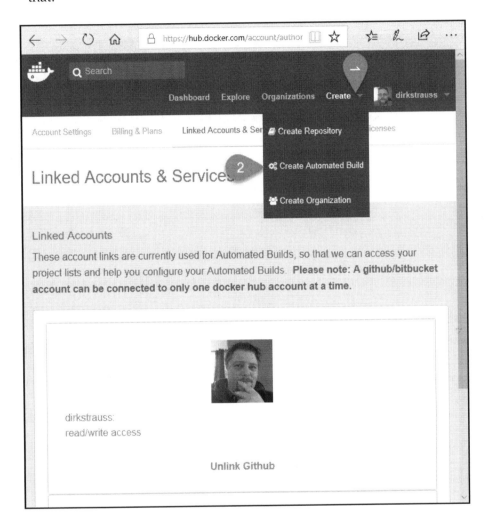

9. You then want to click on the **Create Auto-build Github** option:

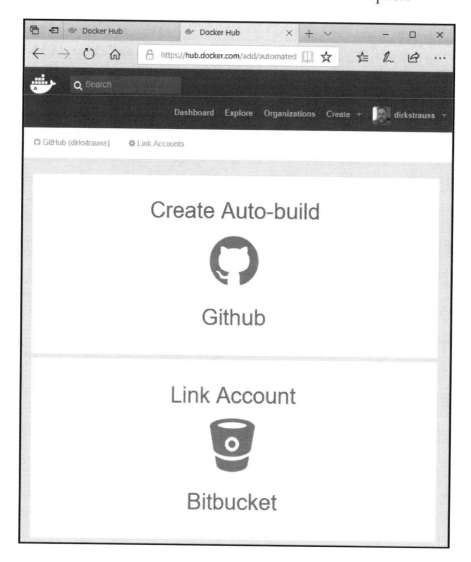

This will display a list of all the available repositories in your GitHub account. I previously checked in the DockerApp project to my GitHub account, so this is what we will be selecting:

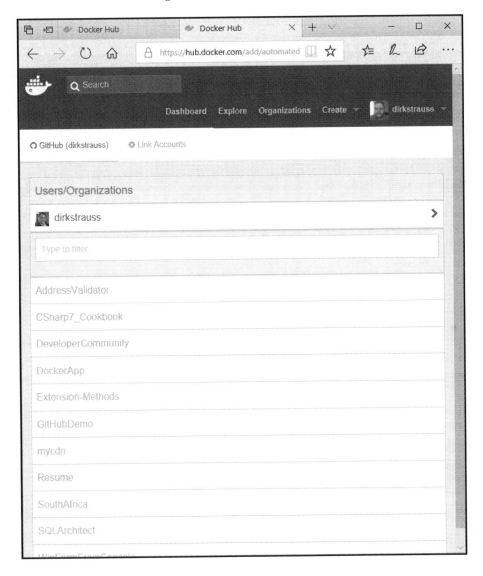

10. You can now go and define additional information here as needed, or you can keep it as default. It is up to you. When you are done, click on the **Create** button:

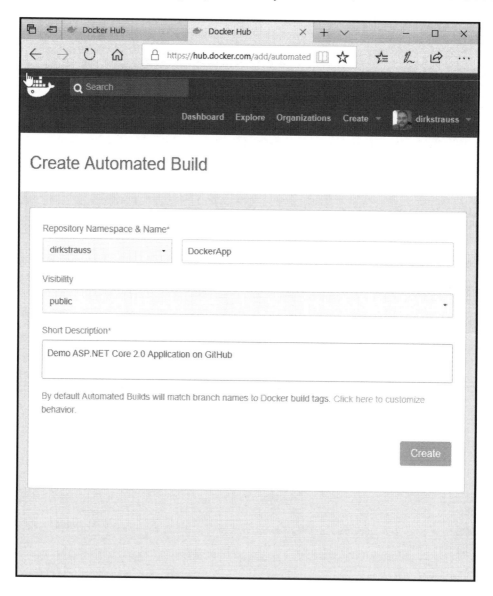

Our automated build is now created and ready. So how, precisely, does this automated build work? Well, every time you commit your code to your GitHub repository, Docker Hub will build your project:

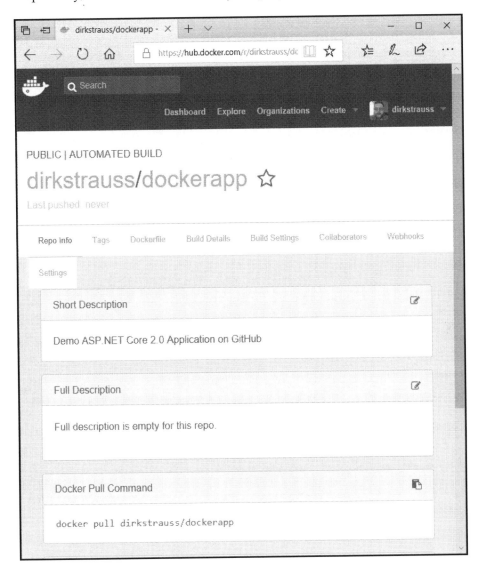

11. To test this, open up your ASP.NET Core application in Visual Studio 2017 and make some changes. Then commit those changes to your GitHub repository. Then click on the **Build Details** link in Docker Hub. You will see that the build has been queued and will complete in a few minutes. To view the build results, just refresh this page after a little while:

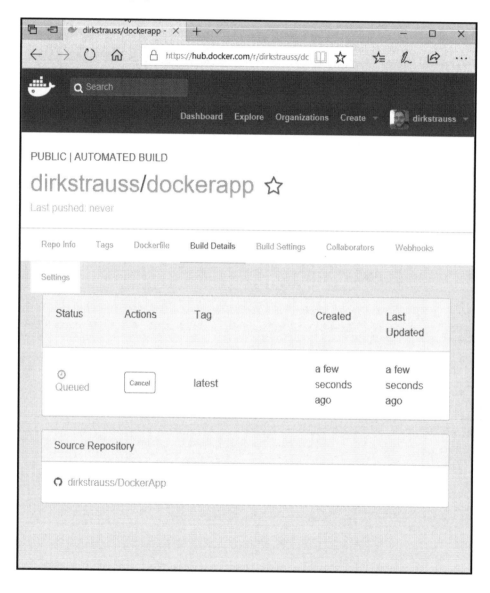

12. After refreshing the page, you will see that an error has occurred. Docker Hub will display the build results for you and you can click on the build result to view the details of the failure.

 I am going to illustrate a few errors that are commonly received during an automated build. I will also show the way I have found to resolve these. I'm not sure whether there will have been changes to the way these work in the meantime but, at the time of writing, these issues presented themselves.

When we look at the cause of the failure, we see that Docker Hub can't find the Dockerfile in the root of the project. Why exactly this is an issue, I don't know. I would have expected Docker Hub to recursively walk the tree structure of your project to find the Dockerfile location. Nevertheless, this is quite easy to fix:

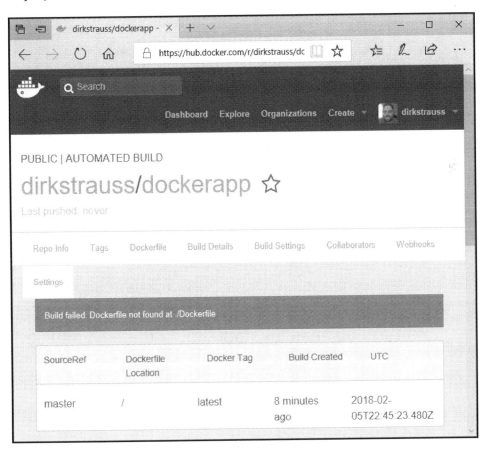

I simply made a copy of my Dockerfile and copied it to the root of the solution. I then checked in my code again to GitHub:

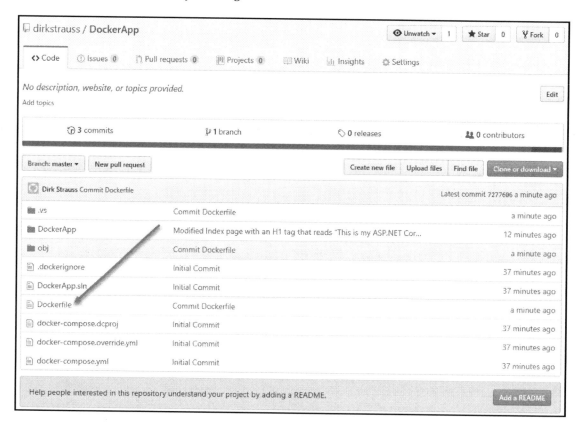

13. If you refresh your automated build page, you will see that it is building the project again:

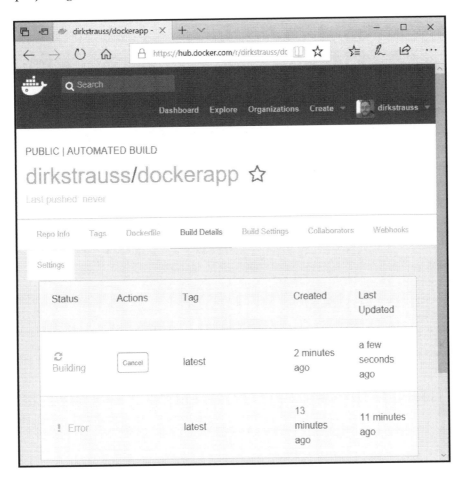

14. This time around, another error presented itself. Clicking on the error entry once again takes you to the error details:

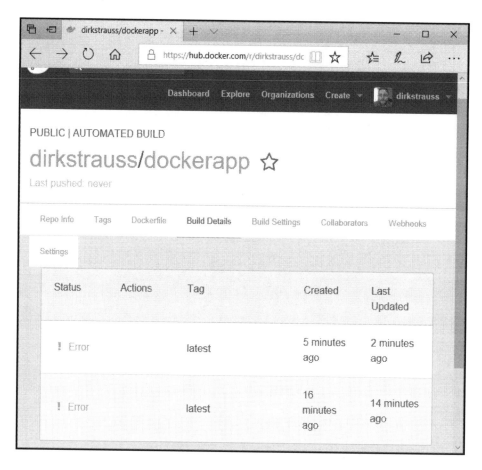

This time, it shows that the cause of the error is the fact that we have targeted Windows OS in our project instead of Linux:

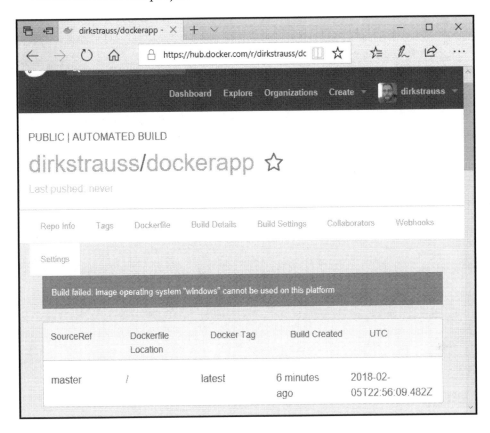

The error is listed as follows:

```
Build failed: image operating system "windows" cannot be used
on this platform
```

15. To fix this issue, we need to modify the Dockerfile. The Dockerfile for Windows will look as follows:

```
FROM microsoft/aspnetcore:2.0-nanoserver-1709 AS base
WORKDIR /app
EXPOSE 80

FROM microsoft/aspnetcore-build:2.0-nanoserver-1709 AS build
WORKDIR /src
COPY *.sln ./
```

```
COPY DockerApp/DockerApp.csproj DockerApp/
RUN dotnet restore
COPY . .
WORKDIR /src/DockerApp
RUN dotnet build -c Release -o /app

FROM build AS publish
RUN dotnet publish -c Release -o /app

FROM base AS final
WORKDIR /app
COPY --from=publish /app .
ENTRYPOINT ["dotnet", "DockerApp.dll"]
```

16. **Modify it to use** `aspnetcore:2.0` **instead of** `aspnetcore:2.0-nanoserver`:

```
FROM microsoft/aspnetcore:2.0 AS base
WORKDIR /app
EXPOSE 80

FROM microsoft/aspnetcore-build:2.0 AS build
WORKDIR /src
COPY *.sln ./
COPY DockerApp/DockerApp.csproj DockerApp/
RUN dotnet restore
COPY . .
WORKDIR /src/DockerApp
RUN dotnet build -c Release -o /app

FROM build AS publish
RUN dotnet publish -c Release -o /app

FROM base AS final
WORKDIR /app
COPY --from=publish /app .
ENTRYPOINT ["dotnet", "DockerApp.dll"]
```

17. Once again, commit your code to GitHub to initiate the automated build:

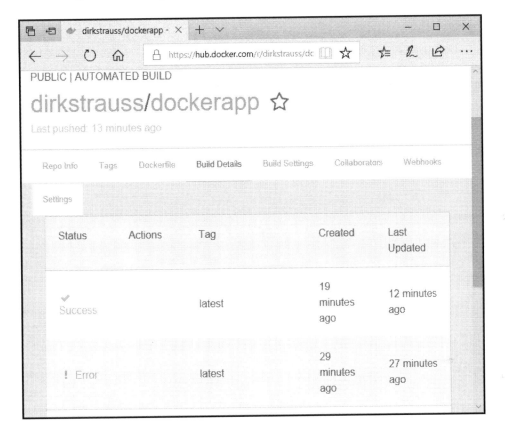

This time around, you will see that the build succeeds.

 For more information on which OS to target with .NET containers, see the following Microsoft
document: `https://docs.microsoft.com/en-us/dotnet/standard/micros ervices-architecture/net-core-net-framework-containers/net- container-os-targets`.

18. We now have a successful automated build of our GitHub project. Swing back to the **Repo Info** tab and make a note of the Docker pull command:

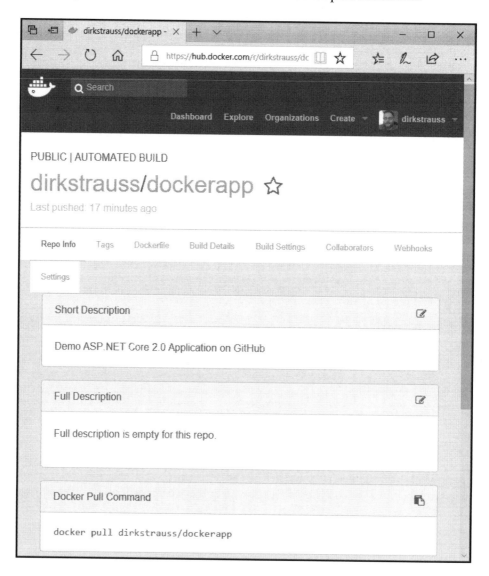

The Docker repository for your image is at `dirkstrauss/dockerapp` and the Docker pull command is `docker pull dirkstrauss/dockerapp`.

19. Run Windows Command Prompt as Administrator, enter the Docker pull command, and press the *Enter* key:

```
Administrator: Command Prompt                                    —    □    ✕

C:\WINDOWS\system32>docker pull dirkstrauss/dockerapp
Using default tag: latest
latest: Pulling from dirkstrauss/dockerapp
                                  723254a2c089: Pull complete
afa846f8a696: Pull complete
ce639c98964c: Pull complete
381459bd1248: Pull complete
4489c120821f: Pull complete
524bdf601083: Pull complete
059a8af1ccbe: Pull complete
Digest: sha256:2c67e0f4689eaf2ba7301b317ba5b206d27a7bb7e42dc10330dc7bf57aa4a015
Status: Downloaded newer image for dirkstrauss/dockerapp:latest

C:\WINDOWS\system32>_
```

You will see that you will start to pull the image down to your local computer.

If, when pulling the Docker image, you receive the error message **Error response from daemon: Get https://registry-1.docker.io/v2/: net/http: request canceled while waiting for connection (Client.Timeout exceeded while awaiting headers)**, simply restart Docker by right-clicking the Docker icon in the taskbar, clicking on **Settings**, and then clicking on **Reset**, and then **Restart Docker**. If you receive an error along the lines of **Image operating system "linux" cannot be used on this platform**, you need to switch back to a Linux container. See the following URL for more information: `https://github.com/docker/kitematic/issues/2828`.

20. We now need to run the container by entering `docker run -d -p 5000:80 [image-repository]`, which binds the container to port 5000:

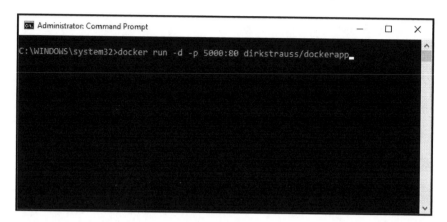

21. If you want to see whether the container has started, run the following command:

```
Docker container ls
```

You can now see the container ID, as well as other information about the running container:

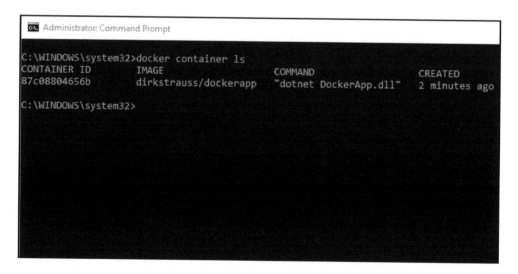

22. What we now want to do is run the ASP.NET Core application we checked in to GitHub in the browser. To do this, we need to find the IP address. On Windows 10, we need to look for the IP address of the DockerNAT, and for this we need to run the following command:

    ```
    ipconfig
    ```

    You will see that the IP address defined is 10.0.75.1 and this is the IP address that our container will be running at:

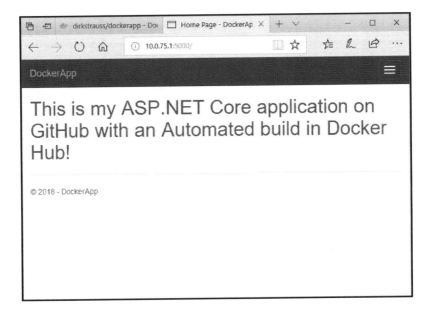

23. Open up your browser and enter the IP address and port number as 10.0.75.1:5000 and hit *Enter*. Your ASP.NET Core application will pop into your browser window in all its glory:

Setting up GitHub with Docker Hub to perform automated builds may seem like a bit of a hassle at first, but the benefits for dev teams are numerous. It allows you to always be working with the latest build of your project.

Summary

In this chapter, we had a look at installing Docker on your Windows 10 Pro machine. We also had a look at what Docker is and the benefits to developers. We then took a look at troubleshooting the setup of Docker on your local machine when the firewall seems to be the blocking issue. Then, we took Docker and created an ASP.NET Core MVC application that had Docker support added from the start. We also looked at how to add Docker support to existing applications. Finally, we set up Docker to integrate with GitHub and perform automated builds. We also had a look at how to pull the container from Docker Hub and run it in a container on your local machine.

Docker containers and Docker Hub are tools that developers can use to make their work much easier. The power of collaborating with such popular platforms such as GitHub and Docker leads to benefits that will increase productivity and profitability. Docker takes away all those compatibility headaches of deploying your application across several machines.

There is still a lot to learn regarding Docker, much more than a single chapter can illustrate. Go forth and explore the power of Docker.

Other Books You May Enjoy

If you enjoyed this book, you may be interested in these other books by Packt:

Learning Angular for .NET Developers
Rajesh Gunasundaram

ISBN: 978-1-78588-428-3

- Create a standalone Angular application to prototype user interfaces
- Validate complex forms with Angular version 4 and use Bootstrap to style them
- Build RESTful web services that work well with single-page applications
- Use Gulp and Bower in Visual Studio to run tasks and manage JavaScript packages
- Implement automatic validation for web service requests to reduce your boilerplate code
- Use web services with Angular version 4 to offload and secure your application logic
- Test your Angular version 4 and web service code to improve the quality of your software deliverables

Dependency Injection in .NET Core 2.0
Marino Posadas, Tadit Dash

- Understand the concept of DI and its implications in modern software construction
- Learn how DI is already implemented in today's frameworks.
- Analyze how DI can be used with current software to improve maintainability and scalability.
- Learn the use of DI in .NET Core
- Get used to the possibilities that DI offers the ASP.NET Core developer in different scenarios.
- Learn about good practices and refactoring legacy code.

Leave a review - let other readers know what you think

Please share your thoughts on this book with others by leaving a review on the site that you bought it from. If you purchased the book from Amazon, please leave us an honest review on this book's Amazon page. This is vital so that other potential readers can see and use your unbiased opinion to make purchasing decisions, we can understand what our customers think about our products, and our authors can see your feedback on the title that they have worked with Packt to create. It will only take a few minutes of your time, but is valuable to other potential customers, our authors, and Packt. Thank you!

Index

Made in the USA
San Bernardino, CA
09 March 2019